REFLECTIONS OF THE RAV

Lessons in Jewish Thought

VOLUME ONE

REFLECTIONS OF
THE RAV

Lessons in Jewish Thought

VOLUME ONE

adapted from Lectures of

RABBI JOSEPH B. SOLOVEITCHIK

by

RABBI ABRAHAM R. BESDIN

KTAV Publishing House, Inc.
Hoboken, N.J.

First Published 1979
Second Impression 1980
Revised Edition 1981
Revised Edition 1993

Library of Congress Cataloging-in-Publication Data

Besdin, Abraham R.
    Reflections of the Rav : lessons in Jewish thought / adapted from
lectures of Joseph B. Soloveitchik by Abraham R. Besdin. -- 2nd rev.
ed.
      p. cm.
    Includes bibliographical references and index.
    ISBN 0-88125-432-0
    1. Judaism. I. Soloveitchik, Joseph Dov. II. Title.
BM45.B47 1992
296.3--dc20   92-32035
                                              CIP

Reflections of the Rav, Volume One, was originally published in 1979 by the
Department for Torah Education and Culture in the Diaspora of the World
Zionist Organization in Jerusalem.

The support of the Memorial Foundation for Jewish Culture is
gratefully acknowledged.

Manufactured in the United States of America

CONTENTS

Photo by Irwin Albert

וְדַם עֵנָב תִּשְׁתֶּה חָמֶר ‏(דברים לב: יד)

אלו אגדות שמושכות לב האדם כיין ‏(ספרי, האזינו יד)

PREFACE

Some Talmudic sages specialized in the study of Halakhah, Jewish Law, and were not as much involved with Aggadah, the non-legal areas of Rabbinic teaching. Halakhah deals with the Biblical commandments and encompasses the Oral Law which, like the Biblical text, was received from Moses. Other Talmudic scholars were known as *Rabbanan DeAggadeta* (Sages of the Aggadah), because their primary teaching was in the realm of ethics, philosophy, and theology of the Torah. They aimed to inspire, guide, and sanctify Jewish life.

Several eminent scholars of the Talmud, however, such as Rav of Babylonia and Rabbi Yoḥanan in Palestine, were accomplished in both fields. Their mastery of Aggadah was as extensive as their brilliance in Halakhah. Both Halakhah and Aggadah are components of Torah, reflecting complementary aspects of Divine teaching. The former governs human behavior, while the latter deals with underlying attitudes, values, and one's religious frame of mind. The Sages, therefore, compared Halakhah to meat and Aggadah to wine, suggesting that a wholesome meal should combine basic nutrition and the fare for spiritual uplifting.

Rabbi Joseph B. Soloveitchik, in our day, typifies the Torah sage who has achieved world renown in both fields. His Halakhic *shiurim* are acknowledged as unsurpassed in their breadth of knowledge and analytical depth. The Rav, as Rabbi Soloveitchik is reverently and affectionately known by his *talmidim* and admirers, is also a brilliant expositor of Aggadah. He holds large

9

audiences spellbound as he weaves together insights from the Talmud, Midrash, Kabbalah, and contemporary sources. The versatility of his knowledge and the freshness of understanding he brings to most subjects are widely recognized in scholarly and lay circles. In addition, he is endowed with a charismatic personality and a dramatic eloquence which invest his talks with the compelling power of a unique experience.

The Rav is unique in our age. Following Maimonides as his model, he is not only a giant in Torah in the Brisk tradition of incisive learning, but is also conversant with the frontiers of knowledge of Western civilization, its scientific achievements, its humanistic pretensions and its philosophical presumptions.

It is the basic thesis of the Rav that the Jew need not ghettoize himself intellectually, and insulate himself from general society. He can belong to both worlds, the holy and secular, secure in the singularity of the Torah and the halachic way of life. The Halacha operates in the practical realm of reality and an insular withdrawal from the pragmatic world is contrary to the spirit of the Torah.

I have attempted, in this work, to project some aspects of the Aggadic thinking of the Rav. Each chapter is a thematic reconstruction derived from lecture-*shiurim* delivered over the course of many years at conclaves of the Rabbinical Council of America and to the students and the Rabbinic alumni of Yeshiva University. The Rav's presentations are usually lengthy and complex, consisting of an overall thesis with a multiplicity of secondary themes and an abundance of supportive material. His audiences follow his words with intense interest and intellectual pleasure. These delights, however, have not been accessible to wider circles of students and general readers.

My primary objective in composing this text is to make the salient ideas of the Rav's *hashkafah* more readily available.

These essays are not literal transcriptions of the Rav's presentations. Rather, they are reconstructions in which texts and ideas, often in the Rav's own felicitous language, are organized and formulated in a manner suitable for the general reader. Those who are puzzled in their efforts to understand the full teachings of the Rav are advised to extend their knowledge by studying his writings, which are listed in the Partial Bibliography found in the back of this volume.

I have, at all times, been aware of the awesome responsibility involved in any attempt to preserve the authenticity of the Rav's ideas. It is with much trepidation, but also with feelings of rare privilege, that I have brought this work to public attention. I caution the reader, however, that all weaknesses discerned in the text, whether substantive or stylistic, are to be ascribed solely to my faulty transmission and interpretation. I pray that such instances are minor and infrequent.

I would like to express my gratitude to those who assisted me in bringing this volume to fruition:

To Rabbi Leonard Oschry, who most conscientiously labored through the manuscript, making valuable suggestions; to Mr. Julius Berman, for his sage counsel, patient encouragement, and unfailing helpfulness; to Mr. Moshe Ishon and Mr. Avner Tomaschoff, directors of the American Office and English Section, respectively, of the Torah Education and Culture Department of the World Zionist Organization, for their overall cooperation.

To my beloved brother, Rabbi Morris J. Besdin, Director of the James Striar School of Yeshiva University, I wish to express my life-long appreciation for the privilege of brotherly love and friendship. As a genuine Talmid Ḥakham, an outstanding pedagogue, and a most precious human being, his influence and guidance have been most valuable to me. And אחרונה אחרונה חביבה, I wish to express my indebtedness and appreciation to my beloved wife, Elana, whose encouragement and support were

indispensable in the preparation of this volume. We thank God
for our children, Adeena Lee, Hillel and Bonnie, and Alisa
Miriam, and we pray that we may be blessed "to see our
children and children's children occupied with Torah and mitzvot."

Abraham R. Besdin

Sivan 5738

מוקדש לזכרו הטהור של אחי, רעי מורי ורבי הרב משה בה״ר אליעזר צבי בית־דין זצ״ל

גדול צערי על מותו ללא עת של אחי, מורי ורבי האהוב,
הרב משה בית־דין זצ״ל, שהלך לעולמו בשבת חול המועד
פסח תשמ״ב. ביראת כבוד אני מקדיש את חיבורי זה לזכרו
הברוך. תהי נשמתו צרורה בצרור החיים

אברהם בית־דין

תשרי תשמ״ג

12

CHAPTER I

THE THREE BIBLICAL NAMES OF GOD

Man cannot perceive God's real essence, "for man may not see Me and live" (Ex. 33:20).[1] The human mind cannot encompass the infinite. We know Him, however, through His deeds, as they affect us in the world. These are His attributes, His *middot*. As the Midrash states: "God said to Moses, 'You wish to know Me [lit. "My Name"]? I am known by My deeds'" (Ex. R. 3).[2]

The first three Divine names in the Bible are *Elohim* (God), *Havayah* (Eternal, a substitute expression used to avoid writing or pronouncing the Tetragrammaton, which it represents), and *ADNY* (Lord, Master, Owner; *aleph, daled, nun, yud*). *Elohim* is used exclusively in the creation chapter of Genesis.[3] *Havayah* is added in the second chapter, which unfolds God's involvement with human history (2:4).[4] In a later chapter (15:8), Abraham uses the name *A-D-N-Y*, which evoked the following laudatory comment of our Sages (Ber. 7a/b):

"R. Yoḥanan said: Since the day that God created the world, no one had called God *ADNY* until Abraham came and called Him *ADNY*, as in the verse, '*ADNY, Havayah* [O Lord, Eternal], how shall I know that I shall inherit it [the land]?" (15:8). In an earlier verse Abraham, pleading for a child, said, "*ADNY, Havayah,* what can You give me, considering that I am childless?" (15:2).[5]

R. Yoḥanan suggests that the generations prior to Abraham were deficient, having failed to perceive the *adnut* (ownership) dimension of God's attributes. Perhaps, had Adam and the generation of the flood known of God's *adnut*, they would have been deterred from sinning. What do these Divine names signify, and what is the special perception implied in the name *ADNY?*

The Name Elohim

The Divine name *Elohim* denotes that God is the Creator of the world. Semantically, it connotes omnipotence, *ba'al hakohot*, the source of infinite energy and power, the original architect and engineer. *Elohim*, however, does not indicate an ongoing relationship of God with His creation. In the first chapter of Genesis, where only *Elohim* is employed, Adam and Eve are listed only incidentally. They are called *zakhar unekevah*, male and female, instead of Adam and Eve. They are simply part of the general creation of inanimate and animate matter. The second chapter, however, deals with a created, already complete world, when it became necessary that He sustain the world in continued existence and that He manifest a concern in man, the apex of creation. This is conveyed by the name *Havayah*, which signifies His continued association with the world.

Elohim tells us that God is the Creator, but we are still uninformed about the relationship of God to the creation after its emergence. What happened thereafter? The Deists believed that after creation the world moved on its own impetus, though even they conceded that God was the original Creator.

Looking at a magnificent, imposing edifice, we can discern that the architect was a genius, possessed of a creative imagination, capable of combining and molding materials: steel, wood, brick, and mortar. His structure is the realization of an idea, a vision, a philosophy. But once completed, the building maintains no continuing relationship with the architect and builder. They pass on to other tasks. *Elohim* signifies Creator and builder; *Havayah* signifies a continued association. Deists believe in *Elohim;* theism begins with *Havayah.*

The Name Havayah

The name *Havayah*, composed of four letters, *yud, heh, vav, heh* (the Tetragrammaton), is singularly distinct from God's other names. The latter are derived from His attributes, His actions as they manifest themselves to man. *Havayah*, however, pertains to His essence, which is Being and is, therefore, called *Shem Hameyuḥad*, "the Singular Name" (Sifre, Num. 143), or *Shem Hameforash*, "the Clearly Expressed Name" spoken by the High Priest on Yom Kippur; later called "Ineffable Name" because it was not otherwise to be pronounced (Yoma 39b; Sotah 37b).[6] This suggests a heightened holiness and a distinctness from other names. There is a special majesty associated with this name and a great dread of uttering it because it denotes God Himself, and not merely some aspect of our perception of Him. While the other names are common nouns which may also be used for created things (e.g., *"elohim"* for judges, *"adoni"* for "my master", etc.), the Tetragrammaton (*Havayah*) is applied exclusively to God.

Havayah denotes Eternal Being, existence, and is an abbreviated form of *hayah, hoveh, veyiheyeh,* which affirms that His existence embraces the total past, the present, and the infinite future. God is existence and the world is sustained only by its being an extension of His existence or, more correctly, it shares in His Being.[7] His existence is independent and not contingent. This means that the world is sustained by God, who "in His goodness, renews the creation every day, continually." [8] Thus, God is not only the Creator (*Elohim*) but also the Sustainer (*Havayah*).

15

In the High Holy day *piyut* (liturgical poem) *Imeru l'Elohim*, God is described as *sovel elyonim vetaḥtonim*, "He carries the upper and lower regions of the world [so to speak] on His shoulders." He can drop them if He wishes and the universe would return to nothingness. The existence of the world depends on His continuous association with it. To exist is to find oneself in the embrace of God, like a newly born baby carried in its mother's arms. It is crucial that the baby still be held and nursed: if dropped, it will die.

The Formulation of Maimonides

Maimonides began his *magnum opus*, the *Mishneh Torah*, with a formulation of the first Article of Faith. "The essential foundation and the pillar of all wisdom is to know that there is a First Being, *matzui rishon*, who bestowed existence on all that is; and all that exist in all realms draw their being from the real source of all existence" (Hil. Yesode Hatorah 1:1).[9]

It is strange that Maimonides avoided using the Biblical terms for creation, *bore*, *nivra*, and *beri'ah*, preferring the terms *matzui*, *mamtzi*, and *nimtza*. Why this evident predilection for contemporary philosophical terms instead of Biblical terminology? Apparently, Maimonides felt that *beri'ah* and its derivatives can be misleading; it could suggest only a "one-time" act of Divine creation, after which He detached Himself from the world. If this inference were made, all of Judaism, the Torah and *mitzvot*, would collapse! The word *matzui* or *mamtzi*, however, clearly states that God continues to watch, to tend, and to nurture the world, that its continued existence is contingent on His existence. Indeed, a combination of each first letter of the first four words of Maimonides' formulation, *Yesod Hayesodot*, *Ve'amud Haḥokhmot*, spells out the name *Havayah*, to emphasize the understanding of God as the Sustainer and not merely as the Creator.

16

The Name ADNY

The word *ADNY* denotes "lord," "master", and "owner," in a proprietary and juridical sense. It proclaims that God is the Lord of the manor, as in the verse, "The earth and all its fullness belong to the Lord, the entire world and its inhabitants" (Ps. 24:1).[10] To own property implies the right to restrict or to deny its use to others. This is what R. Yitzhak, as quoted in the opening sentence of Rashi's Torah commentary, stated: that the primary purpose of the creation chapter was to inform us that God is the *Adon,* the Master of the universe, and that the basis of the Jewish claim to the Holy Land is that its Owner gave it to them. "He created it and gave it to whom He pleased." R. Yitzhak insisted that *adnut* is implicit in the creation chapter, even though the name *Elohim* is used exclusively.

In juridical terms, God acquired ownership of the world through the *kinyan* of creation, an Halakhic principle of legal acquisition.[11] An artisan, given the raw materials from which to fashion a vessel, acquires ownership of the increase in its value which accrued through his craftsmanship. The raw materials belong to the original owner; the artisan owns the creative transformation which he superimposed upon the materials, only to the extent of the increase in its value. Once the artisan is paid for his work, the owner acquires full ownership over his object.

If this be so in the case of an artisan who works with raw materials belonging to someone else, how much more is it true in the case of the Divine Creator who created the *homer hiyuli,** the original raw materials, as well, and is therefore not only a *Yotzer,* artisan, but also a *Bore,* Creator.

---

* *Hyle* was described by ancient thinkers as a formless, primordial substance. See Chapter III.

Adam's Failure

We suggested earlier that the awareness of God as *Adon* might have deterred Adam from his sin. What precisely was his sin? In Christian literature, the *etz hada'at* (tree of knowledge) is considered a demonological tree whose mysterious fruit possessed an unnatural potency. Eating it transformed man's nature, causing his fall and corruption. *Ḥazal*, however, saw nothing unnatural in the tree. They suggest that it was an ordinary plant, the fruit of which was either grapes, figs, wheat or an *etrog* (Gen. R. 15).[12] If so, why was the first couple so adversely affected by such commonplace food?

The answer is that the prohibition was intended to teach Adam the concept of *adnut*, that God is not only the world's Creator and Sustainer, but also its Owner. *Vayetzav Hashem Elohim* was a restrictive command intended to teach man that all benefits and pleasures are gifts of God, who offers them selectively and conditionally. They are privileges that are granted, not prizes freely to be taken. Adam viewed the world as ownerless property, *hefker*. He accepted that God was the Creator and Sustainer; this was indisputable to him. But he was unwilling to concede that God had retained proprietary rights over His creation; he refused to recognize any "no trespassing" restrictions. Rather, Adam claimed for himself *carte blanche* rights to partake as he pleased.

This, therefore, was his sin, the crime of *gezelah*, robbery; he took that which was not his. *Adnut* insists that life and all its benefits stem from God and are granted only to the extent that we accept His will. We must be ready to surrender, to restrict our appetites, to control our fantasies. If we take possession contrary to His will, we are usurpers and thieves. The change in Adam's situation was due to his punishment, and not to the fruit of the tree.

Adam and Eve were only asked to refrain from eating the

fruits of one tree. "Of every tree of the garden you are free to eat; but as for the tree of knowledge of good and evil, you must not eat of it" (Gen. 2:16, 17).[13] In enticing Eve, the serpent (the evil inclination, *yetzer ha-rah*, B. Bat. 16a/b), however, exaggerated God's prohibition as extending to all trees: "You shall not eat of any tree of the garden" (*ibid.*, 3:1).[14] He demagogically intimated that God wants man to forsake the world, to eschew all pleasures, and to be continually bound by "do's" and "don'ts." He sought to arouse Eve's sense of autonomy and rebelliousness.

God, however, does not wish man to be ascetic; instead, vast areas of indulgence in life remain open for him. This explains why the verse prohibiting one tree is preceded by the emphasis that "of every tree of the garden you *may eat*." God's prohibitions are relatively minute and are meant solely to induce man to acknowledge His *adnut*, as the Owner and Master. The Torah regards man as both a natural and a spiritual being, and recognizes his need for pleasure. God wants him, however, not to allow his pleasures to become unbridled hedonism, with self-indulgence as the highest value. In abstaining from the fruit of "one tree," man acknowledges a relationship with, and an accountability to, Him.

The same concept applies to the laws of the Sabbath, with respect to which the Torah states: "Six days may you labor and do all your work, but the seventh day is the Sabbath of the Eternal, your God" (Ex. 20:9).[15] Here, too, the positive permitting of work on six days, during which man can accomplish all his needs and attain all his ambitions (*kol melakhtekha*) is emphasized, in contrast to the one day when labor is prohibited. In the dimension of time, God asks only one day in seven. Similar ratios are reflected in other *mitzvot* of the Torah.

Thievery is the Primary Sin

The pre-flood generation, *dor hamabbul*, we are told, "was

corrupt before God and the earth was filled with lawlessness [*hamas*]" (Gen. 6:11).[16] Our sages defined ḥamas as the sin of robbery, wrongful gains acquired through violence, *gezel* (Rashi). Why, we may ask, was the ultimate corruption of this generation defined as robbery? Were they not guilty of more heinous crimes like idolatry, murder, and gross immorality (Rashi, 6:11)? The very same question may be posed regarding the sinful city of Nineveh, which was judged as deserving destruction. After Jonah's preaching, the king exhorted the people to penitence: "Yea, let everyone turn away from his evil ways and from the *hamas* that is in their hands" (Jonah 3:8).[17] Once again, why was thievery singled out from amongst all their decadence?

Similarly, in the Yom Kippur *Ne'ilah* service, we implore God for forgiveness for all our iniquities, "that we may cease to engage in robbery [*oshek*]".[18] We do not undertake to cease eating *terefah*, worshiping idols, committing immorality, or any other type of sin. There are so many other sins—those enumerated in the *Al Het* confessional for instance—which could have been mentioned.

The answer is that all sinning involves thievery. When we indulge in what is forbidden, we are, in effect, taking that which is not ours. This concept may be even further extended. When we use our tongue to slander, we rightfully lose our right to use this organ henceforth. When our hands engage in wrongful deeds, our eyes in lasciviousness, our intelligence in deception, our free will in choosing evil, we, as a result, lose our further rights, *zekhuyot*, over these organs and faculties. "The soul is Yours and the body is Your work," we acknowledge in our penitential prayers.[19] In our daily morning blessings, we thank God for such gifts as eyesight, the ability to stand upright, to walk, to discern, to be free, to observe *mitzvot*. All that we presumptuously call "ours" is really "His." We may use these gifts conditionally, for the period of our lifetime, only with His concurrence and in accordance with His stipulations. When we sin, these *zekhuyot*, privileges, are forfeited and nullified. Their continued utilization is larceny. The great gift of *teshuvah* (repentance) is that it allows us to reacquire our rights over our lives, our faculties and, once again, to partake rightfully of life's gifts.

All sinning emanates from a denial of God's *adnut*, His right to restrict and to deny. Modern man, in particular, insists that he is free, that, indeed, all restrictions are repressions and do harm. *Adnut*, however, insists that man be humbled before God, that he recognize the Master who bestows all gifts. This is the basic rationale behind all the *berakhot* we recite before we partake of life's bounties.[20] Life is a gift and a privilege to be used only for holy ends. When we surrender our rights of un-inhibited indulgence, we, in effect, acknowledge a Higher Power who is Master over all.

When Abraham asked for a child and for the assurance of a national territory for his descendants, he understood that such gifts are bestowed by God. They are not to be taken freely but reverently to be beseeched. It was Abraham, therefore, who introduced the name *ADNY* and thereby enunciated the basic Jewish *hashkafah* of God as *Adon*.

הערות לפרק 1

1   כי לא יראני האדם וחי (שמות לג, כ).

2   א״ל הקב״ה למשה, שמי אתה מבקש לידע ? לפי מעשי אני נקרא (שמ״ר ג).

3   בראשית ברא אלהים (בראשית א, א).

4   ביום עשות הוי״ה אלהים ארץ ושמים (שם, ב, ד).

5   א״ר יוחנן משום ר״ש בן וחי; מיום שברא הקב״ה את העולם, לא היה אדם שקראו להקב״ה אדון עד שבא אברהם וקראו אדון שנאמר: ויאמר, אד—ני הוי״ה, במה אדע כי אירשנה (שם, טו, ח) (ברכות ז:); אד—ני הוי״ה, מה תתן לי ואנכי הולך ערירי (שם, טו, ב).

6   ראה רמב״ם, מורה נבוכים, א, סב.

7   הנמצא אשר הוא הנמצא, כלומר המחויב המציאות (שם, א, סג).

8   המחדש בטובו בכל יום תמיד מעשה בראשית (שחרית).

9 יסוד היסודות ועמוד החכמות: לידע, שיש שם מצוי ראשון והוא ממציא כל הנמצא וכל הנמצאים משמים וארץ ומה שביניהם, לא נמצאו אלא מאמתת המצאו (רמב״ם, הל׳ יסודי התורה א, א).

10 לה׳ הארץ ומלואה, תבל ויושבי בה (תהלים כד, א).

11 אומן קונה בשבח כלים (ב״ק צח:) (פ׳, אומן קונה את השבח בשנוי המעשה וכי מחזירו, הרי זה כמוכר את השבח שהיה שהיה לו).

12 מה היה אותו האילן שאכל ממנו אדם וחוה ? ר״מ אומר חטים היו . . . ר׳ יהודה בר אלעאי אמר, ענבים היו . . . ר׳ אבא אמר אתרוג היה . . . ר׳ יוסי אומר תאנים היו (ב״ר טו).

13 מכל עץ הגן אכל תאכל. ומעץ הדעת טוב ורע לא תאכל ממנו (בראשית ב, טז, יז).

14 אף כי אמר אלהים לא תאכלו מכל עץ הגן (בראשית ג, א).

15 ששת ימים תעבד ועשית כל מלאכתך ויום השביעי שבת לה׳ אלהיך (שמות כ, ט, י).

16 ותשחת הארץ לפני האלהים ותמלא הארץ חמס (בראשית ו, יא).

17 וישבו איש מדרכו הרעה, ומן החמס אשר בכפיהם (יונה ג, ח).

18 קץ ומחילה וסליחה על כל עונותינו למען נחדל מעושק ידנו (נעילה).

19 הנשמה לך והגוף פעלך (סליחות).

20 כל הנהנה מן העולם הזה בלא ברכה, כאלו גוזל להקב״ה (ברכות לה:).

CHAPTER II

IMITATING GOD—THE BASIS OF
JEWISH MORALITY

Some modern scholars claim that Judaism has no binding dogmas and that it is concerned solely with deeds. They regard Judaism as a purely rational and this-worldly faith which is unencumbered by a complex theology and is primarily humanistic in its purpose. This understanding, however, is simplistic and erroneous. We do have principles of Jewish faith, *ikkare hayahadut*, which are implicit in the Torah and have been formulated and codified in the Talmud and by later scholars.[1] In addition, the deeds prescribed by our faith are both ritualistic and humanistic.

The lifestyle of the religious Jew is based on certain underlying theological assumptions about God and His role in history. Clearly, the belief that He is the Creator and Sustainer of the universe, Who revealed His Law to Israel at Mt. Sinai, has profound practical implications for the Jew and for all humanity. That man is accountable to God for his deeds and that he is expected to realize a spiritual purpose in his life transform him from a highly developed animal into a transcendental being. Most certainly, then, Judaism does affirm basic faith principles.

Unlike many other faiths, however, Judaism does not regard these faith convictions as redemptive in and of themselves. Judaism is a *mitzvah*-oriented faith which insists that one's religious convictions be translated into virtuous deeds. Without the underpinnings of faith, there can be no motivation or rationale to live a life of religious observance. We are not content, however, to have faith confessions remain theoretical. Instead, they become moral challenges and exhortations to man. They express themselves through norms of human behavior and are endowed with practical significance, stimulating us either to do or to abstain, to engage or to withdraw. A faith conviction may be theologically or philosophically significant, but what is primary is the moral principle and practice that emerges from it.

Beyond the clearly prescribed legal precepts of the Torah there are vast areas in which one's moral duty is not precisely defined. Here, the basic guide of the Torah is to emulate Godly ways, *hitdamut la'El—imitatio Dei*. The Talmud states:

> Why does it say (Deut. 13:5): "One should walk after God"? Is it possible to walk after the Shekhinah? Is He not like a consuming fire (*ibid.*, 4:24)? Rather, it means that one should imitate His ways. As God clothed Adam and Eve (Gen. 3:21), so should we clothe the naked; as He visited the ailing (Rashi, Gen. 18:1), so should we visit the sick; as He comforted Isaac after Abraham's death (Rashi, Gen. 25:11), so should we comfort mourners; as He buried Moses (Deut. 34:6), so should we care for the dignity of the dead (Sotah 14a).[2]

Our conception of God is thus translated into a code of human behavior.

Maimonides clearly illustrates this point. He writes (Hil. Yesode Hatorah 7:1) that it is a fundamental principle of our faith to accept that God does speak to man through prophecy,[3] and he immediately converts this article of faith into a moral challenge: it is the ultimate duty of man to make himself worthy of prophecy, for God will not communicate with "trees and stones." He adds: "And prophecy will not be bestowed except upon one who possesses the very greatest wisdom, is of the highest ethical character . . . who is master of his impulses and emotions, and has broad and incisive understanding, etc." In his *Guide for the Perplexed* (2.32), the ideal of prophecy is even further developed. By describing the qualities which invite God's prophetic communication, Maimonides sets forth a human ideal and model towards which all should aspire. Thus, an article of faith becomes a moral exhortation.

The Creation Chapter as a Moral Lesson

The convertibility of faith principles into moral directives may be implicit in the Creation story of Genesis 1. Why does the Torah devote an entire chapter to the story of creation when, actually, all that emerges is a story which is unclear, incomplete, enigmatic, half-told, and half-concealed? The mystery of creation is thereby magnified, rather than dispelled. Even the chronology of creation as indicated in the text cannot be taken literally, as Rashi and others have indicated.[4]

Naḥmanides adds:

> The process of creation is a deep mystery, not to be under-
> stood from the verses, and it cannot truly be known except
> through the tradition going back to Moses, our teacher,
> who received it from the mouth of the Almighty, and those
> who know it are obligated to conceal it . . .[5] There is no
> great need of these narratives to inform us that God is the
> Creator . . . For people who believe in the Torah, it would
> suffice without these verses. They would believe in the
> general statement mentioned in the Decalogue, "for in
> six days God made heaven and earth, the sea and all that
> is in them, and rested on the seventh day," and the knowl-
> edge of the process of creation would remain with in-
> dividuals as a tradition from Moses, who received the law
> on Sinai together with the Oral Law.[6]

(In the opening sentence of Rashi's commentary on the Torah,

REFLECTIONS OF THE RAV

R. Yitzḥak is quoted as asking the same question. Rashi, however, answers it differently.)

Perhaps this elaborate emphasis in the Book of Genesis on God's creation was meant to be converted into a moral challenge to man, that as God created, so should man. The foundation of our morality is: "And you shall walk in His ways" (Deut. 28:9),[7] that we imitate God. Man, like God, is often faced with *tohu vavohu* (utter desolation) and he does not know where to begin. He doubts his ability to say *Yehi or* ("let there be light"). It seems that the world can never be illuminated, such is the prevailing gloom (*ḥoshekh*). Yet man is bidden by the principle of *imitatio Dei* to create, to be a *shutaf* (partner) in *Yetzirah*, fashioning form out of chaos. Of course, man does not create *ex nihilo*, as did God, though at times it seems to man that his task is as formidable as if it were *yesh me'ayin* (from absolute nothing).

Man must be creative in both the material (*eretz*) and the spiritual (*shamayim*) realms. There are diseases to conquer (*verapo yerape*, Ex. 21:19), rivers to control, miseries to extirpate (*vekhivshuha*, Gen. 1:28). Conquering and settling Eretz Yisrael, *kibbush veyishuv ha'aretz*, are also *mitzvot* of *yetzirah*. The Torah tells us that particular territories were assigned to each nation, not only to the Jews, for them to develop according to their creative genius, while Eretz Yisrael was assigned to the Jews (Deut. 32:8, 9).[8]

There is also the mandate to be creative in the spiritual realm. To build a yeshivah in inhospitable territory is a form of *Yehi or* ("Let there be light," Gen. 1:3). Indeed, education in fulfillment of "And you shall teach them diligently to your children" (Deut. 6:7)[9] is creativity *par excellence*. A formless, undirected child is transformed into a refined Torah scholar. An undisciplined child, without any identity, a *tohu vavohu*, is gradually changed into a spiritual personality. Introducing a child to the Biblical narratives about Abraham and Sarah, and later on to a Talmudic discourse such as *hazamah* and *hakḥashah* (dealing with the exposure of false witnesses) is an act of fashioning a soul, the highest level of *yetzirah*. This is similar to God's creation for He, too, is called *hamelammed Torah le'ammo Yisrael*, "Who teaches the Torah to His people Israel" (Morning Blessings). This is the spiritual dimension of parenthood, even as *peru urevu* (the commandment to bear children) is physical *yetzirah*.

Thus Genesis 1 challenges man to create, to transform wilderness into productive life; thereby, an article of faith becomes a moral principle.

The Midrash as a Moral Lesson

Our basic premise that faith concepts are convertible into moral principles may also be implicit in many Midrashim. For example, in *Bereshit Rabbah* 3:9, Rabbi Abbahu depicts God as not only creating (*beri'ah*), but also as recreating, rebuilding after destructions (*yetzirah*). Rabbi Abbahu taught the principle of multiple creations: "And there was evening and there was morning, the first day" (since the sun was not yet created, how could there be morning?). Says Rabbi Abbahu: This indicates a time arrangement prior to this [Biblical] creation; that God built [previous] worlds and destroyed them, built worlds and destroyed them, until He said, "This world pleases Me and the others did not please Me." [10] Apparently, regarding earlier worlds, we may paraphrase "And God saw all that He created and proclaimed them *not* good," a judgment which sufficed to make them disappear. Here we have God not only creating, as in the Biblical text, but also recreating, rebuilding after destructions.[11]

What does Rabbi Abbahu teach? Surely it makes no sense to ascribe to an omniscient God, the *En Sof* (Infinite), the need to experiment before achieving His ideal. God could immedi-

27

ately have created a *ki tov* world (worthy of His approval).
Only man needs experiment because of his difficulty in translating
mental conceptions into physical realities. Like Edison and other
scientists in their experiments, he tries various approaches before
he achieves satisfactory goals. This is the nature of the scientific
method; it cannot be otherwise because man is finite and imperfect. But this surely does not apply to God.

Rabbi Abbahu apparently wanted to teach the concept of
multiple creations, that our world came into being in various
stages. His description of the process, however, of God's dis-
pleasure with previous worlds and His final satisfaction with
this world was intended to provide man with a moral lesson
and was not to be understood literally. As God creates and
recreates (actually refashions, *yetzirah* not *beri'ah*), so too,
should man be ready to rebuild and reconstruct, even as previous
structures collapse. Thus, even a rabbinic concept of faith may
be translated into a norm of human behavior.

To build initially is difficult, but to rebuild is even more challenging. One can erect structures if one has the basic talent,
commitment, and raw materials, but to reconstruct after the destruction of previous achievements is most difficult. Energies, resources, sleepless nights, endless devotion painstakingly expended
are all gone to waste, uprooted as if by a hurricane. But we
are bidden to start over again with faith and resourcefulness,
as God did. Rebuilding a business after bankruptcy is much
harder than building it initially. The Torah clearly conveys this
point: "And if your brother becomes poor ... then you shall
uphold him" (Lev. 25.35). Rashi adds: "Do not forsake him
so that he falls down altogether, when it would be difficult
to raise him, but uphold him from the very moment when he
starts falling." [12] To restore a person after his collapse is most
difficult.

This is precisely what we are continually called upon to do
in Jewish history, to resist succumbing after total destructions

and instead continually to rebuild new worlds, even as God did. The State of Israel itself was erected out of the ashes of the Holocaust. The revival of Torah in Israel and America after its annihilation in Eastern Europe was an act of recreation. To the verse, "the sun rises and the sun sets" (Eccles. 1:5), the Midrash adds, "before the sun of this [settlement] sets, the sun of the other rises."[13] Our sages understood the recreative principle as applying not only to individuals but also to *worlds* and settlements of the Jewish people.

The Talmud tells us (Yev. 62b) that, after Rabbi Akiba's twenty-four thousand pupils died either in battle or through a plague in the brief period between Passover and Lag Ba'Omer, the world seemed desolate. All the energies, discipline, commitment, knowledge, and *hashkafah* which Rabbi Akiba had implanted in these pupils over many years were destroyed in a three-week period. A sense of total shock numbed all of Jewry at the loss of such vast intellectual and spiritual resources. It was a case of *tohu vavohu*. Rabbi Akiba, though then an old man, we are told, rebuilt Torah Jewry and restored the crown of Torah to its previous glory. We do not know precisely how he did it, but the fact that we today are still studying his teachings testifies that he imitated God, in the manner described by Rabbi Abbahu.[14]

This, then, is what the Torah requires of man: to act, to create and, where necessary, to recreate, even as did the Divine Creator.

הערות לפרק 2

1 סנהדרין צ.; ר' סעדיה גאון — "אמונות ודעות"; רבנו בחיי — "חובת הלבבות"; רמב"ם — "שלשה עשר עקרים"; ר' יהודה הלוי — "כוזרי".

2 אמר רבי חמא ברבי חנינא: מאי דכתיב, "אחרי ה' אלקיכם תלכו" (דברים יג, ה). — וכי אפשר לו לאדם להלך אחר שכינה ? והלא כבר נאמר "כי ה' אלהיך אש אוכלה הוא" (שם, ד, כד). אלא להלך אחר מדותיו של הקב"ה. מה הוא מלביש ערומים, דכתיב, "ויעש ה' אלהים לאדם ולאשתו כתנות עור וילבישם" (בראשית ג, כא), אף אתה הלבש ערומים. הקב"ה ביקר חולים דכתיב, "וירא

אליו ה' באלני ממרא" (שם, יח, א), אף אתה בקר חולים. הקב"ה ניחם אבלים,
דכתיב, "ויהי אחרי מות אברהם ויברך אלהים את יצחק בנו" (שם, כה, יא), אף
אתה נחם אבלים. הקב"ה קבר מתים דכתיב, "ויקבר אותו בגי" (דברים לד, ו),
אף אתה קבור מתים (סוטה יד.).

3 מיסודי הדת לידע שהאל מנבא את בני האדם. ואין הנבואה חלה אלא על חכם
גדול בחכמה, גבור במדותיו, ולא יהא יצרו מתגבר עליו בדבר בעולם, אלא
הוא מתגבר בדעתו על יצרו תמיד. והוא בעל דעה רחבה נכונה עד מאד. וכו'
(רמב"ם, הל' יסודי התורה ז, א).

4 ולא בא המקרא להורות סדר הבריאה לומר: שאלו קדמו. שאם בא להורות כך,
היה לו לכתוב, "בראשונה ברא את השמים" וכו' (רש"י, בראשית א, א).

5 חגיגה יא:

6 שמעשה בראשית סוד עמוק, אינו מובן מן המקראות, ולא יוודע על בוריו אלא
מפי הקבלה עד משה רבנו מפי הגבורה, ויודעיו חייבין להסתיר אותו . . . לכך
אמר רבי יצחק שאין להתחלת התורה צורך בבראשית ברא. והספור במה שנברא
ביום ראשון ומה נעשה ביום שני ושאר הימים, והאריכות ביצירת אדם וחוה,
וחטאם ועונשם, וספור גן עדן וגרוש אדם ממנו, כי כל זה לא יובן בינה שלימה
מן הכתובים וכל שכן ספור המבול והפלגה, שאין הצורך בהם גדול. ויספיק
לאנשי התורה, בלעדי הכתובים האלה, ויאמינו בכלל הנזכר להם בעשרת
הדברות, "כי ששת ימים עשה ה' את השמים ואת הארץ את הים ואת כל אשר
בם וינח ביום השביעי", ותשאר הידיעה ליחידים שבהם הלכה למשה מסיני עם
התורה שבעל פה (רמב"ן, בראשית א, א).

7 והלכת בדרכיו (דברים כח, ט).

8 בהנחל עליון גוים, בהפרידו בני אדם, יצב גבלות עמים, למספר בני ישראל. כי
חלק ה' עמו, יעקב חבל נחלתו (שם, לב, ח, ט).

9 ושננתם לבניך (שם, ו, ז).

10 אמר ר' יהודה ב"ר סימנו: יהי ערב אין כאן כתוב, אלא ויהי ערב. מכאן שהיה
סדר זמנים קודם לכן. אמר ר' אבהו: מלמד שהיה בורא עולמות ומחריבן עד
שברא את אלו. אמר, דין הניין לי, יתהון לא הניין לי (ב"ר ג); ראה פ' ר' אבהו
על פסוק "ואלה המשפטים" (שמות רבה ל).

A kabbalistic interpretation of this Midrash may be found in G.G. 11
Scholem, *Major Trends in Jewish Mysticism* (Schocken House, N.Y.,
1941), p. 266.

12 וכי ימוך אחיך ומטה ידו עמך, והחזקת בו (ויקרא כה, לה). רש"י — אל
תניחהו שירד ויפול ויהיה קשה להקימו, אלא חזקהו משעת מוטת היד וכו'.

13 וזרח השמש ובא השמש (קהלת א, ה) — עד שלא השקיע שמשו של [זו], הזריח
שמשו [של זו] (קהלת רבתי א, י).

14 שנים עשר אלף זוגים תלמידים היו לו לרבי עקיבא . . . וכולן מתו בפרק אחד,
מפני שלא נהגו כבוד זה לזה והיה העולם שמם עד שבא רבי עקיבא אצל
רבותינו שבדרום ושנאה להם ר"מ ור' יהודה ור' יוסי ורבי שמעון ורבי אלעזר בן
שמוע והם הם העמידו תורה אותה שעה (יבמות סב:).

30

CHAPTER III

THE WORLD IS NOT FORSAKEN

There are moments in history and in the life of the individual when it seems as if God has relinquished all concern with the course of human affairs. The Torah calls this state *Hester Panim* (lit. "hiding the face") and describes such periods as fraught with terrors. Man feels forlorn and helpless in the face of life's fearful possibilities. Actually, God never withdraws from His creation. All existence depends on His continued association. What, then, does *Hester Panim* mean? We will attempt to explain it in the context of the two stages of Divine creation, as outlined by Naḥmanides.

Boré and Yotzer

A *boré* is one who creates *yesh me'ayin*, something out of nothing. A *yotzer*, in contrast, fashions *yesh miyesh*, something out of something else. Only God can be a *Boré* (Creator); He miraculously brought the world into being, by creation *ex nihilo*, out of nothing. Man can never be a creator; he can only be a *yotzer*. He must have the material before he can fashion his product.

Naḥmanides described the process of the creation of the world as follows:

> We have no expression in the sacred language for bringing forth something out of nothing except the word *bara*. What-

31

ever exists [today] under and above the sun was not made from nothing at the outset. Initially, God brought forth from total and absolute nothingness a very thin substance which was intangible. This substance, which the Greeks called *hyle* (matter), possessed the potentiality to be fashioned into various forms (to be shaped into our reality). The *hyle* was created by God [as a *Boré*].) After the *hyle*, God no longer created; He now fashioned (as a *Yotzer*) everything from it into a finished condition.[1]

When a potter shapes a vase out of clay, he is not really creating; he is fashioning. He is giving form to amorphous clay which existed before he started his work. Though he be a gifted craftsman, his product cannot exceed the potentialities inherent in the clay. The size of the vase cannot be larger than the amount of clay will allow; its artistic pattern will be affected by the quality of the raw material. All these external considerations limit the craftsman's options. Moreover, there need not be any continuing relationship between the potter and his vase. Upon completion, it may be sold or given away, with the artisan passing on to other tasks. This is the *modus operandi* of the *yotzer* who produces one object from another.

God's initial act, however, was *creatio ex nihilo*, that of a *Boré*. The liturgical hymn *Adon Olam* proclaims, "Lord of the world, He reigned alone, while yet the universe was naught." [2] This affirms that before God created the world, there was only God and nothing else. God is unlike a human artisan who can only produce from raw materials. The word *ayin*, as in *yesh me'ayin*, is somewhat misleading. There really was no *ayin*, no emptiness, before creation. There was only a *yesh*, God, Who, the Zohar says, "filled the entire universe." [3] We use the word *ayin* because there is no other way of conveying the idea that there was no preexistent, primordial matter before creation.

Naḥmanides, who described the world as coming into being

in two stages, insisted that the initial *hyle* itself was created by God. This *hyle* was described by ancient thinkers as a formless and chaotic substance and may be conceived, in modern terms, as either a type of energy or loosely floating atoms. At this point the *beri'ah* ended. Thereafter, God fashioned the world into the reality we know today; this was the *yetzirah* described in Gen. 1:2 ff.

The Secular World Dissents

The ancient Greek philosopher Plato refused to accept the possibility that physical matter, the *hyle*, could be created by a God Who is spiritual. Plato, therefore, insisted that God could be only a *Yotzer*, a Fashioner, not a *Boré*, a Creator. Aristotle also believed that matter existed coeternally with God.

The Torah principle, however, as taught to us by tradition and as formulated by Maimonides, Naḥmanides, Yehudah Halevi and others, affirms that God created the world *yesh me'ayin* and that no matter, even *hyle*, existed previously. Since this creation emanated from God, His association with it is intimate and continuous and it reflects aspects of His holiness. Indeed, the world could not endure for an instant without His support, for its continued existence shares in His existence.[4]

The Midrash (Gen. R. 1) records a debate between an ancient philosopher and one of our Sages on this very subject. The philosopher challenged Rabban Gamliel: "Your God was only a great fashioner (not a Creator). He had raw materials which helped Him (hence there was no *ex nihilo* creation)." "What were these [materials]?" the Rabbi asked. He replied, *"tohu* (unfoimed), *vavohu* (void), *ḥoshekh* (darkness), *mayim* (water), *ruaḥ* (wind), and *tehomot* (deep) [which are mentioned in Gen. 1:2 prior to God's first declaration, "Let there be ..."]." The Rabbi retorted angrily, "With each of these, the word *beri'ah* is found" (in various Scriptural verses, cited

33

by the Midrash, signifying that these essences were also created *ex nihilo* and were not preexistent).[5]

We have not progressed much since ancient days in persuading the secular world of *yesh me'ayin*. Despite the compelling evidence of the "big bang" theory, which alone seems logically defensible, scientists still insist that particles of matter always existed. In actual fact, the tools of science are incapable of deciphering the nature of creation. All of science deals with matter and energy. These resulted from creation and did not exist beforehand. Actually, creation is a metaphysical, not a scientific, problem.[6]

And so the Torah continues to find itself at loggerheads with most of the secular world with respect to *yesh me'ayin*.

Religiously, it matters greatly whether or not we believe in *yesh me'ayin*. If all matter was created by God, then He is Omnipotent, Master of the universe which He directs in accordance with His will and which is responsive to His purpose. God can perform miracles, reveal Himself at Mt. Sinai, and direct history towards a Messianic end. Creation is also an assurance of His enduring involvement with the world and with man, whose very existence depends on His continuous support. *Yesh miyesh,* however, posits a dualism, the eternal existence of something besides God, which is governed by its own inner laws and nature and over which God may have only limited control. His relationship to such a universe would be like a potter to his vase. Such a finite God is not the God of Israel.

Hester Panim and Middat Hadin

We cited the view of Naḥmanides that the world had come into being in two stages, first the *beri'ah* from which the amorphous *tohu vavohu* (*hyle*), emerged; subsequently, the *yetzirah,* the fashioning of the world into the stable shapes and patterns that we know today. This understanding may help us explain the distinction between two types of Divine punishment, *Hester Panim* and *Middat Hadin,* particularly as they apply to the Holocaust and to the State of Israel.

In Deut. 31:17, the Torah describes the ultimate punishment of *Hester Panim*:

> Then My anger will flare up against them in that day and I will abandon them and *hide My face from them,* and they shall be devoured and many evils and distress shall befall them; so that they will say in that day, "Are not these evils come upon us, because our God is not in our midst?" [7]

Hester Panim involves a temporary abandonment of the world, a suspension of His active surveillance, as Rashi clearly explains, "as though I do not see their distress."

But here we face a difficulty. According to Maimonides, the world exists only because it shares in God's existence; if He were to withdraw His support or approval, the world would instantaneously recede into nothingness. The world is not self-sustained but is contingent on His continued sharing of His existence.[8] Yehudah Halevi (Kuzari 3:11) is even more explicit:

> Creation is unlike other formed objects. When a craftsman, for example, makes a mill, he departs from it upon completion because the mill can function without him. But the Holy One, blessed be He, created limbs and invested therein energies and nurtures them continually without respite. And if He were to remove His solicitude and guidance only for one instant, the whole world would be lost.

If this be so, *Hester Panim* should cause the world to cease to exist. How do we reconcile *Hester Panim* with God as the necessary Sustainer of all existence?

God's Involvement and Withdrawal

There are two levels of Divine punishment, *Middat Hadin* and *Hester Panim*. The former involves measure for measure punishment, commensurate with one's sins. It does not signify God's withdrawal; on the contrary, it reflects His involvement and concern, intended to stimulate *teshuvah* (repentance). *Middat Hadin*, therefore, never inflicts annihilation or total extermination, *kelayah*.

Hester Panim, however, is a temporary suspension of God's active surveillance. He turns His back, so to speak, on events and leaves matters to chance. Under such circumstances, the usual vulnerability of the Jew invites the threat of total extermination. This is strikingly conveyed by the words *vehayah le'ekhol*, "they shall be devoured." What ensues is not circumscribed by considerations of measure for measure, and the magnitude and severity can be devastating. Without God's governing control, events may simply go berserk.

Hester Panim, the Torah indicates, is related to Israel's waywardness and may be regarded as an ultimate punishment. It is terrifying because it signifies rejection. A child can bear a father's reprimand or punishment stoically, but to be totally ignored and treated as *persona non grata* in one's own home is a frightening experience.

Hester Panim may be explained as a temporary and partial reversion of the world to its pre-*yetzirah* state when *tohu vavohu* (*hyle*) prevailed, a period without physical patterns, a state of chaotic sub-existence. God's moral law, as we know it, was similarly inoperative and inapplicable in a setting so unformed and unstable. *Hester Panim* is not a rejection of the original *beri'ah*; this would destroy the world. Instead, it is the undoing of the restraints and controls of *yetzirah* while God still remains the Sustainer of creation. With *teshuvah*, the Torah assures us, the *yetzirah* state of God's close surveillance can be restored.

The Asarah Haruge Malkhut and the Holocaust

The *Asarah Haruge Malkhut* were victims of *Middat Hadin*, not *Hester Panim*. It was a measured *onesh*, but it indicated God's involvement, *gezerah hi milefanai*. It is related in the *Eleh Ezkerah* piyyut of the Yom Kippur *Musaph* service that, when the angels protested against the torturing to death of the Sages, a heavenly voice replied: "If I hear further protest, I will force the world to revert to water. I will reduce the world to *tohu vavohu.*" [9] God threatened the *tohu vavohu* of *Hester Panim* if the *Middat Hadin* of controlled retribution were not accepted.

The Holocaust, in contrast, was *Hester Panim*. We cannot explain the Holocaust but we can, at least, classify it theologically, characterize it, even if we have no answer to the question, "why?" The unbounded horrors represented the *tohu vavohu* anarchy of the pre-*yetzirah* state. This is how the world appears when God's moderating surveillance is suspended. The State of Israel, however, reflects God's return to active providence, the termination of *Hester Panim*.

That Israel is being subjected to severe trials in its formative years does not negate the miraculous manifestations of Divine favor which have been showered upon the State. Clearly, this is *Middat Hadin*, not *Hester Panim*. Jewish history has always moved ahead in a circuitous and indirect path. When the Israelites left Egypt, we are told, "God did not lead them by way of the land of the Philistines, although it was nearer" (Ex. 13:17).[10] Nevertheless, it was God who led them and they eventually did reach the Promised Land.

The Psalmist vividly captures the world's dependence on God's closeness with the words: "[when] You hide Your face, they vanish: You withdraw their breath, they perish and return to the dust. [But when] You send forth Your spirit, they are created; and You renew the face of the earth" (104:29, 30).[11]

הערות לפרק 3

1 הקב"ה ברא כל הנבראים מאפיסה מוחלטת ואין אצלנו בלשון הקדש בהוצאת
היש מאין אלא לשון ברא ואין כל הנעשה תחת השמש או למעלה הווה מן האין
התחלה ראשונה, אבל הוציא מן האפס הגמור המוחלט יסוד דק מאד, אין בו
ממש אבל הוא כח ממציא מוכן לקבל הצורה ולצאת מן הכח אל הפועל והוא
החומר הראשון נקרא ליונים היולי, ואחר ההיולי, לא ברא דבר אבל יצר ועשה,
כי ממנו המציא הכל והלביש הצורות ותקן אותם (רמב"ן, בראשית א, א).

2 אדון עולם אשר מלך בטרם כל יציר נברא (פיוט).

3 איהו ממלא כל עלמין (זוהר פ' פנחס).

4 המחדש בטובו בכל יום תמיד מעשה בראשית.

5 פילוסופוס אחד שאל את רבן גמליאל. א"ל, צייר גדול הוא אלוהיכם. אלא שמצא
סממנים טובים (מיני חומר קדום) שסייעו אותו (והעולם לא נברא באין גמור).
א"ל, ומה הם ? א"ל, תוהו, ובוהו וחושך ורוח ומים ותהומות. א"ל, תיפח רוחיה
דההוא גברא ! כולהון כתיב בהן בריאה (ב"ר א).

6 Recent astronomical evidence has considerably altered science's traditional resistance to creation *ex nihilo*. Dr. Robert Jastrow writes:
"Adverse evidence has led to the abandonment of the steady-state
theory by nearly everyone, leaving the big-bang theory exposed as
the only adequate explanation of the facts... All these lines of evidence point to the fact that the universe had a beginning. A few
scientists dared to ask, 'What came before the beginning?' Edmund
Whittaker, a British physicist, wrote a book on religion and the new
astronomy called 'The Beginning And The End' in which he said,
'There is no ground for supposing that matter and energy existed
before and were suddenly galvanized into action. For what could
distinguish that moment from other moments in eternity? It is simpler
to postulate creation *ex nihilo*, Divine will constituting nature from
nothing'. Some even bolder asked, 'Who was the Prime Mover?' The
British theorist, Edward Milne, wrote a mathematical treatise on re-
lativity that concluded by saying, 'As to the first cause of the Universe,
in the context of expansion, that is left to the reader to insert, but our
picture is incomplete without HIM'... The world had a beginning
under conditions in which the known laws of physics are not valid
and as a product of forces or circumstances we cannot discover...
Science cannot answer these questions because, according to astro-
nomers, in the first moments of its existence the universe was com-
pressed to an extraordinary degree and consumed by the heat of fire
beyond human imagination. The shock of that impact must have
destroyed every particle of evidence that could have yielded a clue

to the cause of the great explosion ... The scientist's pursuit of the
past ends in the moment of creation"

(R. Jastrow [Director of Nasa's Goddard Institute for Space
Studies; author of *Until the Sun Dies*]: *New York Times Magazine*,
June 25, 1978).

7 וחרה אפי בו ביום ההוא, ועזבתים, והסתרתי פני מהם והיה לאכל, ומצאהו רעות
רבות וצרות, ואמר ביום ההוא הלא על כי אין אלהי בקרבי, מצאוני הרעות
האלה (דברים לא, יז); רש"י — "והסתרתי פני" — כמו שאיני רואה בצרתם.

8 ואם יעלה על הדעת שהוא אינו מצוי, אין דבר אחד יכול להמצאות (פ' ולא
יוכלו להתקיים אף רגע בלעדיו) (רמב"ם, הל' יסחדי התורה א, ב).

9 ענתה בת קול משמים. אם אשמע קול אחר, אהפוך את העולם למים, לתוהו ובוהו
אשית הדומים. גזירה היא מלפני. קבלוהו (פיוט, אלה אזכרה).

10 ויהי בשלח פרעה את העם ולא נחם אלהים דרך ארץ פלשתים, כי קרוב הוא
(שמות יג, יז).

11 תסתיר פניך יבהלון, תסף רוחם יגועון. ואל עפרם ישובון. תשלח רוחך, יבראון,
ותחדש פני האדמה (תהלים קד, כט, ל).

CHAPTER IV

MAN IS VULNERABLE

Nature is governed by immutable physical laws which God ordained at the time of creation. These laws are discovered through scientific research. Nature always conforms to these laws; they are universally uniform. In all of creation, however, man is unique; only he has an intellect and free will. Though he was given a Divine Law that is to govern his behavior, man has also been granted the capacity to choose and, if he wishes, to disobey God's commandments.

Maimonides writes that:

> ... the human species had become unique in the world—there being no other species like it in this respect, namely, that man, of himself and by the exercise of his own intelligence and reason, knows what is good and what is evil and there is none who can prevent him from doing that which is good or that which is evil ... Let not the notion, expressed by the foolish gentiles and most of the senseless among Israelites, pass through your mind that, at the beginning of a person's existence, the Almighty decrees that he is to be either righteous or wicked ... wise or foolish, niggardly or generous, and so with all other qualities ... There is no one that coerces him or decrees what he is to do ... Accordingly, it follows that it is the sinner who has inflicted injury on himself; and he should

therefore weep for and bewail what he has done to his soul . . . it behooves us to return in a spirit of repentance . . . for we have the power to do so (Hil. Teshuvah 5:1, 2).[1]

Even as we emphasize man's free will, we are also aware that so much of what happens in life is not of man's making. He does not choose the family into which he is born and reared nor the society whose values will have such an impact upon him. He makes choices, yet major aspects of his life seem to be governed by capricious, chance events and circumstances beyond his control. He is a vulnerable creature whose serenity may suddenly be jarred by overpowering temptations, peculiar turns of events, unexpected political coups, an economic collapse, a terminal illness, or traumatic shocks. The Book of Kohelet portrays this unnerving uncertainty of man's life in these words: "For man also knows not his time; as the fishes that are taken in an evil net, even so are the sons of man snared in an evil time when it falls suddenly upon them" (Eccles. 9:12).[2] The key word above, *pitom* ("suddenly"), characterizes the vulnerability of man to events which befall him and which are not of his choosing.

This tension between man as chooser and man as victim of circumstances affects him in many ways. It is the basis of his plea for forgiveness on Yom Kippur for, otherwise, why should God give him a second chance? It is also an inducement to him to be humble, since fortune is fickle and can suddenly change. Finally, the uncertainty of man's life is the motivation for many Biblical precepts and Rabbinic enactments and is the primary motive for prayer, as man seeks assurance and sustenance from the Almighty.

Why Does God Forgive Sinners?

How does God relate Himself to the sinner who has knowingly defied the *mitzvot* of the Torah but now earnestly regrets his

41

rebelliousness? Judaism teaches the doctrine of *teshuvah*, repentance, whereby the sinner is granted forgiveness and the chance to rebuild his life on a higher spiritual plane. This is an act of *hesed*, lovingkindness, on the part of God, who seeks not man's punishment but his rehabilitation. Yom Kippur is particularly propitious for the achievement of atonement, especially for grievous sins.[3] In the days of the Temple, a dramatic ritual prescribed by the Torah, called the *Avodah*, constituted the climactic moment of the Yom Kippur day.

To the uninformed the *Avodah* must have appeared a very strange ritual. The Talmud classified it as a *hukkah*, a Divine imperative, which the Jew is bidden to observe, even though it defies his human comprehension.[4] On the other hand, multitudes of worshippers filling the Temple courts were deeply stirred by this ritual. It reflected their state of mind and their desperate yearning for forgiveness. Accordingly, we will suggest an explanation of the *Avodah*, in terms of its impact on the participants, by contrasting the awesome observance of Yom Kippur with the joyful celebration of Purim, as prescribed by Rabbinic enactment.

The Yom Kippur Avodah

For the Yom Kippur sacrificial Temple service (*Avodah*) two male goats were required. "And Aaron shall place lots upon the two goats; one marked for the Eternal and the other marked for Azazel"[5] (Lev. 16:8). The word *Azazel* is defined by the Gemara (Yoma 67b), the Septuagint, and Rashi as a precipitous and flinty rock, a towering peak, from which the goat was hurled to its destruction.[6] The goat marked for *Azazel* means, then, "the one that is sent away, dismissed, or entirely removed." The Talmud elaborates: "The two male goats for Yom Kippur are required to be alike in appearance, in size, and in value and were to have been bought at the same time"

(Mishnah, Yoma 6, 1; Gemara, 62a).[7] Though they resembled each other in every respect like identical twins, their destinies were antithetically dissimilar; one was "unto the Lord" (*Lashem*) and was sacrificed on the altar, the other was sent away to Azazel.

How were their destinies decided? Rashi describes the ceremonious casting of lots:

> He placed one goat at his right and the other at his left. He then put both his hands into an urn and took one lot in his right hand and the other in his left. These he placed on them (one on each of them). The goat upon which fell the lot bearing the inscription *"Lashem"* was for the Lord and that bearing "for Azazel" was later sent forth to Azazel (Rashi, Lev. 16:8).[8]

Analogy to Purim

The *Ba'ale Hakabbalah* (Kabbalah exponents) discovered mystical associations between *Purim* and *Yom Kippurim*, the only difference between the two in the Hebrew spelling being the initial *kaf* in *Kippurim*. *Yom Kippurim*, then, would signify "a day like Purim." A strange association! To suggest that Yom Kippur is like Purim, to compare the boisterous Purim to the awesome Yom Kippur, a raucous celebration to a solemn observance! In what way, then, does Yom Kippur resemble Purim?

The Dual Character of Purim

We usually think of Purim in terms of indulgence and merry-making, to the point of forgetfulness and the dulling of the senses. Actually, Purim is also a day of introspection and prayerful meditation. The Megillah is both a Book of Thanksgiving and a Book of Distress and Petition. The narrative relates two stories, of a people in a terrifying predicament and also of their great exhilaration at their sudden deliverance.

Since it is impossible to juxtapose contradictory moods into one day, our Sages instituted the Fast of Esther for the thirteenth of Adar in anticipation of Purim. They advanced the supplication aspect of Purim to the preceding day, when *selihot* (penitential prayers) and *Avinu Malkenu* ("Our Father, Our King, we have sinned before Thee") are recited and a mood of solemn penitence prevails. The Fast of Esther and Purim are integrally connected—unlike Passover and *Ta'anit Bekhorim* (Fast of the First Born), where the latter does not form part of the festival and is an extraneous addendum. The Fast of Esther, however, is a genuine Purim day; it reflects the foreboding fear and prayer of the Jews on the thirteenth of Adar as they gave battle to their enemies. Purim day itself celebrates the victory which followed, the sudden miraculous salvation of the people. The joining of a fast day and a feast day bespeaks the dual character of Purim.

Perhaps the feature common to both Purim and Yom Kippur is that aspect of Purim which is a call for Divine compassion and intercession, a mood of petition arising out of great distress. While the Fast of Esther reflects the terror of the threatening physical extinction of the people, the prayerful mood of Yom Kippur emerges out of a sense of spiritual anxiety and the desperate need for reconciliation with God.

Casting of Lots Signifies Uncertainty

Purim and Yom Kippur are also alike in another respect. Both involve the casting of lots (*goral*), a characteristic of games of chance. As for the Purim *goral*, it determined the date chosen by Haman for the destruction of the Jews (Esther 3:7, 9:24, 26). Indeed, the very name *Purim* means "lots." What, we may ask, is so significant about the method that Haman employed to choose a date? Why should the holiday itself be so named? It seems only a tangential and insignificant detail of the Purim story.

The Megillah is a book of contradictions. It is filled with events that are unreasonable, even absurd, coincidental, pure chance. At one moment the Jews live in security in Persia; at the next, they face destruction. Mordecai is threatened with execution; then, suddenly, he is the Prime Minister. Irrational events and moods transform fear into festivity; and entire situations are suddenly reversed. Purim, therefore, epitomizes the instability, uncertainty, and vulnerability which characterize human life generally but particularly govern the destiny of the Jews. Thus, the name *Purim* (*goral*) expresses the erratic capriciousness of events. It alerts the Jew to the sudden turns of fortune, lurking dangers, the fickleness of life, even as the *goral* itself seems to operate through blind chance.

Theologically, God forgives man's sinfulness precisely because He acknowledges human vulnerability to changing fortunes, pressing circumstances, and the intrusion of the unexpected. Otherwise, sinful man would always stand condemned before his Maker. As Eliphaz said to Job, "Can mortal man be just before God; can a man be pure before his Maker?" (Job 4:17).[9] Similarly, we read, "If You, O Lord, should note iniquities, O Lord, who shall remain standing?" (Ps. 130:3).[10] The mitigation of His judgment is due to God's recognition that man is subject to pressures and temptations, and is gullible, easily persuaded. Man can be brainwashed by a society which is intellectually agnostic, by the lure of intoxicating pleasures and by the appeal of political and social ideologies which disguise themselves as redemptive (liberating). Such was the overpowering appeal of communism to many idealists, who saw in it the messianic utopia for mankind.

One individual may be saintly because he was reared in

noble surroundings; another succumbs to evil because his home background lacked moral instruction and inspiration. The two may be as alike as twins, with similar dispositions, but the difference in their environments has affected their personalities. Should all sinners, then, be deemed equally guilty? Is not much of man's waywardness due to his susceptibility to external pressures? He finds himself almost overwhelmed by situations not of his own making, and by chance circumstances which propel him in various directions. It is because of this that man can stand before the Heavenly Bar of Justice, hoping for compassion and forgiveness. Despite his free will and his accountability for his deeds, man enters his plea before the Almighty, claiming that he is not the author and designer of the worldly pressures that were too powerful for him to resist. These subverting temptations were thrust upon him by *goral* circumstances.

The Goral Significance of the Avodah

The two male goats were identical, as we previously explained, but their fates led them in opposite directions, as determined by chance (*goral*) decisions, entirely beyond their control. The casting of lots decreed which was to go *Lashem*, to be sacrificed within the Temple, and which to *Azazel*, to be cast out of the camp of Israel, ignominiously to be destroyed. The secret of atonement is thus indicated in the ceremonious casting of the lots. It reflects the basis for the penitent's claim to forgiveness, that his moral directions were similarly influenced by forces beyond his control, that his sinning was not entirely a free and voluntary choice. Only the Almighty can evaluate the extent of human culpability in situations which are not entirely of man's making. Only God knows to what extent a man was a free agent in making his decisions. The *Avodah* is thus a psychodramatic representation of the penitent's state of mind and his emotional need. Only by entering such a plea can man be declared "not guilty."

Yom Kippur is in this respect like Purim, both involving a *goral*. The compelling intrusion of the unknown and irrational is basic to man's existential condition and it is precisely this weakness which qualifies him to receive God's compassionate forgiveness on Yom Kippur.

Awareness of Uncertainty Leads to Humility

Man's susceptibility to accidental turns of fortune is not necessarily a tragic condition. It can also be the source of ethical virtues and nobility of human character. An awareness of one's vulnerability induces humility, which dispels arrogance and pride. We become aware of the instability of our condition. Maimonides regarded humility as the highest ethical quality of man. Though he consistently counseled the golden mean, *shevil hazahav*, with respect to other human characteristics, he suspended this balance of moderation when speaking of humility, citing the dictum in *Avot* 4:4, "be humble exceedingly" [11] (Hil. De'ot 2:3).

How is this humility achieved and why should one seek to be self-effacing, especially in the case of people who have obviously succeeded where others have failed? How honest can the profession or practice of such humility be? Why does a successful man not have a right to pride? The answer is that personal triumph and success lead to arrogance, aggressiveness, and ethical insensitivity. But the awareness of one's vulnerablity, the knowledge that fortune is fickle, that there ever lurks a hovering threat which can transform our condition —these considerations induce us to be humble and enhance our ethical character. Thus, from an ethical standpoint, vulnerability can cleanse, purge, and ennoble man; it is a spur towards better conduct.

There Are No Accidents

We have spoken of an irrational *goral*, random events in nature and human life. This can easily be misunderstood. Actually, Judaism rejects any belief in a deterministic *mazal* or in a blind *goral*. We do not believe in fate as did the Greeks, who saw everything affected by absurd, unalterable, and ruthless decrees which emanated from the remote unknown. Such fate often clashes with the yearnings of man and crushes his hopes and aspirations, irrespective of his ethical behavior. This, to the Greeks, was the source of human tragedy. Man becomes a helpless pawn in the hands of inexorable forces which cannot be thwarted, even by the gods.

Judaism, even as it knew and tried to comprehend catastrophic events which cruelly destroy man's dreams and hopes, could not accept the existence of the ultimately irrational in human life. Events which we label as accidents belong to a higher Divine order into which man has not been initiated. Not decrees of fate, but rather reasons beyond our comprehension, operate in such instances. We have been granted the opportunity of gaining insights and of accumulating scientific knowledge about the regular course of events and physical nature, but we are excluded from the realm of *goral* understanding. The relationship between the individual and his environment eludes our grasp. To God there are no accidents, though they often appear so to us. Essentially, this is the reply which God gave to Job, who sought to reconcile his painful plight with his faith in God's justice. There is no deterministic fate; all operates on a transcendental plane which is beyond the grasp of man's finite mind.

Vulnerability in Halakhah

There are numerous religious laws, *halakhot*, which seek to minimize the dangers to life. For example, "When you build a new house, you shall make a parapet for your roof, so that you do not cause blood to be shed, if any man fall therefrom" (Deut. 22:8).[12] The Talmud extends this regulation to include all uncovered pits and other obstacles which can cause accidental injury to others. Man's vulnerability also extends into the spiritual realm, where he is continually susceptible to subversion. In areas of religious observance our Sages prescribed, "And make a [protective] hedge for the Torah" (Avot 1:1),[13] thus indicating that regulatory "fences," precautionary restrictions, be enacted around basic religious laws because man's attention is often distracted by temptation.

According to Ḥazal, the primary motivation for prayer is derived from man's feeling of *tzarah*, distress or desperation, and of *tzorekh*, need.[14] Abraham and Isaac prayed for children (Gen. 15:2, 25:31); Jacob prayed for protection from his brother Esau (*ibid.*, 32:11 ff); Moses prayed for Miriam's restoration to health (Num. 12:13). The fragile state of one's condition is a stimulant to prayer. Our *Amidah* is filled primarily with petitions reflecting life's menacing uncertainties. Even if one is rich, one prays for material sustenance, *parnassah*; even if one enjoys robust health, one pleads for healing *refu'ah*. Why? The answer is that man is vulnerable and his present blessings may be transformed a few moments later. Complacent satisfaction about one's good fortune is unrealistic; there lurks in the shadows the possibility of sudden reversal. "In the evening one retires with tears, but joy comes in the morning" (Ps. 30:6),[15] and the reverse is equally possible. There can be no wholehearted praise and thanksgiving, *shevaḥ vehodayah*, without an awareness that we may suddenly be reduced to petition, *teḥinah*. There can be no sense of need, *tzorekh*, no matter how desperate one's plight, without *shevaḥ vehodayah* for God's blessings and our faith in His eventual redemption.

The existential vulnerability of man, we have shown, is the theological foundation of repentance and atonement, as expressed through the *Avodah* of Yom Kippur. It also induces

49

humility and prayerfulness. This is what our Sages meant when they declared: "Everything is in the hand of Heaven, but man still possesses moral freedom" (Ber. 33b).[16] It is only in the larger realm of *goral* circumstances, which belong to a Divine order into which man has not been initiated, that man's free choice ceases to operate.

הערות לפרק 4

1 הן מין זה של אדם היה יחיד בעולם, ואין מין שני דומה לו בזה הענין; שיהא הוא מעצמו, בדעתו ובמחשבתו, יודע הטוב והרע ועושה כל מה שהוא חפץ, ואין מי שיעכב בידו מלעשות הטוב והרע... אל יעבור במחשבתך דבר זה שאומרים טפשי אומות העולם ורוב גלמי בני ישראל, שהקב"ה גוזר על האדם מתחילת ברייתו להיות צדיק או רשע. אין הדבר כן... נמצא זה החוטא, הוא הפסיד את עצמו, ולפיכך ראוי לו לבכות ולקונן על חטאיו... ראוי לנו לחזור בתשובה ולעזוב רשענו (רמב"ם, הל' תשובה ה, א, ב).

2 כי גם לא ידע האדם את עתו, כדגים שנאחזים במצודה רעה וכצפרים האחוזות בפח כהם יוקשים בני האדם לעת רעה כשתפול עליהם פתאם (קהלת ט, יב).

3 יומא פו. — שאל ר' מתיא בן חרש וכו'.

4 ואת חוקותי תשמרו (ויקרא יח, ד), דברים שהשטן (רש"י — יצר הרע) משיב עליהן (ואומות העולם משיבין עליהן) ואלו הן: אכילת חזיר, ולבישת שעטנז, וחליצת יבמה, וטהרת מצורע, ושעיר המשתלח. ושמא תאמר מעשה תוהו הם, ת"ל אני השם (שם) אני ה' חקקתיו ואין לך רשות להרהר בהן (יומא סז:).

5 ונתן אהרן על שני השעירים גורלות, גורל אחד לה' וגורל אחד לעזאזל (ויקרא טז, ח).

6 עזאזל הוא הר עז וקשה, צוק גבוה (שם, רש"י).

7 שני שעירי יום הכפורים, מצותן שיהיו שניהן שוין במראה, ובקומה ובדמים ובליקחתן כאחד (משנה, יומא ו, א; גמרא סב.).

8 מעמיד אחד לימין ואחד לשמאל ונותן שתי ידיו בקלפי ונוטל גורל בימינו וחברו בשמאל, ונותן עליהם את שכתוב בו "לשם", הוא לשם. ואת שכתוב בו "לעזאזל", משתלח לעזאזל (רש"י, ויקרא טז, ח) (יומא לט).

9 האנוש מאלוה יצדק, אם מעשהו יטהר גבר (איוב, ד יז).

10 אם עונות תשמר יה, ה' מי יעמוד (תהלים קל, ג).

11 מאד, מאד הוה שפל רוח (פרקי אבות ד, ד) (רמב"ם, הל' דעות ב, ג).

12 כי תבנה בית חדש, ועשית מעקה לגגך, ולא תשים דמים בביתך (דברים כב, ח).

13 ועשו סיג לתורה (אבות א, א).

14 והיא מצוה על צרה שתבא על הצבור, לזעוק לפניו בתפלה ובתרועה... ונאמר שהיא מצוה לעת הצרות שנאמין שהוא, יתברך ויתעלה, שומע תפלה והוא המציל מן הצרות בתפלה ונעקה (רמב"ן, ספר המצות, מצוה ה').

15 בערב ילין בכי ולבקר רנה (תהלים ל, ו).

16 אמר רבי חנינא: הכל בידי שמים חוץ מיראת שמים (ברכות לג:).

CHAPTER V

THE TORAH WAY OF JUSTICE

When was the first time that, among the children of Israel, cases were tried in accordance with Torah Law? In Ex. 18:13 we read: "And it was on the next day [*mimahorat*] that Moses sat judging the people; and the people stood about Moses from morning until evening." [1] Rashi explains that "the next day" refers to the day after Yom Kippur when, after a forty-day absence, Moses had descended from Mt. Sinai. Rashi calculates that from the sixth of Sivan, when the Decalogue was revealed, until the tenth of Tishri (Yom Kippur) there was no opportunity for Moses to administer Torah judgment. Nahmanides also associates this first *mishpat* ("judgment," i.e. court session) with Yom Kippur, but he suggests that it did not necessarily take place on the very next day; it was the first available day thereafter. [2]

The Word "Mimahorat"

Whenever the Torah uses the word *mimahorat*, it seeks to relate two days by comparing or contrasting them. It may signify that the second day marks a drastic change from the preceding shameful day; the day before had been negative and destructive, while today is positive and worthy. In this instance, it is the second day which is compared favorably and is primary; the day before was unworthy. The word *mimahorat*, however, can also indicate the reverse, namely, that it was the first day which was special because of its heightened significance and holiness. This superior day may overflow and affect the next day as well, so potent was its inspiration. The second day is thereby enhanced and achieves status, being closely related in time to the *kedushah* of the preceding day. Here, it is the first day which is primary.

Let us cite illustrations of both meanings of *mimaḥorat*. In its account of the sin of the golden calf, the Torah relates: "The next day [*mimaḥorat*], Moses said to the people, 'You have been guilty of a great sin' . . . when the people heard this harsh word, they mourned penitently" (Ex. 32:30; 33:4).[3] The yesterday witnessed orgiastic merrymaking and wild dancing before the idol.[4] The *mimaḥorat*, however, brought a sobering, a regaining of perspective and *teshuvah*. Hence this day's worthiness is noted in contrast to yesterday's shame.

In our text dealing with *mishpat*, it is clearly the reverse. It was Yom Kippur which represented a pinnacle experience of holiness. Its inspiration overflowed into the next day and suffused the mundane, civil litigation of the contending parties. This, we believe, is the implication of Rashi's and Naḥmanides' association of these two days: the first *mishpat* in Jewish history and the first Yom Kippur.

The Impact of Yom Kippur

On that historic tenth day of Tisʰri, Moses descended from the mountain with the new Tablets of the Law and with the eagerly-awaited report, *salaḥti kidevarekha*, that Jews had been forgiven the sin of the *egel hazahav* (golden calf). We can well imagine the feeling of being cleansed and reconciled with God which the news generated among the people. The heavy burdens of guilt and rejection were dramatically lifted and the people of Israel were now assured of God's continued presence and providence. This was, indeed, a peak moment of religious fervor.

The very next day, according to Rashi (or shortly thereafter, according to Naḥmanides), Moses convened the first
Jewish court in history. Surely, the religious-emotional impact
of Yom Kippur—with its message of forgiveness and Divine
mercy—overflowed into this day. In the afterglow of Moses'
descent and God's forgiveness, the spirit of joy and gladness
must have brought all Jews together in brotherly love. The
antagonists were no longer disposed to vanquish each other,
but to be reconciled; not to emerge triumphant, but to be at
peace with their fellow man. The lesson of the historic association of these two days is that every future *mishpat*, whenever
it takes place during the course of the year, should reflect the
qualities which governed this first, model *mishpat*. Every *mishpat*
should see itself associated with the spirit of Yom Kippur.

The Concept of Pesharah (Arbitration)

When does a *mishpat* rise above the heated rivalry of two
contenders and reflect, instead, the spirit of Yom Kippur? This
is clearly achieved when both parties choose to resolve their
conflict through *pesharah* (arbitration), rather than through
the verdict of a court (*din*). Rabbi Joshua, son of Korḥa,
said: "Settlement by arbitration is a *mitzvah* (Sanh. 6b).[5] Maimonides elaborates: "It is a *mitzvah*, at the outset, to offer the
contenders the option: 'Do you prefer *din* or·*pesharah* to resolve
your conflict?' If they choose *pesharah*, so be it. And a
court which always settles cases by *pesharah* is praiseworthy"
(Hil. Sanh. 22:4).[6]

Din pits one party against the other. The *dayyan* analyzes
the relevant facts of the case and applies the appropriate legal
sanctions as prescribed by the *Ḥoshen Mishpat* (civil and criminal
code). The law is administered with cold impartiality and its
decisions are dictated by objective data. One party emerges
the victor; his case is vindicated. The plea of the other is denied.

Discord and resentment persist even as the court docket is cleared and the case is closed. The legal issue has been resolved, but human bitterness continues to fester.

In *pesharah*, however, social harmony is the primary concern of the *dayyan*. The fine points of the law and the determination of precise facts are of secondary importance. The goal is not to be juridically astute but to be socially healing. The psychology of the contenders, their socio-economic status and values, as well as the general temper of society, are the primary ingredients employed in the *pesharah* process. These considerations are evaluated within the broad halakhic parameters of the *Hoshen Mishpat*, and the final resolution of the conflict is a delicate and sensitive blending of both objective legal norms and subjective humanistic goals. For this reason, *pesharah* is the preferred alternative.

Pesharah differs striklingly from its application in Roman or modern civil law. The latter regard arbitration as contradictory to juridical action and as an extra-legal procedure. The judge may recommend out-of-court reconciliation, but he must eliminate himself from the process because a judge's role is that of a jurist, not a humanist. He is compelled to implement the law within well-defined bounds. In *Halakhah*, however, *pesharah* is a juridical procedure presided over by the *dayyan*; it does not contradict the law but is its preferred and finest fulfillment. That *pesharah* is very much a legal procedure is attested to by the strict halakhic requirements which govern its operations; it is not an informal and arbitrary agreement. The commitment to arbitration is initiated by a *kinyan*, a legal act, which obligates both parties to abide by the outcome and establishes the status of the presiding court (*pesharah tzerikhah kinyan*). Also, like all *din* cases, *pesharah* can only take place during daylight (*en danin balayelah*). Numerous other strictures establish the legal structure wherein *pesharah* operates.

How Can We Justify Pesharah?

A compelling question arises: On what authority did the Sages allow and even prefer *pesharah*, which is influenced by psychological and social considerations, and which may often contradict the *halakhah*? The execution of impartial and equitable justice (*din*) is a Divine commandment, and the *halakhah* is the means whereby this justice is realized. How can *Ḥazal* nullify a Torah commandment?

The Talmud (Sanh. 6b) justifies the institution of *pesharah* on the basis of two Biblical verses. Both verses are needed because each contributes a different consideration. Justice, the verses insist, does not operate in an ivory tower of isolation. It must help to attain other worthy ideals, namely *shalom*, social harmony and peace, and *tzedek*, righteousness. Justice combined with *shalom* serves the socio-ethical needs of man and society. Justice tempered by *tzedek* affirms a metaphysical truth concerning man. Only through *pesharah* are *shalom* and *tzedek* combined with *mishpat*.

Mishpat and Shalom

The first verse reads: "Execute the judgment of truth and peace in your gates" (Zech. 8:16). The Talmud explains: "Surely, where there is strict justice [*mishpat*] there is no peace. And where there is peace, there is no strict justice! But when do justice and peace coincide? Only in *pesharah* . . ." [7]

Where there is strict adherence to *din*, there is justice but no *shalom*, because one of the parties is humiliated and antagonized. The immediate issue is resolved but the conflict persists, with ensuing social discord. The secular judge is seemingly indifferent to this failure since justice, not harmony, was his objective. *Shalom* is for social workers and psychologists to attain; it is beyond his jurisdiction. The Torah, however, wants the

55

dayyan to be not only a magistrate but a teacher and a healer. He should seek to persuade both parties to retreat from their presumed points of advantage, and he should preach to them about the corrosive personal and social effects of sustained rancor. His responsibility is primarily to enlighten, rather than to render decisions on points of law.

The first verse, therefore, projects the social welfare of society and the happiness of individuals as primary ideals, as being truly a higher form of justice. *Pesharah* is socially and morally preferred, even if the strict *din* is neutralized. In its highest sense, justice obtains when people are reconciled.

Mishpat and Tzedek

The second verse states: "And David executed justice and righteousness toward his people" (II Sam. 8:15). The Talmud explains: "Surely, where there is strict justice [*mishpat*] there is no righteousness [*tzedek*], and where there is righteousness there is no justice. But when do justice and righteousness coincide? Only in *pesharah!*" [8]

This verse is concerned with the attainment of *tzedek*. In Aristotelian logic, there is a law of contradiction which states that a thesis and its antithesis cannot both be valid. This means that if A and B are mutually exclusive and contradictory, then if A is right, B must be wrong. Conversely, if B is right, A must be wrong. Both A and B cannot be simultaneously right. It follows from this logic that, when two litigants present opposing claims, only one can be right. Strict logic demands the application of *din* whereby the claim of the righteous party will be vindicated while the other party will be discredited.

The *halakhah*, however, believes that absolute right and wrong can be realized only in heaven. In dealing with imperfect man, we posit that no man is totally wrong or right and that, in the case of the litigants, both are partially right and wrong.

The application of *din* can only take account of obvious surface conditions; it fails to perceive subtleties underneath, which dilute our certainty about the right and the wrong of the litigants. Each has some responsibility for the situation and is partially guilty of the misunderstanding, for misleading innuendoes, and for contributing indirectly to a climate in society which places others at a disadvantage. Strict justice deals with plain facts and salient reality; real responsibility, however, goes much deeper and is obscured from the scrutiny of the court. Metaphysically, no one is entirely absolved in situations of conflict.

Tzedek, therefore, is truly realized only through *pesharah,* which declares the parties both winners and losers. Thus, *pesharah* is not only socially desirable, as the first verse claims, but it is also morally just. The principle of *tzedek* demands that *mishpat* reflect the existential condition of man's inevitable imperfection.

In the above spirit, Moses explained to his father-in-law, Yitro, the unique Torah way of justice. "And I judge between a man *(ish)* and his neighbor *(re'ehu)*" (Ex. 18:16).[9] Why, asks the *Mekhilta,* does the verse employ two different terms, *ish and re'ehu?* Wouldn't *ben ish le'ish* or *ben re'a lere'a* have been more appropriate?

Apparently, the terms refer to two types of persons. *Ish* connotes any man; *re'a* suggests neighborliness, a person concerned about others. The *Mekhilta,* therefore, explains that *ben ish* deals with *din* without *pesharah*; a representative *ish* would insist on the strict enforcement of the law. *Re'ehu,* however, refers to a gentle, conciliatory person who would prefer *pesharah* as a means of achieving amity with his fellow man. In the latter case, both parties depart from the court as friends.

Every *mishpat,* we said, should regard itself as being related to Yom Kippur. On Yom Kippur day we all stand in judgment before the Almighty, seeking to be absolved of our guilt. What kind of judgment shall it be, *din* or *pesharah?* At first, we fearfully approach the Heavenly Court, pleading: "Do not enter

57

into judgment with us, for in Thy sight no man alive is free of guilt." [10] *Din* will find us all wanting. But as Yom Kippur proceeds, we desperately implore God to judge us in the spirit of *pesharah*. We ask, "You, O Lord, extend Your helping hand to sinners, Your right hand is extended to receive repentant sinners," [11] praying that His awareness of our imperfections will assuage the severity of the judgment. Hopefully, what will result will be harmony and reconciliation.

הערות לפרק 5

1 ויהי ממחרת, וישב משה לשפט את העם, ויעמד העם על משה מן הבקר עד הערב (שמות יח, יג) (רש״י — מוצאי יום הכפורים היה... ומהו ממחרת? למחרת רדתו מן ההר... ומשנתנה תורה עד יוה״כ, לא ישב משה לשפט את העם).

2 אין הכונה שיהיה ממחרתו ממש... אבל הכונה לברייתא הזו לומר שהיה זה אחר יום הכפורים, כי אין להם יום פנוי למשפט מיום בואם להר סיני עד אחר יוה״כ של שנה ראשונה הזאת (רמב״ן, שם).

3 ויהי ממחרת ויאמר משה אל העם, אתם חטאתם חטאה גדולה... וישמע העם את הדבר הרע הזה ויתאבלו (שמות לב, ל; לג, ד).

4 ויקמו לצחק (שם, לב, ו) — רש״י — יש במשמע הזה גלוי עריות... ושפיכת דמים.

5 רבי יהושע בן קרחה אומר: מצוה לבצוע (סנהדרין ו:).

6 מצוה לומר לבעלי דינין בתחלה: בדין אתם רוצים או בפשרה? אם רצו בפשרה, עושין ביניהן פשרה. וכל בית דין שעושין פשרה תמיד, הרי זה משובח (רמב״ם, הל׳ סנהדרין כב, ד).

7 אמת, ומשפט שלום שפטו בשעריכם (זכריה ח, טז). והלא במקום שיש משפט, אין שלום. ובמקום שיש שלום, אין משפט. אלא, איזהו משפט שיש בו שלום, הוי אומר, זה ביצוע (סנהדרין ו:).

8 ויהי דוד עשה משפט וצדקה (שמואל ב׳ ח, טו). והלא כל מקום שיש משפט, אין צדקה, וצדקה, אין משפט. אלא איזהו משפט שיש בו צדקה, הוי אומר, זה ביצוע (סנהדרין ו:).

9 "ושפטתי בין איש ובין רעהו" (שמות יח, טז). בין א י ש , זה הדין שאין בו פשרה, ובין ר ע ה ו , זה הדין שיש בו פשרה, ששניהם נפטרים זה מזה כרעים (מכילתא).

10 אל תבא במשפט עמנו, כי לא יצדק לפניך כל חי (סליחות).

11 אתה נותן יד לפושעים וימינך פשוטה לקבל שבים (נעילה).

58

CHAPTER VI

THE PROFUNDITY OF JEWISH FOLK WISDOM

Scholars often tend to dismiss the unlearned condescendingly, regarding them as incapable of clear perceptions or correct opinions. This disparagement is undoubtedly justified in fields of specialized knowledge which require many years of detailed study. In the realm of science or of *Halakhah,* the ignorant are sorely handicapped. There are, however, other aspects of the understanding of life and its values where simple, but earnestly searching people often intuitively grasp essential truths. This is particularly the case with devout Jews who, though formally unlearned, may absorb from the Torah atmosphere in which they live profound and valid perceptions of the basics of Judaism.

Ḥazal (Sanh. 7a) paid special tribute to the aphorisms of common folk. Samuel, Dean of the Academy of Nehardea and one of the foremost scholars of his day, noted the expressions of folk wisdom emanating from people in the market-place, related them to Biblical verses, and thereby gave them the support of Torah. The Talmud cites a series of seven aphorisms, each of which is introduced with the words, "There was one who used to say..."[1] The authors of these aphorisms were not scholars; had they been, their names would have been recorded, as is the usual practice of the Talmud. They could not trace their aphorisms to Scripture, because they did not know the Bible. Samuel, however (and Rav Huna in the seventh aphorism), felt impelled to anchor this folk wisdom in the Bible and, thereby, ascribed to them a Scriptural basis.

Two questions arise. Why did such illustrious scholars as Samuel and Rav Huna feel inclined to give credence and authority to folk adages which emanated from the non-learned, non-*massorah* community? Secondly, this Aggadic section dealing with folklore follows an halakhic discussion in the Academy on the relative merits of *din*, court cases decided by strict objective law, and *pesharah*, arbitration which emerges out of the subjective reasoning of the judge, the *dayyan*. Was there any rational justification for the legal discussion to be interrupted by this Aggadic Interlude dealing with folk wisdom? It is likely that Samuel and Rav Huna introduced these popular adages in order to fortify their position in the *din-pesharah* legal controversy. Otherwise, we are unable to explain why these Sages made the effort to trace them to Scripture. Must Torah and folk wisdom be identical? Surely, there was a good reason for their taking non-Torah metaphors and transforming them into Torah lessons.

Respect for Intuitive Wisdom

What emerges is that the *Ḥazal* had great respect for the intuitive metaphors of the common man who, though formally uneducated, absorbs truisms from the Torah setting in which he lives. The observant, godfearing Jew, who never had the opportunity or the intellectual ability to study Torah, often manages to grasp perceptions which are well grounded in the tradition. This idea is supported by the following: Rabbi Simlai said:

> The fetus in the womb is taught the entire Torah; his gaze penetrates the mysteries of the entire universe; as he is

born, an angel taps him on the mouth, causing him to
forget all the Torah he had learned (Nid. 30b).[2]

Why was it important to teach the fetus material it cannot possibly carry over into life? Why teach what will soon be forgotten?

Rabbi Simlai is apparently saying that every Jew comes into
the world with a natural responsiveness to Torah teaching.
Every Jew begins with a share in Torah which was vested
in him before his birth and, though he is made to forget
it, it is preserved in the deep recesses of his soul, waiting to
be awakened by study and a favorable environment. Scholars,
of course, convert this latent knowledge into actual living
knowledge; but the simple Jew also has a share. Some members
of the *Massorah* community are scholars whose knowledge
is well formulated and codified, while others, though unlearned,
may be endowed with inspired and intuitive Torah wisdom. Once
the basic tenets are implanted in them, they express these
principles unconsciously in the form of adages and folk wisdom.
On the last day of his life, Moses, exhorting the children of
Israel to be loyal to the Torah, said, "These commandments are
neither'hidden nor distant from you ... but are very close to
you, within your mouths and hearts" (Deut. 30:11, 14).[3] When
a Jew studies Torah, he finds it native to his spiritual personality
and he responds to it readily. It is an act of recollecting, recaptur-
ing, bringing to the surface what was once learned and forgotten. The Torah did not impose upon the Jews some extraneous
matter, foreign to their natures. Rather, Torah study and
practice awaken the Jewish memory and we recall that which
is inherent in the Jewish soul and is often reflected in the
everyday folk wisdom of the Jewish people.

This is why Samuel and Rav Huna sought to find Torah lessons in the popular folk sayings of the people.

But what connection is there between the intuitive wisdom
of common people and the preceding *halakhah* disputations on

the relative merits of *din* and *pesharah?* When a *dayyan* renders his decision in legal cases, he is applying the laws and regulations of the *Hoshen Mishpat,* the halakhic code on civil and criminal cases. He establishes the facts and he adduces the appropriate laws to resolve the dispute. His role is clear: to be objectively impartial. But what guide does the *dayyan* employ in *pesharah?* He will decide to compromise and reconcile the contradictory claims of the claimants and to render both litigants part-losers and part-winners. On what considerations does he base his *pesharah* decisions, which have the same binding authority as *din verdicts? The verse, "Elohim* [the name of God as judge, *shofet*] stands in the congregation of God [the courts] (Ps. 82:1),[4] applies not only to cases of *din,* but to *pesharah* as well. The *dayyan* in a *pesharah* case also represents God's will.

In a *pesharah* case the *dayyan* forms his judgment out of his conscience, his sense of justice, fairness, and charity. He employs his *da'at Torah,* his sense of Torah fairness, stemming from his intuitive sense of rightness. His is a humane approach, reflecting Torah sensitivity and his love of his fellow man. Recording a discussion of this topic in the Academy, the Talmud paused for a brief Aggadic interlude which certified that not only Torah scholars but even the unschooled, common people are capable of intuitive Torah perceptions which are found to be rooted in Scripture. The scholars, of course, deal with halakhic matters and formulate their intuitive understanding in legal and learned terminology. The common folk are content to express their perceptions in adages which sometimes parallel Torah teaching.

Analyzing Three Aphorisms

We will present a sampling of aphorisms to illustrate the kind of folk wisdom which our Sages accredited as intuitive Torah perception.

1. *Secret of Jewish Survival.* The first Aggadic adage reads:

> There was one who used to say, "Happy is he who is
> capable of ignoring abuse; he will escape a hundred evils."
> Said Samuel to Rav Judah: "This is implicit in the verse,
> 'As one lets loose a stream of water, so is the beginning of
> strife' (Prov. 17:14)." [5]

The numerical value of the letters of the Hebrew word *madon*,
signifying "strife", amounts to 100. Now just as the simple act
of removing a barrier allows a mighty stream of water to gush
forth, so does the mere abandonment of restraint, the replying
to abuse, let loose a torrent of strife that will bring a hundred-
fold evil. Samuel, then, enjoined the vilified person to ignore
the abuse and thereby prevent a hundred evils. Strife, therefore,
should be avoided at all costs, even at the price of insult and
abuse.

This aphorism must be understood in a broader sense; otherwise Samuel would not have taken note of it. How does one
maintain a stoical self-control in the face of provocative abuse?
Basically, it depends on the strength of one's value system.
Those who continually crave approval and approbation are
unable to bear being slighted or ridiculed. Insecure and uncertain about their own convictions and values, they slavishly
submit to public judgments and criteria of the masses in respect
of what is good or bad, sacred or profane. When insulted, they
imagine that the whole world is reproving and humiliating them.
Disaster threatens and their hurt is unbearable. They have no
inner resources to withstand the onslaught. The basis of their
self-respect, public opinion, is collapsing. Their self-identity and
image of themselves are being questioned.

For the religious Jew, to dismiss abuse requires a sense of
confidence and self-regard which is rooted in his faith in his
own value system, enabling him to say, "I don't need the
approval of men. I only need that God approve my motives

and deeds. That is enough!" The truly good and pious man lives his life in an inner-directed manner and is neither corrupted nor deflected by the mass immorality surrounding him, the irreligious and immoral pressures of the general society which often looks down on him. To repel the vulgarity in language and conduct that is rampant in the modern world, it is necessary to stand firm on one's own convictions and ignore the jeering scoffers of our generation.

This inner assurance born of one's faith is particularly vital for our Jewish people, who are everywhere enveloped by cultures which are unsympathetic to and often abusive of our religious way of life. To persevere in our claim to all of Eretz Yisrael, despite the inability of most of the world to recognize what we feel and know to be true and valid, requires a conviction that is sustained by an absolute faith in the ultimate justice of our cause. The Jew has, at different times in our history, been subjected to daily insult and humiliation; he was regarded as sub-human, a member of a Divinely accursed people which was preserved by God in order to demonstrate the validity of the dominant faith. But the Jew dismissed all the pomp and power of the Church as unworthy of his serious consideration. Consequently, Jewish religious life continued to flourish with a profound sense of its ultimate worth. In our modern pluralistic society, the task may seem easier but, because of the closer intermingling of groups, we need even more to possess an inner pride and the conviction that ours is the true faith in order to maintain our way of life. To face world abuse, and yet to persist unflinchingly, is the secret of Jewish survival.

2. *Divine Retribution.* The second adage reads:

There was a man who used to say, "A thief is not killed for stealing two or three times." Said Samuel to Rav Judah: "This is also implied in a Scriptural passage, 'Thus, has the

Lord said, for three transgressions of Israel and for the fourth, I will not turn away their punishment'[6] (Amos 2:6). This folk saying is basically acknowledging, in the words of Rashi, that 'if one commits a sin two or three times but was not punished, do not wonder; punishment will surely come at the end.' "

Maimonides explains that the individual sinner, the *yaḥid*, is punished not when he commits a sin twice, but when he commits the sin a third time and his sins exceed his good deeds; a community, a *tzibbur*, goes unpunished for perpetrating a transgression three times, but receives its retribution upon the fourth time.[7] This explains the "two and three times" in the verse in Amos; "two" refers to the individual and "three" to the community.

Why the difference between the individual and the community? Apparently, God does not necessarily punish the occasional sinner. He punishes the sinner who, through repetition, shows that he has become addicted to the sin. This follows the principle of *ḥazakah*, a repetitive behavior pattern, which demonstrates that the person has adopted a value system that is sinful. We assume that it is much easier for an individual to become corrupted than an entire community. The individual is regarded as a sinner and deserving of punishment upon his third violation; the ethos of an entire community, however, cannot be regarded as corrupt until the fourth. This distinction is derived from the *halakhah*, where the number of repetitive acts which create a *ḥazakah* varies with different situations and contexts (Yev. 64b).

Samuel noted that this popular maxim deals with a fundamental principle of Jewish faith, that of reward and punishment, *sakhar va'onesh*. The greatest problem confronting the believer is the frequent suffering of the righteous and prospering of the wicked. It is difficult to reconcile this fact with God's justice and with

our belief in Divine retribution. The Talmud (Ber. 7a)[8] quotes
Moses as posing this dilemma to the Almighty, as did many
prophets thereafter. This is also the central theme of the Book
of Job, which the Sages included in our Scriptures. The delayed
coming of reward or punishment perplexes many believers
and contributed to the apostasy of the Tanna, Elisha ben Avuya.
When a crime, perpetrated two or three times, does not incur
immediate retribution, many assume that retribution will never
come. This is the significance of the adage for which Samuel
provided textual support. Retribution will come, Judaism teaches,
even if it is delayed.

We previously cited the verse in Amos 2:6 which, in its
entirety, reads as follows:

> Thus says the Lord: For three transgressions of Israel, and
> for the fourth, will I not turn away their punishment: for
> their sale of the righteous (Joseph) for silver, and the
> needy for the price of sandals.[9]

This verse introduces the chapter which is read as the *Haftarah*
to the *Sidrah, Vayeshev*, which tells the story of Joseph and
his brothers. It is generally accepted that the thematic connection between the *Haftarah* and the Torah reading is in the
second half of the verse, which refers to the crime of the
brothers against Joseph. The *Targum Yerushalmi* avers (Gen.
37:28) that the compensation received by the brothers for the
sale of Joseph only sufficed to purchase a pair of sandals.

We may, however, find a connection between the first part
of the verse as well, in its reference to retributions which are
often delayed. The brothers, in selling Joseph, assumed that
no one would ever discover their crime, that Joseph would
either die in captivity or be assimilated into a foreign culture. Twenty-three years later, the entire episode seemed to
have been forgotten. Who could ever imagine that the brothers
would one day be called to account for their crime? That is

why, when Joseph revealed himself, they were stunned into silence and frightened by him (Gen. 45:3),[10] not for fear of punishment but by their discovery that their calculations were wrong and that, eventually, retribution is exacted.

The appropriateness of the *Haftarah*, therefore, is now seen to lie in the entire verse, the first part as well. It speaks precisely of the events in the *Sidrah*, the delayed but inevitable retribution which the brothers had to face.

3. *Faith in Man is Idolatry.* The Aggadic adage reads:

> There was another who used to say: "The man upon whom I relied lifted up his club and rose against me." Samuel said to R. Judah: "This is illustrated in the Biblical verse, 'Yea, even the man that should have sought my welfare, in whom I trusted, who ate my bread, has lifted up his heel against me' (Ps. 41:10)." [11]

The Torah frequently warns us that man is prone to be deceitful.[12] The Zohar excerpt, *Berikh Shemeh*, which we recite prior to taking the Torah scroll from the ark, contains the sentence, "Not in man do I place my faith, nor on any angels do I rely, but upon the God in heaven." [13] This teaches that only in God may we have faith; man will frequently disappoint us.

We may trust man, have confidence in him, but we may not have faith in him. Faith connotes absoluteness and no man is worthy of absolute faith. Faith is only applicable to God. For two thousand years we have had faith in the Divine promise to the Patriarchs and to the Prophets that Eretz Yisrael would belong to their descendants in perpetuity. This faith carried us through centuries of turmoil and agony. The reconstitution of the State of Israel in our day is a vindication of that faith.

But the promises of men, even the finest and most well-meaning, are subject to frailties of character and capriciously changing circumstances. To believe totally in man borders on idolatry and inevitably invites calamity. Idolatry is not only the worship of objects of metal or wood; the most dangerous idolatry is the idolization and deification of man.

The Torah has confidence in man. We are forbidden to harbor unwarranted suspicions or to hurl unsubstantiated charges. We may never assume that others are lying. On the contrary, Jewish courts accept that witnesses who are subjected to halakhic scrutiny are truthful; otherwise, we would never act on the strength of their testimony. Similarly, oaths, when administered by courts, determine the outcome of civil litigation; we do not suspect perjury. But this is trust and confidence, not faith which ascribes an absolute integrity to fallible man.

The incisive validity of this judgment was demonstrated during the war years when the President of the United States refused to bomb the railroad system leading to the crematoria and concentration camps. American Jewish leaders accepted the transparent rationalization of the State Department that intervention would have hampered the war effort. Why did American Jews not act like Mordecai who, when he heard the evil decree, "went into the center of the city and shouted bitterly and loudly" (Esth. 4:1)? [14] Why weren't there public demonstrations, with mass tearing of garments, as Mordecai did, to awaken Jewish leadership and to arouse the conscience of Christian America? Had we responded like Mordecai, would President Roosevelt have acted as callously as he did? Perhaps we should add another *al het* to our Yom Kippur confessional, "for the sins we have committed in being unresponsive to the cries of our brethren in Europe who were being brutally slaughtered."

Apparently, what inhibited Jewish action was the faith that American Jews had in the President; their adulation bordered on idolatry. But for this idolatry, millions of Jews would probably have been saved. President Roosevelt was a great leader for America, but he was a disaster for the Jews.

If he had been president in 1948, Israel would probably not have come into being, so mesmerized were we by our faith in him. The *Hashgaḥah* chose Harry Truman to be the instrument of God's purpose. We had trust and confidence in Truman, but we never exalted our regard for him. Our relationship was, therefore, healthy and our critical vigilance in protecting Jewish rights did not falter.

These are some of the necessary truths which Samuel felt impelled to emphasize by associating them with Biblical verses. He recognized that the folklore of unlearned Jews frequently reflects profound Torah wisdom. Accordingly, by citing them in the Academy, Samuel accredited them as part of the necessary truths of the Torah tradition.

הערות לפרק 6

1   ההוא דהוה קאמר ואזיל (סנהדרין ז.).

2   דרש ר' שמלאי: למה הולד דומה במעי אמו ? . . . וצופה ומביט מסוף העולם
עד סופו . . . ומלמדים אותו כל התורה כולה . . . וכיון שבא לאויר העולם, בא
מלאך וסטרו על פיו ומשכחו כל התורה כולה (נדה ל:).

3   כי המצוה הזאת אשר אנכי מצוך היום לא נפלאת היא ממך ולא רחקה היא . . .
כי קרוב אליך הדבר מאד בפיך ובלבבך לעשותו (דברים ל, יא, יד).

4   אלהים נצב בעדת אל בקרב אלהים ישפט (תהלים פב, א).

5   ההוא דהוה קאמר ואזיל, טוביה דשמע ואדיש חלפוה בישתיה מאה. א"ל שמואל
לרב יהודה, קרא כתיב, "פוטר מים, ראשית מדון" (משלי יז, יד), ריש מאה
דיני (פ' רש"י — אשריו ששומע חרפתו ושותק ומרגיל בכך . . . הלכו להם
בשתיקתו מאה רעות שהיו באות עליו על ידי התגר).

6   ההוא דהוה קאמר ואזיל, אתרתי תלת גנבא לא מיקטל. א"ל שמואל לרב יהודה:
קרא כתוב, "כה אמר ה', על שלשה פשעי ישראל ועל ארבעה לא אשיבנו"
(עמוס ב, ו) (פ' רש"י — כלומר, אם עובר אדם עבירה פעמים ושלש, ולא באה
עליו פורענות, אל יתמה, דאתרי תלת גנבא לא מיקטיל וסופו ללקות באחרונה,
שם).

7   בשעה ששוקלין עונות אדם עם זכיותיו, אין מחשבין עליו עון שחטא בו תחלה
ולא שני, אלא משלישי ואילך . . . אבל הצבור — תולין להם עון ראשון, שני
ושלישי, שנאמר, "על שלשה פשעי ישראל ועל ארבעה לא אשיבנו", וכשמחשבין
להם על דרך זה מחשבין להם מרביעי ואילך (רמב"ם, הל' תשובה ג, ה).

69

8 אמר לפניו, רבש״ע, מפני מה יש צדיק וטוב לו ויש צדיק ורע לו ; יש רשע
וטוב לו, ויש רשע ורע לו ? (ברכות ז.).

9 על שלשה פשעי ישראל ועל ארבעה לא אשיבנו, על מכרם בכסף צדיק, ואביון
בעבור נעלים (עמוס ב, ו).

10 ולא יכלו אחיו לענות אותו, כי נבהלו מפניו (בראשית מה, ג).

11 ההוא דהוה קאמר ואזיל, גברא דרחיצנא עליה, אדייה לגזיזיה וקם. א״ל שמואל
לר׳ יהודה, קרא כתיב, ״גם איש שלומי אשר בטחתי בו, אוכל לחמי, הגדיל
עלי עקב״ (תהלים מא, י).

12 אני אמרתי בחפזי, כל האדם כזב (תהלים קטז, יא).

13 בריך שמה . . . לא על אנש רחיצנא, ולא על בר אלהין סמיכנא. אלא באלהא
דשמיה (זוהר, פ׳ ויקהל).

14 ויצא בתוך העיר ויזעק זעקה גדולה ומרה (אסתר ד, א).

CHAPTER VII

PRAYER AS DIALOGUE

There are four media through which man reaches out to God, transcending his finiteness and communicating with infinity. These are the intellectual, *limmud* (study); the emotional, *ahavat Hashem* (love of God); the volitional, *shemirat hamitzvot* (observance of the Torah commandments); and prayer, *tefillah*.

Intellectual

The human mind reflects the infinite mind of God; to know is to identify with His knowledge, to partake of it and, in effect, to identify with Him. To know, either through the *limmud* of Torah or the study of science, is a Divine act; it is a joining with the intellect of God. A child shares the knowledge of his father; this is a form of identification. It is God who bestowed knowledge upon man, *atta ḥonen le'adam da'at*. Studying and acquiring knowledge is not an independent act; it involves the sharing of Divine knowledge. In this experience there is a fusion of the finite with the infinite; thinking of an object means merging with the essence of that object, *aḥdut hamaskil vehamuskal*; our minds absorb the characteristics of that object.

God reveals Himself in the cosmic (natural), as well as in the moral (Torah), order.[1] Thus, in discovering through *limmud* the workings of the cosmic and moral order, we approach the knowledge of God Himself. Thinking in terms of eternal truth is an act of craving for God. In *Hilkhot Teshuvah* (10:6), Maimonides says: "It is known and certain that the love of God becomes imbedded in the heart of man only if he has a proper and continuous mental awareness of Him ... and according to the knowledge will be the love." [2] Maimonides maintains that even emotional *ahavah* is dependent upon one's intellectual perception. Thus, the intellectual exploration of God's moral and cosmic order is a bridge spanning the gap between men and God.

Study of the cosmic order through science produces *hokhmah* (secular knowledge); study of the moral order is Torah (Divine wisdom); man's intellect probes both realms. Both are expressive of God's knowledge. The study of Torah usually leads man closer to God. The study of science has not always done so successfully; yet it need not produce any injurious effects on faith, and it can and has bolstered the religious commitments of many individuals.

Emotional

Through our hearts, we achieve a *devekut* (cleaving) with Him in a mystical reaching out of the spirit. Here the heart, not the mind, predominates in ecstatic and passionate love of God; man thereby transcends the finite world and reaches his Creator. We mentioned previously that Maimonides felt that an intellectual effort must exist in order to bring forth the emotional transport. In *Hilkhot Yesode Hatorah* (4:12), he amplifies this point:

> When a man ponders these matters and understands all creation ... and he becomes aware of the wisdom of God which is manifest in all creation, he feels additional love for God and his soul and body crave to love Him. [3]

Yehudah Halevi (Kuzari, 4), however, maintains that the

emotional, visionary experience is a stronger link than the abstract, intellectual experience. Through ethical preparation, intuition, not intellectual knowledge or conceptual thinking, man renders himself fit for emotional communion with the Deity. The God of Abraham was apprehended, not merely comprehended. God to him was a supreme reality, a totally emotional and not abstractly intellectual experience. The God of Aristotle, in contrast, is only comprehended, as a distinct, abstract and remote idea; there is no direct and totally embracing experience but, rather, one mediated by the intellect. The Book of Psalms, as a religious work *par excellence*, reflects the emotional and immediate experience of God's reality and providential presence.

The emotional experience represents man's yearning to return to his origin and source. Man seeks to attach himself to his origin like "a tree planted by streams of water" (Ps. 1:3), *ke'etz shatul al palge mayim,* a tree attached to its source of life. This concept is a metaphysical support for the idea of the fatherhood of God, that we are all His progeny and derive from Him. In the hymn of Hannah, *Tefillat Ḥannah,* the word *tzur* (rock) is used: "Neither is there any rock like our God," *ve'en tzur ke'Elohenu* (I Sam. 2:2). God is the Creator, the originator of all; man is part of God, as a stone is part of a larger rock. *Teshuvah* means return to one's metaphysical origin and *tefillah,* too, means a return to one's wellspring. Ḥassidim, especially, emphasized the importance of this concept.

The emotional communion is non-normative. In a normative experience we are obliged to act, to perform dutifully in submission to a commandment. The emotional experience is spontaneous, not a volitional act; it bursts forth out of an inner need, not in response to an outer norm requirement. It is unintentional and unplanned; it springs out of an instinctive search for God. It is an adventurous plunge into infinity, with man playing almost a passive role as he is carried forth, almost propelled, and overwhelmed.

This being so, how can such an experience be prescribed and controlled by the *Halakhah*, which seeks to impose precise regulatory controls governing time and manner? How can the *Halakhah* be reconciled with spontaneous emotionality? We go even further. We know that the *Halakhah* prescribes norms which can express themselves only through the emotions, such as *ahavat Hashem*, love of God; *yirat Hashem*, fear of God; *bitaḥon BaShem*, confidence in God. How can law dictate emotions which, by their very nature, are spontaneous, which defy coercion or regulation? Yet we know that the *Halakhah* does set up norms for these experiences.

The answer is that the norm creates the mood and setting which allow for the spontaneous overflow of emotions. The norm is an educational tool, a guide which organizes our personalities and heightens our sensitivities. It does not dictate the emotion; it molds man and his circumstances and thereby stimulates the emotional outpouring. In addition, the norm also serves as an *ex post facto* judge in analyzing the experience, defining it, refining it, and providing it with a rational understanding. It serves to make the experience, the spontaneous gush of emotions, a part of our larger selves, and helps to integrate it into our total personalities. Otherwise, it would represent an unrelated mystical transport, something that happened to us, rather than something that is part of our identity. It is merged into the total personality which is also possessed of intellect, will, memory, and imagination. This *ex post facto* self-analysis is prescribed by both Maimonides and Halevi.

The emotional experience is non-normative because it is spontaneous. It is not something we must or should do; it just happens. At first glance, the intellectual medium, previously described, seems normative because it cannot be spontaneous. By its very nature the intellectual quest, in science or philosophy, must be organized and planned, with set goals and with clearly defined means of research. In actuality, however, this is not so.

It is also non-normative. It is a response to a need; it is impelled from within by simple, irrepressible curiosity. The *etz
hada'at*, tree of knowledge, represents an act of inquisitiveness
rooted in our very being. Its implementation depends upon the
adoption of certain standards, but its essential thrust emerges
from within. Thus it is not a submission to an external imperative.

We may further add that intellectual activity is stifled when
it is prescribed or compelled from without; creativity is stunted
when governments, for instance, intervene. Even *limmud Torah*
should not only be motivated by a desire to comply with a
Divine imperative, but rather to accomplish, to explore, to
comprehend the great mystery which intrigues the mind. Ideally,
we study Torah not to please God but to satisfy our thirst.
Reb Ḥaim of Volozhin defined *Torah lishmah* as study for the
sake of acquiring knowledge; our impetus should be cognitive
intellectual curiosity. (Studying Torah *shelo lishmah* has, as its
purpose, impressing others.) As a practical observation, it may
be added that those who study Torah *leshem mitzvah* rarely
become *talmide ḥakhamim*. For this reason, *Talmud Torah* does
not require *kavvanah*, a feeling of compliance with the Divine
will. We do not study in order to achieve *devekut*; the subjects
of the *Gemara* are not necessarily ecstatically motivating. Thus,
the intellectual medium, like the emotional, is non-normative. It
springs uncontrollably from within.

Volitional

Man approaches God through the exercise of his moral will,
by arriving at ethical decisions. The main objective of *Halakhah*
is to achieve performance, to bend man's will to accord with
God's; this is the normative realization of halakhic theory. This
medium is obviously normative for it is directed and controlled
and therefore requires *kavvanah*. Its purpose is to raise man

to a spiritual personality, to guide his drives and biological instincts, to endow them with meaningful content, and to convert mechanical, psychological laws into patterns of sacred living. In a word, to achieve *kedushat haguf,* sanctification of man's physical life.

While Christianity felt that the carnal body is corrupt and beyond redemption, Judaism fused the body and mind and recognized the soul as the harmony-activating factor of the body. The transformation of the body, its sanctification, could not be achieved by *limmud,* because only the mind is involved in the intellectual process. Similarly, ecstatic emotion (*ahavah* —mysticism) does not consciously involve the body in its communion experience. The latter may affect the body, as in singing, dancing, swaying; but these psychosomatic overtones involve the body only as an adjunct, in a secondary role. Only in the volitional media, where the whole person acts in response to a spiritually defined norm, are both body and soul in a parity of worship.

The will makes the ethical decision; the body implements and executes; through his will, man becomes master of his body. The moral act starts with the will, but is only completed by the body through *mitzvot ma'asiyot,* actual *mitzvah* performances. This is a unique feature of Judaism, to proclaim the will as all-powerful, sufficient to transform the whole of life.

The ethicist drive (moral will) is motivated by the desire to make man's will like God's will. Bergson and Schopenhauer also extolled the role of the will. But to Schopenhauer, the will was blind, instinctive, a drive to doom and self-destruction. His was a philosophy of pessimism. To Bergson, the will was the more optimistic *élan vital,* an intuitive apprehension. In Judaism, however, the will is moral.

The will precedes thought, and, when morally motivated, will even oppose self-preservation as an ideal, as with martyrdom. Intellect is important in *limmud Torah,* but the crowning achievement is the free-will decision determining man's deeds. Aristotle's will is a businessman's will: the will to succeed, to adjust, to get along, to achieve happiness; it is pragmatic and utilitarian. In Judaism, the will is selfless; it is moral.

Serving God through ethics is a Jewish concept: "walking humbly with your God" [4] (Micah 6:8) means to walk humbly with people according to God's norms. Pagans invented mechanical, irrational cults to placate their deities, because their gods were irrational. Thus, the Grecian cults were devoid of ethical content; their gods had no concern with morality. In the Torah, God speaks to man in rational terms about the moral life. The Decalogue is devoid of ritual prescriptions. Even the *hukkim* are not rites, but rather acts of submission and compliance, involving the concept of total surrender to God. This is rational, as with a son who complies with his father's behest in the performance of an act which is incomprehensible to him.

The Jewish people is a people of the committed: an entire group exercising its freedom to commit itself to a life of *mitzvah* performance.

The Uniqueness of Prayer

We wish to designate prayer as an autonomous realm, as distinct from the previous three. The three media are one-directional, they are unilateral acts performed by man. Man transcends his finitude, but God does not respond by meeting him halfway. In prayer, however, we have a dialogue, which is bilateral and reciprocal. Man climbs the mountain toward God while He descends, figuratively, from the mountain top. Two hands embrace, as in a handshake. "And the Lord came down upon Mt. Sinai, on the top of the mountain; and the Lord called Moses to the top of the mountain and Moses went up" (Ex. 19:20).[5] The prayer of Solomon suggests the mutuality of prayer: "And incline unto the prayer of Your servant and to his supplications, O Lord, my God . . . that Your eyes may be open towards this house [Temple] night and day" (I Kings 8:28). In prayer, both God and man move. In the other three media, man moves but God does not.

Prayer, we said, is a dialogue, not a monologue. A dialogue exists when one person addresses another, even if the other is temporarily silent. In prophecy, God speaks and man is silent; in prayer, there is the reverse situation. We have the assurance that He is a *shome'a tefillah* (that He hears our prayers), even if He does not accede to our wishes. He is not necessarily a *mekabbel tefillah* (responsive to our specific requests). History records that when prophecy ceased after Haggai and Malakhi, the *Anshe Keneset Hagedolah*, the Men of the Great Assembly, continued the dialogue by instituting formal prayer. The words of the Torah continue to talk to us even as we respond through prayer.

In praying, we do not seek a response to a particular request as much as we desire fellowship with God. Prayer is not a means for wheedling some benefit from God. Despite our prayer, *vekabbel berahamim uveratzon et tefillatenu* ("Accept our prayer in mercy and favor"), it is our persistent hope that this may be fulfilled, but it is not our primary motivation. Our Sages felt that the acceptance of our prayers is beyond our understanding and is governed by unknowable considerations. We do not really understand why some prayers are accepted and others rejected. Nevertheless, prayer in the sense of petition, *tehinnah*, does play a central role in our *Shemoneh Esreh*, as will be explained later.

Dialogue means communication, engagement, and interaction. When we pray, God emerges out of His transcendence and forms a companionship with us; the Infinite and finite meet and the vast chasm is bridged. We cannot all achieve the intimacy with God which Moses attained: "And the Lord spoke to Moses face to face, as one man speaks to another" (Ex. 33:11).[6]

The ideal communion in prayer is signified by the word *adekha* (unto you), as in *shome'a tefillah, adekha kol basar yavo'u*, "O, You Who hear prayer, to You does all flesh come" (Ps. 65:3).[7] The word *el* (to) connotes direction and distance; the word *ad* (unto), however, suggests that the distance has been covered and the gap bridged. In *teshuvah* (repentance), the word *ad* in *shuvah Yisrael ad Hashem Elohekha*, "Return, O Israel, unto the Lord your God" (Joel 14:2), has the same connotation.

The Vilna Gaon defined *melekh*, King, as signifying kingship by consent of those ruled, both entering the relationship freely; subjects willingly pledging their fealty. A *moshel*, a ruler, however, implies an absolute monarch. In the first three media, God is a *moshel*; there is no community experience; man seeks a seemingly unapproachable absolute monarch. In prayer, however, we have a *melukhah*, a community relationship.

The material content of prayer is not unique; it partakes of elements of the first three media, primarily of the emotional. What is unique is its form, its dialogue aspect. Prayer may be defined as the objectivating agency or medium of expression for the other three media.

Is Prayer Biblically Mandatory (Mide'Orayta)?

There is an important difference of opinion between Maimonides (Rambam) and Nahmanides (Ramban) (see *Sefer Hamitzvot*, 5). Maimonides regarded prayer as a *hiyyuv min-Hatorah*, as ordained by the Torah. He derived this view from the verse, "And to serve Him [*le'ovdo*] with all your heart" (Deut. 11:13).[8] The words "to serve Him" connote worship through prayer. Just as the edict, *kedoshim tiheyu*, "Be you holy" (Lev. 19:2), is a generalized ideal which finds its application in specific norms spelled out in the Torah, so is the *le'ovdo* a general precept, whose qualified norm and means of fulfillment is *tefillah*. Maimonides regarded prayer as one of the fundamental principles of Judaism, according it fifth place in the *Sefer Ha-mitzvot* (listing of the 613 precepts), after the belief in God's existence, His unity, the obligation to love Him and to fear Him —all these being obligatory aspects of our relationship with God.

Naḥmanides, however, did not acknowledge *tefillah* as a Biblically required norm: "It is a privilege to pray and it is one of the merciful attributes of the Creator that He hears and responds whenever we call unto Him. The verse, 'And to serve Him with all your heart', refers to worship in general, and not specifically to *tefillah*. It urges that our worship be sincere and wholeheartedly directed unto Him." [9]

Naḥmanides, therefore, insisted that the obligation to pray is *miderabbanan*, rabbinically prescribed, and he cited many Talmudic sources to support that view. However, even Naḥmanides conceded that, *be'et tzarah*, in times of great distress, the *mitzvah* of prayer is *mide'Orayta*, Biblically required. Such moments warrant our recognition that God is our only salvation. He wrote: "It is a *mitzvah* to plead fervently with God through prayer and *teru'ah* (shofar blasts) whenever the community is faced with great distress . . . for it is a *mitzvah* to affirm. in moments of distress our belief that the Holy One listens to prayers and intervenes to grant aid." [10]

Naḥmanides surely viewed prayer as being part of the Jewish historical experience—before the Temples were built, during their existence, and after their destruction. Abraham, Isaac, Jacob, and Moses prayed to God, and the children of Israel in Egypt directed their pleas heavenward. Its performance, however, is Biblically mandatory only when one is under duress; it is not otherwise an obligatory daily *mitzvah*.

The views of Maimonides and Naḥmanides can be reconciled. Both regarded prayer as meaningful only if it is derived from a sense of *tzarah*. They differ in their understanding of the word. Maimonides regarded daily life itself as being existentially in straits, inducing in the sensitive person feelings of despair, a brooding sense of life's meaninglessness, absurdity, lack of fulfillment. It is a persistent *tzarah*, which exists *bekhol yom*, daily. The word *tzarah* connotes more than external trouble; it suggests an emotional and intellectual condition in which man sees himself as hopelessly trapped in a vast, impersonal universe, desolate, without hope. Certainly, the Psalmist's cry, *min hametzar karati Yah*, "Our of my straits, I have called upon the Lord" (118:5), refers to an inner, rather an externally induced, state of constriction and oppression.

Out of this sense of discomfiture prayer emerges. Offered in comfort and security, prayer is a paradox, modern methods of suburban worship and plush synagogues notwithstanding. The desire for proximity of wife and children at services comes from a need for security and comfort. Real prayer is derived from loneliness, helplessness, and a sense of dependence. Thus, while Naḥmanides dealt only with "surface crisis," public distress, *tzarot tzibbur*, Maimonides regarded all life as a "depth crisis," a *tzarat yaḥid*.

These two types of *tzarah* vary in many aspects. The "surface *tzarah*" of Naḥmanides is an external crisis which arises independently of man. It emerges out of the environment and usually appears suddenly. Our plight is discernible to the eye; we see it, feel it, suffer pain and anxiety. One need not be a reflective, introspective or a brooding type to perceive this crisis; the simplest person experiences it, whether it be poverty, illness, famine, war, or death. It strikes like a hurricane; the Biblical *tokheḥah*, with its threats of dire punishment if Israel be untrue to its covenant, speaks precisely of this kind of crisis. It may strike a community or an individual. It is a *tzarah* which can be shared with others, through empathy and sympathy.

The "depth *tzarah*" of Maimonides, however, is an inner, personal, clandestine, and undefined crisis which is not readily manifest to the eye; it is perceived only by thinking and sensitive persons who wish to identify with it. It can be evaded, shunted aside by superficial people, who will thereby avoid being affected. Others, however, search for it and willingly accept it. This type of crisis cannot be attributed to man's stupidity, negligence or incompetence, as can the "surface crisis." The "depth crisis" is clearly beyond solution; it is an existential reality, a condition of human existence. It will be felt more poignantly by persons of greater intelligence and imaginative perception; the wiser and more sensitive one is, the greater the crisis. It is rooted in man's essence, his metaphysical origin. It is existential, not social, political, or economic.

The Torah bids man actively to combat and possibly eliminate superficial, external crises. The ills of poverty, disease, and war are debilitating and impair our spiritual freedom. The Torah, however, encourages man to submit to and embrace the experience of the "depth crisis." Thereby does man truly grasp the reality of his condition and become stirred to great heights of the spirit. For this "depth crisis," there is no solution except prayer. "Surface crisis" can be overcome; the existential crisis can only be met by prayer.

Petitionary Prayer—Tehinnah

The Structure of Tefillah. The word tefillah generally refers to any entreaty to God. Halakhically, it refers to the *Shemoneh Esreh* (*Amidah*), which is composed of three parts:

1) *Praises — Shevah —* the first three blessings of the *Amidah* until *Ha'El Hakadosh;* 2) *Petition — Tehinnah* (or supplication) — thirteen (originally 12) central blessings; and 3) *Thanksgiving — Hodayah*—from *Retzeh* until the conclusion—an expression of gratitude, "like one who is withdrawing respectfully from his master." The sequence of moving from *shevah* to *tehinnah* and to *hodayah* is a pattern inspired by the Torah. Maimonides

describes it thus: "And he relates his praises of the Holy One, blessed be He. After that he implores for his needs, with pleas and supplication, and then he renders praise and thanksgiving to God for the good that was given to him" (Hil. Tefillah 1:2).[11]

Although the liturgical text is rabbinic, it is patterned after the prayer of Moses in Deut. 3:24. He began with *shevah* (*attah hahilota*) and proceeded to *tehinnah* (*e'ebrah na ve'ereh*). This procedure is prescribed in the Talmud: "One should always start with praise of God and then proceed to prayer. How do we know this?—from Moses' prayer..." (Ber. 32a). Similarly, in the *Hallel* (Psalms 113–118)—Hymns of Praise recited on the three Pilgrim Festivals and Hannukkah — we begin with praises, "Praise the Lord. Praise, O you servants of the Lord. Praise the name of the Lord" (*Halleluyah, Hallelu avde Hashem; Hallelu et Shem Hashem,* etc.). We then proceed to address petitions in *Lo Lanu,* "Not unto us, O Lord, not unto us, but unto Your Name give glory" (*ki leshimmekha ten kavod*), and also in *Ahavti,* "O Lord, I beseech You, deliver my soul" (*ana Hashem maleta nafshi*). Finally, we move to thanksgiving in *Mah Ashiv,* "What [gratitude] can I render unto the Lord for all His benefits to me?", "I will offer You the sacrifice of thanksgiving" (*zevah todah*), and "O give thanks unto the Lord" (*hodu Lashem, ki tov*).[12] In the marriage blessings we find the same liturgical sequence—praise: "Who has created all things to His glory" (*shehakol bara likhevodo*); petition: "May she who was barren [Zion] find gladness and exultation" (*Sos tasis vetagel ha'akarah*), and also, "O make these lovely companions greatly to rejoice" (*same'ah tesamah re'im ha'ahuvim*); thanksgiving: "Blessed are You ... who created joy and gladness, bridegroom and bride" (*asher barah sason vesimhah, hatan vekalah*) and "Soon, our God, may there be heard in the cities of Judah ... the voice of joy and gladness" (*meherah Hashem Elohenu yishama be'are Yehudah,* etc.).[13]

Petitionary Prayer Analyzed

The word *teḥinnah* suggests an unearned grace, something not due to us. As Rashi says in Deut. 3:23, "All forms of the word *ḥannun* signify an unmerited gift." [14] We prefer *teḥinnah* to *bakkashah*, because the latter suggests a claim, a demand. The principal topic of Jewish prayer is *teḥinnah*; praise and thanksgiving are merely prologues and epilogues. Most of the Psalms are petitionary. Isaac prayed for progeny, *vaye'tar Yitzḥak* (Gen. 25:21); Eliezer said, *hakreh na lefanai* (Gen. 24:12), and other Biblical figures did the same. We petition without offering any apologies; it is most legitimate, but the request is always for *mattenat ḥinnam*, a gift which we do not deserve.

Christians and mystics considered *teḥinnah* an unworthy form of prayer, a cash-and-carry relationship, a form of trade or barter, a sacrifice for a recompense, a self-directed prayer. This was a knotty problem in their theology. At first, Christian prayers were limited to praises and thanksgiving; even the word "bread" in the famous Christian prayer was interpreted as referring to spiritual sustenance. Eventually, Christianity did incorporate petitions for material sustenance, but these were kept in a minor key; their primary requests were for gifts of the soul.

Why is Teḥinnah Emphasized in Judaism?

This is based on our singling out of one particular emotion above all others as the central requisite for prayer, namely, dependence and helplessness. Though contradictory emotions may exist, such as joy, sadness, gratitude, submission, shyness, etc., the feeling of dependence in our state of wretchedness is paramount. In Psalm 121 we read, "I lift up my eyes unto the mountains": the mountains here refer to the temporally powerful who do not really help. "From where will my salvation come? My salvation will only come from God" [15]: this is the *tzarah*, the surface crisis and the depth crisis, which we previously explained in reconciling Maimonides and Naḥmanides.

The Existential Plight

We are aware that our lives commenced and will be terminated without our consent. "You were born involuntarily, and you live involuntarily and you will die involuntarily, and you will in the future render an accounting involuntarily before the Supreme King of Kings, the Holy One, blessed be He." (Av. 4:22).[16]

We lack faith in the justifiability of our existence and we are bereft of an ontic fulcrum. This is a metaphysical experience, not merely psychological or rational, though it may manifest itself on psychological, social or political levels. A pervasive meaninglessness, purposelessness, and an absurdity of life convey themselves to the introspective, sensitive person.

This disapproval of oneself, of one's inherent worthiness, manifests itself in a feeling of boredom, the basic disease of modern man. Man spends millions to escape it, to forget his worries and the emptiness of existence itself. He detests routine and repetition in daily life, although this is a natural phenomenon. He is miserable because he is confined to a cyclic existence, a repetitive life of eating, sleeping, and contrived diversions. Nature itself involves a cyclic repetitiveness, with the sun rising and setting with impersonal regularity and the seasons similarly governed. Students of history over long spans also discern patterns of repetition, the notion of progress being no more than an illusion.

In the words of Kohelet: "All is vanity... one generation passes away and another generation comes, and the earth abides forever... all things toil to weariness... that which has been is that which shall be... and there is nothing new under the sun." [17] Man, in desperation, travels far to seek new experiences,

85

variety; but all results in futility. Even work becomes tiresome: "By the sweat of your brow shall you eat bread" (Gen. 3:19). The sameness and monotony of all life's experiences deprive us of the joy of life. This is the depth crisis of human existence.

Escaping from Boredom

Kohelet enumerates his attempts to escape from this existential emptiness—through pleasure: "I said in my heart, come now, I will attempt mirth and pleasure" (2:1); through the pursuit of knowledge: "For in much wisdom is much vexation, and he that increases knowledge increases sorrow" (1:18); through work: "And I detested all my labor, etc." (2:18); through material accumulation: "He that loves silver shall not achieve satisfaction" (5:9). He sought novelty, but this paled and his need was insatiable; immersion in work, once a pinnacle was achieved, would, he hoped, exhilarate him. But it did not. Instead, he became more ensnared and enslaved.

Constancy and Change

In Greek philosophy, there is a difference of opinion on the essence of being. Parmenides is the apostle of identity, constancy; the world of modern science is Parmenidian—constant, quantitative, unchanging; the world of thought, abstraction, also deals with constants. Heraclitus described the world as in continual flux, ever changing. The apprehended world (in contrast to the comprehended world) is Heraclitian, namely, the sentious: colors, smell, light, the qualitative, the aesthetic. While the cognitive world, the scientific, the world construed by abstraction is constant, the world with which we are consciously in contact, however, is fluctuating, aesthetic. The constant world, created by abstraction, is a parallelism to our sentious, qualitative world. This constitutes a conflict in the human personality, to reconcile the cognitive-constant with the aesthetic-flux.

Conclusion

The existential depth crisis and the state of alienation and boredom which ensue are unresolvable except through prayer. Primarily, because prayer is a dialogue, it differs from the other media of communion. It involves an interrelationship with God which can dispel the existential restlessness and unhappiness of man. In this respect, prayer is a unique experience.

הערות לפרק 7

1 The two *berakhot* prior to the *Shema* refer to these two Revelations in the *Yotzer Or* and the *Ahavah Rabbah*.

2 דבר ידוע וברור, שאין אהבת הקדוש ברוך הוא נקשרת בלבו של אדם עד שישגה בה תמיד כראוי ... אינו אוהב הקב"ה אלא בדעת שידעהו, ועל פי הדעה תהיה האהבה ... לפיכך צריך האדם ליחד עצמו להבין ולהשכיל בחכמות ותבונות המודיעות לו את קונו כפי כח שיש באדם להבין ולהשיג (רמב"ם, הל' תשובה י, ו).

3 בזמן שאדם מתבונן בדברים האלו ומכיר כל הברואים ... ויראה חכמתו של הקב"ה בכל היצורים וכל הברואים — מוסיף אהבה למקום ותמצא נפשו ויכמה בשרו לאהב המקום, ברוך הוא (רמב"ם, הל' יסודי התורה ד, יב).

4 והצנע לכת עם אלהיך (מיכה ו, ח).

5 וירד ה' על הר סיני אל ראש ההר ויקרא ה' למשה אל ראש ההר. ויעל משה (שמות יט, כ).

6 ודבר ה' אל משה פנים אל פנים כאשר ידבר איש אל רעהו (שמות לג, יא).

7 שמע תפלה, עדיך כל בשר יבאו (תהלים סה, ג).

8 מצות עשה להתפלל בכל יום שנאמר: "ועבדתם את ה' אלהיכם" (שמות כ"ג, כ"ה). מפי השמועה למדו שעבודה זו היא תפלה, שנאמר, "ולעבדו בכל לבבכם" (דברים י"א, י"ג). אמרו חכמים, איזו היא עבודה שבלב, זו תפלה (משנה תורה, הל' תפלה א, א).

9 ודאי כל ענין התפלה אינו חובה כלל אבל הוא ממדת חסד הבורא, יתברך, עלינו ששומע ועונה בכל קראנו אליו ועיקר הכתוב "ולעבדו בכל לבבכם", מצות עשה שתהיה כל עבדתנו לאל יתעלה בכל לבבנו, כלומר, בכונה רצויה שלימה לשמו (רמב"ן, ספר המצות ה).

87

10 והיא מצוה על צרה שתבא על הצבור, לזעק לפניו בתפלה ובתרועה... ונאמר
שהיא מצוה לעת הצרות שנאמין שהוא יתברך ויתעלה שומע תפלה והוא המציל
מן הצרות בתפלה וזעקה (רמב״ן, שם).

11 ומגיד שבחו של הקב״ה ואח״כ שואל צרכיו שהוא צריך להם בבקשה ובתחנה
ואח״כ נותן שבח והודיה לה׳ על הטובה שהשפיע לו כל אחד לפי כחו (רמב״ם,
הל׳ תפלה א, ב).

12 שבח: הללויה, הללו עבדי ה׳, יהי שם ה׳ מבורך מעתה ועד עולם. תחינה: למה
יאמרו הגוים איה נא אלהיהם. אנא ה׳ מלטה נפשי. הודיה: מה אשיב לה׳ כל
תגמולוהי עלי. לך אזבח זבח תודה. הודו לה׳ כי טוב.

13 שבח: שהכל ברא לכבודו; תחינה: שוש תשיש ותגל העקרה, שמח תשמח רעים
האהובים; הודיה: אשר ברא ששון ושמחה, חתן וכלה, מהרה ה׳ אלהינו ישמע
בערי יהודה ובחוצות ירושלים, קול ששון וקול שמחה וכו׳ (שבע ברכות).

14 אין חנון בכל מקום אלא לשון מתנת חנם (רש״י, דברים ג, כג).

15 אשא עיני אל ההרים, מאין יבא עזרי. עזרי מעם ה׳ עשה שמים וארץ (תהלים
קכא, א, ב).

16 ועל כרחך אתה נולד... חי... מת... עתיד לתן דין וחשבון לפני מלך מלכי
המלכים, הקדוש ברוך הוא (אבות ד, כב).

17 הבל הבלים... דור הלך ודור בא, והארץ לעולם עמדת... כל הדברים
יגעים... מה שהיה הוא שיהיה... ואין כל חדש תחת השמש (קהלת א).

CHAPTER VIII

MT. SINAI—THEIR FINEST HOUR

When the Torah was offered to the Israelites at Mount Sinai, they responded, "All that the Lord has spoken, we will observe and heed" (*Na'aseh Venishma*) (Ex. 24:7). The word "observe" connotes unqualified obedience and the submission of one's will; "heed" suggests a receptivity of mind and heart and also indicates the willingness to study and to be enlightened. This response of unconditional acceptance evoked great excitement in heaven, the Talmud tells us. Rabbi Elazar said: "When the Israelites gave precedence to 'observe,' *na'aseh*, over 'heed,' *nishma*, a heavenly voice exclaimed. 'Who divulged to my children this secret which only the angels employ?' " (Shab. 88a).[1] Apparently, only the heavenly hosts, who are close to the Divine Presence, respond to God's will without hesitation or reflection; they are never diverted by other considerations. The angels thereupon bestowed two crowns upon each of the Israelites, one for *na'aseh* and one for *nishma*[2] (*ibid.*). What was the significance of *na'aseh venishma* which warranted such heavenly approval and the bestowal of the crowns?

Giving priority to *na'aseh* over *nishma* meant that the Israelites pledged their absolute, unconditional commitment even before they were informed of the content of the Torah or understood the meaning of its commandments. They did this without prior deliberation and critical judgment. They accepted a distinctive and demanding national destiny, for themselves and for their future generations, without prior deliberation and without subjecting the proposition to critical evaluation. Such unqualified, undiscriminating commitments would seem rash and unwise in other spheres of life. The Jews are not known to be a gullible people; they are often inclined to be skeptical and rebellious; they are not easily persuaded. Even the Bible speaks of them as "stiff-necked," *am keshe oref* (Ex. 32:9). What, therefore, motivated their unanimous and unhesitating response, *na'aseh*?

The Bible teaches that in all of creation man is unique; only he was created in God's image. What is this singular, distinguishing characteristic which differentiates man from the animals, plants, and the rest of creation? What endowment reflects the Divine image which is the source of man's status and dignity? Maimonides and other medieval philosophers regarded man's *logos*, his thinking capacity, his ability to acquire knowledge, as man's most singular characteristic. They divided all of creation into four categories: mineral (*domem*), plant (*tzome'ah*), animal (*hai*), and man (*medabber*). Man is called a *medabber* (one who speaks), because speech reflects and conveys human thought; it is a noetic quality and the means whereby we articulate and formulate ideas.

If man's thinking capacity constitutes his singularity, how could God ask man to commit himself to precepts, the rationality of many of which eludes him and of which some actually conflict with his reason? If man's dignity and humanity are rooted in his intellect, would God command a *hukkah*, a *mitzvah* which is beyond human understanding? Why would the angels in heaven salute the *na'aseh venishma* response of the Israelites which, in effect, negated the rational element that is the basis of man's Divine image? To ask man to act without reason is to bid him to be less human, while God created man precisely to be different, to be human.

90

The Ratzon Elyon and the Ratzon Taḥton

We are, therefore, inclined to follow the masters of the Kabbalah, who taught that not man's rationality but his *ratzon elyon* (higher will) constitutes the singular endowment which distinguishes him from the rest of creation. This will makes decisions without consulting the intellect. It is in the center of the spiritual personality and constitutes man's real identity. Man's pragmatic intellect, which weighs pros and cons, is of subordinate stature in man's personality and is called *ratzon taḥton,* the lower, practical will.

The major decisions of man's life are made spontaneously and suddenly, in response to an aboriginal command from within, and are not necessarily dictated by external considerations or conditions, not necessarily affected by pragmatic considerations. They derive from intuitive affirmations which suddenly light up from within. Decisions of faith, of marriage, choice of profession, solutions to financial problems, acts of military genius, and most pivotal resolutions in life are reached intuitively, without addressing any inquiries to the intellect.[3] We are suddenly struck by an incisive insight and with a sense of direction. Later on, the practical intellect is called upon to justify the decision, to remove inconsistencies and to plan implementation.

In fact, only second- and third-level decisions which govern most situations are reached after long consultations. The intellect is inherently wary, slow-moving, computing in terms of loss and profit. To decide by reason is essentially to balance credits and debits, to weigh alternatives, and to measure consequences. This analysis is painstaking and time-consuming. The *ratzon elyon,* however, is intuitive, dynamic, aggressive, and passionate. It bursts forth with fervor and emotional intensity. Its insights and higher affirmations are inspired with the breath of divinity with which every man is endowed. There is no choosing between alternatives; one either accepts it or rejects one's identity. Decisions which are radical in nature, revolutionary, and decisive are extensions of this *ratzon elyon* which can change the direction of one's life. This will transcends man's intelligence and, in most cases, points toward a more exalted ideal. It illuminates the path for the intellect to follow, to elucidate, and to elaborate. Without this *ratzon elyon*, great minds would never have made their revolutionary discoveries in science,[4] religion, and other fields. While science is needed to unravel the mysteries of nature and we use logic to arrive at rational concepts, we rely on an inner illumination to answer pivotal questions. The further one moves from the concrete to the abstract, the more one must seek knowledge from within oneself.

The Kabbalists taught that the *ratzon elyon* belongs to the *Keter Elyon* (the crown, the highest *Sefirah*).[5] A crown rests on top of the head; the brain, underneath, is the seat of *hokhmah*, *binah*, and *da'at* (various levels of mental endowment) which constitute the *ratzon tahton* (the lower will). The crown, however, towers over the intellect; it is not governed or motivated by that which is underneath. It starts with an awareness of the cognitive world, but leaps beyond it. It wills because it wills, defying any attempt to explain the antecedents of the will. It is the real "I" in the human personality.

There are thus two wills: the *ratzon elyon*, the unmotivated will which derives from unknowable inner promptings; and the *ratzon tahton*, the will which is pragmatically motivated by reason or practical considerations. These two *retzonot* merge into an absolute unity, the Kabbalists say, only in the Almighty; within Him there are no conflicts. However, God gave man two *retzonot*, one of which is intelligible and the other unintelligible. These two are often in conflict; they collide and clash and man must choose the one with which he identifies. Should man be true to his inner light or should he respond to practical pro and con considerations? This is a dilemma which confronts us daily. Motivated by the *ratzon taḥton,* man lives in a utilitarian, pragmatic world. He does only what will be to his practical benefit. But if man aspires to greatness, he must identify with the *ratzon elyon,* which is not concerned with worldly success, progress, business profits, and similar considerations. Here, ideals which at times seem impractical predominate. The *ratzon elyon* decides because it decides; it wills because it wills. The mundane, drab, plodding *ratzon taḥton,* however, will only take the safe path and ends in mediocrity; it is guided by cold facts and will take no chances. It lacks elevating vision and the capacity to venture forth boldly.

The Two Retzonot in Halakhah

The concept that there are two levels in man's identity, his genuine self and his pragmatically motivated self, finds its echo in the *Halakhah.* We will cite three such instances.

There is an halakhic principle called *asmakhta,* "assurance," relating to obligations assumed, *hitḥayevut.*[6] A person may assume obligations or liabilities to another party by writing them in a contract or by expressing them verbally before witnesses. Such commitments are binding. If, however, these obligations are assumed subject to a prior fulfillment of certain conditions, the entire agreement may be declared invalid if it falls into the category of an *asmakhta.** Maimonides formulated the principle as follows: "This rule applies to all conditions that people stipulate to each other, even if supported by a deed and made in the presence of witnesses. Thus, if they say, 'Should such and such happen,' or 'If you do this-and-that, I will give you a *mina* [a particular coin],' or 'I will convey this house to you,

---

* The halakhic concept of *asmakhta,* involving conditional transfer of property and the assumption of obligations, is very complicated and is subject to varying interpretations. See *Encyclopedia Talmudica,* Vol. II; Isaac Halevi Herzog. *The Main Institutions of Jewish Law,* II, p. 71.

and if this does not happen, (or, 'If you do not fulfill this condition), I will not convey,' or 'I will not give you this house'—then, even if the transferee has fulfilled the conditions or the contingent event has occurred, the transferee does not acquire title." The reason for this rule is that whoever makes a transaction contingent upon the occurrence of a future event has not resolved to sell, inasmuch as in his mind he still waits for the occurrence of such an event.

In such instances, we assume that the person never truly intended to obligate himself. He was sure that the conditions would not be fulfilled. Therefore, even if they are fulfilled, he bears no liability because there was no initial wholehearted commitment. An *asmakhta* pledge comes from overconfidence. We rule *asmakhta lo kanya*, that his conditional commitment is unenforceable. Why should such an agreement not be binding when it was assumed with the full awareness of all particulars? Why should a legal, contractual obligation be invalidated when such conditional clauses are attached? Certainly, his later claim that he miscalculated, or that he made an error in judgment, is no excuse!

Similarly, the practice of *hattarat nedarim*, the dissolution of vows which later prove difficult to fulfill, also needs explanation. The Torah clearly requires the fulfillment of vows, yet our Sages have deduced from the Torah the practice of dissolution of vows by a *Bet Din* (a court of three, even of non-qualified judges) or one *talmid hakham* (a qualified judge, *mumheh*, competent Talmudic scholar), if this entails unforeseen hardship or other difficulties. On what grounds are such vows absolved when they were clearly freely assumed? Indeed, our *Hazal* suggest that this practice is not explicitly sanctioned by the literal text, *hetter nedarim porehim ba'avir;* yet we practice it. What is its justification?

Our third halakhic instance involves *teshuvah*, where sinners who acted with the full awareness of their wrongdoing, *bemezid,* are nevertheless bidden by God to repent and are granted atonement. Why do sinners and criminals deserve such consideration? How are sin and crime undone? Should not a just God mete out just punishment?—*Hashofet kol ha'aretz lo ya'aseh mishpat?* (Gen. 18:25).

The three halakhic problems become understandable if we acknowledge that the real "I," the genuine center of one's personality, the *ratzon elyon,* was not involved in any of these deeds. What acted hastily and unwisely was the *ratzon tahton,* the surface personality, which is motivated by profit and loss considerations, by lust, greed, pride, and other worldly inducements. The real identity of man is hidden, at times, even to himself. A total commitment in terms of obligation, vow, or transgression was not involved; the real "I" held back and was not responsible.

Yehudah Halevi (Kuzari 4:3) explained this as follows: "To the gifted among His creatures He has given an inner eye [*ayin nisteret*] which sees things as they really are, without any alteration . . . He to whom this has been given is clearsighted indeed. Other people, who appear to him as blind, he guides on their way . . . This eye beholds a grand and awful sight which reveals unmistakable truths."

The Mt. Sinai Response

When God offered the Torah at Mt. Sinai, the Israelites did not ask for a sample, to witness a demonstration, or to accept the Torah for a thirty-day trial period. This would have been the calculated, practical thing to do. In fact, according to the Midrash, God first offered the Torah to other nations—Esau, Ammon, Moab, and Ishmael—but they cautiously responded in pragmatic terms, weighing the value of the Torah in terms of social, cultural, and economic utility.[7] The Jewish response was *na'aseh venishma,* which means "we have decided to commit ourselves and, after that, to understand intellectually." The decision was a leap of faith by the *ratzon elyon,* an intuitive sense of what was valid and imperative. The inner soul of man is capable of such bold visions, to transcend mundane considerations in an heroic embrace of what is or must be. This explains why *Ḥazal* ascribed so much significance to the response. Two crowns, they taught, were bestowed upon every Jew, one for *na'aseh* (the *ratzon elyon*) and the second for *nishma* (the *ratzon taḥton*), the intellect. Which is the superior perception? Obviously, the *elyon,* which transcends man's intellect.

Two Commitments

A religious Jew basically makes two unqualified commitments, and both defy rational justification. In his personal life, he accepts the discipline of all-embracing *mitzvot,* among which are *ḥukkim,* which are intellectually unintelligible, and *mishpatim,* social laws, which in the modern world are often similarly resisted. We stubbornly and lovingly observe these regulations, despite the disdain of the wider society and the implied ridicule of our way of life. We insist on the superiority of our perception of God as Legislator and of the *mitzvot* as sanctifying life.

The second religious commitment of the observant Jew is to the historical destiny of his people. We believe that, despite contradictory historical experiences, fearful holocausts, and the enmity of the entire world, our inexorable movement is towards a Divine *ge'ulah* (redemption), "even though he may tarry," and that, eventually, our people's aspirations will be fulfilled. We refuse to succumb to despair and persist in an irrational faith.

Both religious commitments are expressions of a faith which is beyond logic and practical considerations. To persist in Torah observance nowadays, and to support the State of Israel despite the concerted hatred which envelopes her, require the same kind of uncalculating response of *na'aseh venishma.* We will because we will. This is the faith which initiated our peoplehood and which still sustains us to this day.

No Disparagement of Intellect

To give precedence to the *ratzon elyon* does not imply disparagement of the intellect. Indeed, man is bidden in the Bible to use his mind in order to achieve dominion over nature and, in effect, to combat disease and poverty. The Talmud employs logical analysis in its deliberations, searching for underlying principles and applying them to diverse situations. The first section of Maimonides' classic halakhic code is entitled *Sefer Hamada* (The Book of Rational Knowledge). The intellectual emphasis has always been a distinctive characteristic of Jewish life.

But this intellect must acknowledge its limitations. It is subservient to perceptions of faith. The intellect classifies and applies basic truths which the *ratzon elyon* affirms. This Kabbalistic teaching expresses a cardinal tenet of Judaism. The intellect has boundaries within which it exercises its cognitive powers. The goals of life emanate from within, but the intellect removes inconsistencies, plans implementation, and formulates logical justification. Without the *ratzon elyon*, the Jew could not sustain his commitments to the demanding discipline of *mitzvot* observance and the unshakable faith in our people's future.

הערות לפרק 8

1 אמר רבי אלעזר: בשעה שהקדימו ישראל נעשה לנשמע, יצתה בת קול ואמרה
להן, מי גילה לבני, רז זה שמלאכי השרת משתמשין בו (שבת פח.).

2 דרש ר' סימאי, בשעה שהקדימו ישראל נעשה לנשמע, באו ששים ריבוא של
מלאכי השרת לכל אחד ואחד מישראל קשרו לו שני כתרים אחד כנגד נעשה
ואחד כנגד נשמע (שם).

3 דע... כי ההאמנה... ענין המצוייר בנפש, כשיאמינו בו שהוא כן כמו
שיצוייר.. כי האמונה היא ההאמנה במה שיצוייר שהוא חוץ לשכל כפי מה
שיצוייר בשכל, ואם יהיה עם זאת האמונה שאי אפשר חילוף זאת האמונה בשום
פנים, ולא ימצא בשכל מקום דחייה לאמונה ההיא, ולא לשער אפשרות חלופה,
תהיה אמתית... כמו שצוו החשובים, ונאמר, "אמרו בלבבכם על משכבכם
ודמו סלה" (תהלים ד. ה) (רמב"ם, מורה נבוכים א, נ; בתרגום שמואל אבן
תיבון).

4 "At times I feel certain that I am right without knowing the reason.
When the eclipse of 1919 confirmed my intuition, I was not in the
least suprised" (Albert Einstein, *Cosmic Religion.* p. 7).

5 Name given in Kabbalah to ten creative powers, arranged in a
gradation from the most spiritual to the least.

6 וכן כל תנאין שמתנין בני אדם ביניהן, אע"פ שהן בעדים ובשטר, אם יהיה כך
או אם תעשה כך, אתן לך מנה, או אקנה לך בית זה, ואם לא יהיה או לא תעשה,
לא אקנה לך, ולא אתן לך אע"פ שעשה או שהיה הדבר, לא קנה. שכל האומר
"אם יהיה אם לא יהיה", לא גמר והקנה, שהרי דעתו עדיין סומכת שמא יהיה,
שמא לא יהיה (ולא גמר בלבו להקנותו) (רמב"ם, הל' מכירה יא, ה).

7 ספרי, ברכה; פסיק"ר כ"א; ע"ז ב:.

CHAPTER IX

SURRENDERING OUR MINDS TO GOD

The Israelites were highly commended for responding *na'aseh venishma* at Mt. Sinai. They thereby emulated the response of the angels, who perform their assigned tasks without any questions or doubts. They took upon themselves two types of *mitzvot*, as the Bible states: "And you shall keep My statutes [*hukkim*] and My ordinances [*mishpatim*], which if a man do, he shall live" (Lev. 18:5).[1] "The general object of the Law," Maimonides wrote, "is twofold: the well-being of the soul and the well-being of the body. The well-being of the soul is promoted by correct opinions ... The well-being of the body is established by proper management of the relationships we share with one another" (*Guide for the Perplexed*, 3:27). In the Midrash, Rav teaches: "The Commandments were given only to purify the people therewith ..." (Gen. R. 44:1).[2]

The difference between *hukkim* and *mishpatim* is explained in *Yoma* 67b; "*Mishpatim* are those commandments which should have been written down even if they had not been transcribed in the Torah [since they are in conformity with human feelings of justice and morality]. These are prohibitions of idolatry, immorality, bloodshed, robbery, and blasphemy (Ex. 20). *Hukkim* are all the commandments with which the evil inclination and the heathen find fault [because they seem beyond human comprehension]. They are: the prohibitions against eating pork (Lev. 11:8) and wearing *sha'atnez* (a mixture of wool and linen in garments; Deut. 22:11), *halitzah* (release from the obligation of levirate marriage; Deut. 5:10), the purification of a leper (Lev. 14), the scapegoat on the Day of Atonement (Lev. 16:15–29), and the *Parah Adumah* (ceremony of the red heifer; Num. 19). Lest one be inclined to dismiss them as meaningless ceremonies, Scripture says: 'I am the Lord' (Lev. 18:4); that is to say, 'I, the Lord, have decreed them and you have no right to question them.' " [3]

Generally, *hukkim* seem to be irrational and, if not for the Divine imperative, we would never observe them. We assume a Divine purpose and value, but we cannot fathom them. The *mishpatim*, on the other hand, reflect cultural and humanistic considerations. Yet the force of the Divine command applies to both, demanding observance and unqualified commitment. We intend to analyze the nature of the *hok* and also to explain why the *mishpat* needs the support of the same Divine imperative as the *hok*. Would our social conscience not be sufficient motivation for the *mishpat*?

Analyzing the Hok. Rashi cites a Rabbinic comment on the *Parah Adumah* rite: "It is a decree ordained by Me. You have no right to question it" (Num. 19:2). This suggests that the *hok* can be defined as an absolute norm and an ultimate command, demanding total submission without reservations. It is to be affirmed even if "Satan and the nations of the world taunt Israel," ridiculing its irrationality. The observant Jew accepts the Torah even as a patient follows the prescription of his doctor, taking complex medications and submitting to required surgical procedures. We may seek to understand and make all possible inquiries, but ultimately we accept it on faith. The Lord, Creator and Healer of all flesh, undoubtedly knows what is best for our bodies and souls as well as what is harmful to them.

The *hok* may be said to possess two characteristics. The first is its universal immutability: the fact that a *hok* is independent of situational factors, changing philosophies and ideologies, or shifting practical and economic conditions. All these have no effect or bearing on a *hok*, which persists and retains its value under all circumstances, at all times and everywhere. Obviously, only an absolute faith in God as the Legislator of the *hok* would motivate such acceptance.

Psalm 139:7, 8 can be understood as suggesting the unchanging universality of God and His law: "Whither shall I go from Your spirit [statutes] or whither shall I flee from Your presence [law]?; I ascend to heaven, You are there [and so are Your commands]; if I make my bed in the bottomless depths, behold You are there [and also Your precepts]." [4] As God is universal and eternal, so is His law.

The verb *hakok*, etymologically, signifies the act of carving, engraving, making incisions in a hard surface such as stone or metal. Several verses support this meaning: "Behold, I have graven you (*hakkotikh*) upon the palms of my hands" (Isa. 49:16);[5] "Oh that My words were ... engraven (*yuhaku*) with an iron pen and lead in the rock forever" (Job 19:23, 24).[6] Such engravings are protected against the erosion of time and the elements. Used in religious law, the term signifies that the *hok* is characterized by perpetual validity and is "graven in the rock forever." *Hok* implies "eternity"; it is not a temporary regulation.

The Decalogue was engraved on Two Tablets of stone. Surely God could have used a lighter material, which would have been less burdensome for Moses to carry? Stone, however, conveys the notion of stability and permanence. Faced by the golden calf idolatry (Ex. 32:19), Moses smashed the Two Tablets because the people's backsliding indicated the transience of their commitment. Only forty days before, they had vowed acceptance. The stone, symbolic of the permanence of their commitment, was incongruent with the inconstancy they had displayed.

Nature's laws are also *hukkim*, unalterable and universal. The same Legislator instituted both systems of law, governing physical nature as well as man's deportment. The Bible uses the word *hok* in regard to nature, as in Proverbs 8:29: "When He gave to the sea His decree [*hukko*], that the waters should not transgress His commandment; When he appointed [*Behukko*] the foundations of the earth." [7] Nature is not capricious; it unfailingly abides by God's laws, even as man should in the human realm. There are no exceptions or surprises; nature is reliable and predictable and its laws are universally valid.

Paradoxical Nature of the Ḥok. We have previously described one aspect of the *hok*, its unchanging universality. The second characteristic is its incomprehensibility: it demands the surrender of one's mind and the suspension of one's thinking. It is a total commitment precisely because it requires an abdication of one's reason. The commitment of a child to his parents, however fervent, is not total; it is rooted in the family setting and has many qualifications and reservations. A parent's commitment to a child, however, is instinctive and total; it is irrational and therefore not contingent or conditional. The reason for the *hok* remains a mystery; indeed, the *hok* is often contested by one's thinking mind. Although man is a rational being, the *hok* demands that he violate his reason.

Actually, the immutability of the *hok* is implicit in its paradoxical nature. A *hok* is unchanging because it is not subject to reason. It is in the non-cognitive dimension and is, therefore, not susceptible to change. Only laws which are based on intellect are vulnerable to modification, correction, or reinterpretation. The intellect is able to build and tear down, to create and to destroy; it continually reevaluates and postulates anew. The history of science is a chronicle of the construction and destruction of ideas, theories, affirmations, and negations. The *hok*, however, rises above human reason and motivation. It therefore remains unchanged and is not modified by the attrition of time and mood. The commitment to the *hok*, as we previously explained (Chap. VIII),[8] derives from the *ratzon elyon*. It is a leap of affirmation; it is the inner *neshamah* (soul), the real "I" replying *na'aseh* even before *nishma*.

The religious Jew accepts the entire Torah as a *hok*, both in regard to its immutability and also its unintelligibility. At the conclusion of the daily morning service, we find this affirmation: "I believe with perfect faith that this Torah will not be changed and that there will be no other Torah given by the Creator, blessed be His Name" [8] (Maimonides, *Principles of Faith*). The laws of the Torah are thus above place or time. Moreover, the observant Jew never asks "why?" in regard to *mitzvah* obligations. He may ask "how is it performed?" or "what lessons are to be derived therefrom?" but not "why?" In the face of disaster, in confrontation with stark evil and utter distress, the believing Jew does not question their justice. The classic response of Aaron after the death of his two sons was one of mute silence and acceptance of the heavenly decree [9] (Lev. 10:3). Job asked "why?" and was clearly informed that mortal man cannot grasp the full meaning of events, and so no answer was given to him. To be a loyal Jew is to be heroic, and heroes commit themselves without intellectual reservations. Only one who lacks the courage of commitment will belabor the "why." The *ratzon elyon* makes a commitment of certitude. This is what governed the survivors of concentration camps who, fortified by religious faith, emerged to rebuild their lives.

Why the Divine Imperative for Mishpatim? We have spoken heretofore primarily of the *hok*, the inexplicable precept. In fact, we perform all *mishpatim* (mostly social laws) in the same manner as the *hukkim*. The Torah does not assign separate sections to the *hukkim* and *mishpatim* respectively; they are interspersed throughout Scripture. We make no distinctions between the two as regards the quality and totality of our commitment.

Why, we may ask, is it not enough for the *mishpatim* to be intellectually motivated? Why the need to add a *hok*, a non-*logos* dimension, to social laws which conscience itself dictates?

Apparently, reason is not a reliable guide even with respect to *mishpatim*. There are borderline situations which confuse the mind, and consequently it finds itself helpless in applying its moral norms. Since our intellect must weigh pros and cons and is slow and deliberate in deciding, society starts to nibble away at the edges of marginal, borderline problems. Life must be lived; before our logic can formulate an opinion, society will already have weakened all restraints. Permissiveness will have replaced orderliness and the amoral in man will have emerged triumphant.

For example, the mind certainly condemns murder. This is particularly true of the killing of a young working mother who leaves behind orphaned children. But does this abhorrence of murder also apply when the victim is an old, cruel, miserly woman who in the eyes of society was a parasitic wretch, as in Dostoyevsky's *Crime and Punishment?* May we murder her in order to save a young girl from the clutches of degradation? May euthanasia be practiced to relieve the elderly or terminally ill of further suffering? Here the *logos* hesitates, is uncertain, and imparts no decisive guidance. We can easily rationalize in either direction and no external norm is compelling. As a *mishpat*, a social norm, murder may at times be tolerated; as a *hok*, the prohibition against murder is clear and absolute.

May we kill an infant? Certainly not, the *logos* in the *mishpat* proclaims. But a fetus in the womb confuses the intellect. Is this also murder or does one become a human being only upon emerging from the womb? The confusion is compounded when we consider the womb as a mother-incubator, no different from the hospital's incubator. Perhaps, then, even incubator babies may be put to death. The *logos* can easily be stretched in various directions. If the dominant principle governing the *logos* is that abortion is morally permissible because only a mother has a right to decide whether she wishes to be a mother, then infants may similarly have their lives terminated after birth. What if the child interferes with the promising brilliant career of the mother? The *logos* is confused and our modern secularized world, which only applies the yardstick of logic, is similarly perplexed.

When is one a human being? The authoritative response frequently heard is that two factors must be present: the possession of a genetic code and the capacity to communicate with fellow human beings. The fetus has the first characteristic, but lacks the second. But perhaps, extending the point to an extreme, those two requirements should apply after birth until the child develops intelligible means of communication. We can sense the untenability of this position but, in a like manner, the *logos* will often find itself perplexed; where does mercy end and murder begin?

We have assumed that *mishpatim* are prompted by reason. Yet, in our modern world, there is hardly a *mishpat* which has not been repudiated. Stealing and corruption are the accepted norms in many spheres of life; adultery and general promiscuity find support in respectable circles; and even murder, medical and germ experiments have been conducted with governmental complicity. The *logos* has shown itself in our time to be incapable of supporting the most basic of moral inhibitions.

The Torah, therefore, insists that a *mishpat* be accepted as a *ḥok*; our commitment must be unshakable, universally applicable, and upheld even when our *logos* is confused. Without *ḥok*, every social and moral law can be rationalized away, leaving the world a sophisticated jungle of instincts and impulses. The Torah therefore enjoins: "And thou shalt keep My statutes [*ḥukkim*] and My ordinances [*mishpatim*]" (Lev. 18:5).[10] Only then can we realize *vaḥai bahem* ("he shall live by them"), a support of moral living. Even a *mishpat* can endure only when it is sustained by the *ratzon elyon*, an unmotivated commitment which is impervious to confusing circumstances.

הערות לפרק 9

1 ושמרתם את חקתי ואת משפטי, אשר יעשה אותם האדם וחי בהם, אני ה׳:
(ויקרא יח, ה).

2 רב אומר: לא נתנו המצות אלא לצרף בהן את הבריות (ב״ר מד, א).

3 ת״ר ״את משפטי תעשו״ (ויקרא יח) דברים שאלמלא לא נכתבו, דין הוא
שיכתבו, ואלו הן: עבודת כוכבים, וגלוי עריות, ושפיכת דמים, וגזל, וברכת
השם; ״את חקתי תשמרו״ (שם), דברים שהשטן (רש״י — יצר הרע) משיב
עליהן ואלו הן, אכילת חזיר, ולבישת שעטנז, וחליצת יבמה, וטהרת מצורע,
ושעיר המשתלח ופרה אדומה. ושמא תאמר, מעשה תהו הם, ת״ל, ״אני ה׳״ —
אני ה׳ חקקתיו ואין לך רשות להרהר בהן (יומא סז:).

4 אנה אלך מרוחך, ואנה מפניך אברח. אם אסק שמים, שם אתה. ואציעה שאול,
הנך (תהלים קלט, ז, ח).

5 הן על כפים חקתיך (ישעיה מט, טז).

6 מי יתן אפו ויכתבון מלי. מי יתן בספר ויחקו. בעט ברזל ועפרת לעד בצור
יחצבון (איוב יט, כג, כד).

7 בשומו לים חקו ומים לא יעברו פיו. בחוקו מוסדי ארץ (משלי ח, כט).

8 אני מאמין באמונה שלמה, שזאת התורה לא תהי מחלפת ולא תהי תורה אחרת
מאת הבורא, יתברך שמו (רמב״ם, שלשה עשר עקרים).

9 וידם אהרן (ויקרא י, ג) רש״י — קבל שכר על שתיקתו.

10 ושמרתם את חקתי ואת משפטי, אשר יעשה אתם האדם וחי בהם, אני ה׳
(ויקרא יח, ה).

106

CHAPTER X

DUALITY OF JEWISH COMMITMENT

A religious Jew makes two commitments: to observe the *mitzvot* of the Torah and also to identify with the historical destiny of his people. Both require a leap of faith which is impelled by the *ratzon elyon*, the sovereign, unmotivated will, the essential "I." Both may be regarded as *hukkim* because they involve considerable suspension of one's reason and are not based on practical considerations.

When a candidate for conversion appears before a *Bet Din* (religious court) and declares his intention to join the Jewish fold, he is asked two questions: "What motivates you? Do you not realize that we are a persecuted people, subject to oppression and hatred? Do you feel that your desire is reasonable or worthwhile?" The candidate responds, in effect, *"Af al pi khen"*—"despite these considerations I am determined to convert." This response is similar to the daily affirmation of faith of all Jews who say in their morning prayers, *"Ve'af al pi sheyitmahme'ah, im kol zeh ahakeh lo"*—"though the Messiah and Jewish salvation and vindication be slow in coming, I will nevertheless persist in believing in their imminent realization." The second question deals with the acceptance of the discipline and sovereignty of *mitzvot* such as *kashrut, Shabbat, tefillin,* and *tzedakah,* which characterize our unique way of life. Here the convert makes a commitment to live a lonely life in the larger family of man, becoming a member of a minority people in a society which is

107

often cynical and which in general hardly encourages our distinct way of life.. The *Berit Milah* (circumcision) which a male convert undergoes is a covenant that binds him to the Jewish people; it is a sign of identity with the community of Israel. The *tevilah* (*mikveh* immersion) initiates the *kabbalat ol mitzvot* or assumption of *mitzvah* obligations. This duality of commitment is expressed in the famous words of Ruth: "Your people shall be my people and your God, my God" (1:16).[1]

Which of these is of greater consequence to Jewish survival, the personal *mitzvah* commitment or the national commitment to peoplehood? We are not implying that either may be rejected. Both are required, but which takes precedence?

The Parah Adumah and the Korban Pesah

The Midrash (Ex. R. 19) compares two *hukkim,* the *Parah Adumah* (red heifer) and the *Korban Pesah* (Paschal Lamb sacrifice), and it ascribes a higher value to the *Parah Adumah.* The Torah refers to both as *hukkim*: "This is the statute of the Law [*Parah Adumah*]" (Num. 19.2) and "This is the statute of the *Pesah*" (Ex. 12:43).[2] In what way is the *hok* or *hukkah* of the *Parah Adumah* superior to that of *Korban Pesah*?

The Midrash reads: "The verse in Psalm 119:80 says: 'Let my heart be undivided in [observing] Your statutes, so that I may not be put to shame.' "[3] Because the *hok* lacks the support of reason, it often exposes us to taunting, and the psalmist, therefore, prays to God to strengthen our resolve to adhere to the Divine teachings.

"This [verse]," the Midrash says, "refers to two statutes [since *hukkekha* is in the plural], the *Korban Pesah* and the *Parah Adumah.* In both cases the term *hukkah* [suggesting an absolute command] is used . . . but which of these two statutes is greater? This may be illustrated by the story of two women. They were walking side by side, apparently social equals, but when one escorted the other to her house, it became clear which

was the mistress and which the attendant. Similarly, the *Parah
Adumah* is greater, because all who would eat the *Pesah* need
the ashes of the *Parah* and must go to it, as Scripture states:
'And they shall take for the unclean, of the ashes' (Num.
19:17)." [4] The purifying process of the *Parah Adumah* was a
sine qua non for partaking of the paschal sacrifice and, in
this sense, the Midrash regards the *Parah* as the mistress and
the *Pesah* as the attendant.

(In terms of indispensability, the *Parah* is essential to the
Pesah, but not vice-versa. In terms of purpose, our logic would
suggest otherwise—that the *Parah* serves the needs of the *Pesah;*
it is a means to the *Pesah*, which is the end. Our Midrash, however, is not dealing with purpose but with the element of indispensability. The *Parah* can manage without the *Pesah*, not
the reverse).

Evidently, the Midrash intends to impart a philosophical lesson
which is reflected in the relationship of the *Parah* and the *Pesah*.
Perhaps it is attempting to resolve a dilemma which was perplexing in its day and which is still relevant to ours. We believe
that *Parah* and *Pesah* are meant to represent the two levels of
hukkah or *hok* commitment which we explained previously
(Chap. VIII). These are the individual commitment of the
Jew to the *mitzvah* discipline of the Torah (*mitzvot*), and his
identification with *Keneset Yisrael* and its particular destiny.

The Parah Adumah

The *Parah* ritual represents an act of personal purification, an
individual experience which cleanses the Jew ritually and allows
him to participate in sacred observances. Its efficacy is based
neither on sense nor on reason; it demands obedience and submission, surrender of mind and of will to the Law of God. Such
absolute commitment is necessary to maintain loyalty to Torah
and *mitzvot* even in an environment and society that mock its
observance. The *zot hukkat hatorah* injunction encompasses all

aspects of personal life—food, ethics, sex, business activity, and ritual observance. Only a recognition of the *gezerah hi milfanai*, of the absolute Divine decree, can sustain the life of *mitzvah* obedience.

In the previous chapter we explained that the term *hok* subsumes *mishpatim* as well. A *mishpat*, even when it is based on reason, must be accepted as a *hok*; otherwise, even rational social and moral laws may be corrupted or distorted, as is often demonstrated in our modern secularized society. The *hok* differs from the *mishpat* only in the degree of its intelligibility; both, however, need the Divine imperative to sustain their religious fulfillment.

The Korban Pesah

This *hukkah* deals with the paschal offering and is a corporate group activity. "No alien may eat of it" (Ex. 12:43)[5], but only members of the Jewish community. Here, at this sacrifice commemorating the birth of the Jewish people, the *ratzon elyon* commits the Jew to the collective unfolding of the Jewish historical destiny. Ours is a paradoxical history, with unrealized dreams, unfulfilled hopes and yearnings, supported by an unbounded faith and promise—a history that is both tragic in suffering and glorious in its unyielding loyalty and amazing survival.

One of the unique aspects of our history is surely our capacity to evoke *sinat Yisrael*, the persistent and ever-present hostility which humanity directs at us as a people; it is a strange and inexplicable fact of our history. Another is the contradictory, zig-zagging pattern of our historical past, seeming to violate the geometric rule that "the shortest distance between two points is a straight line." At times, we seem to be approaching our destiny, slowly but surely; suddenly we are deflected, thrust aside or forced to move in the opposite direction. Positions previously achieved are abandoned and the accomplishments of entire generations are wiped away. Whole settlements, *yishuvim*, are annihilated and we find ourselves starting anew. Just as surely, *ge'ulah* once again starts beckoning, inspiring new hopes and movements. This process of historical detours is unlike the history of other nations, which seem, more or less, to be moving in a straight course—from the inception of nationhood to eminence, upon occasion, and to subsequent decline.

This irregular pattern began early in our history. God had promised Abraham that his descendants would inhabit Canaan. Why did they have to endure the servitude of Egypt for hundreds of years and the subsequent confinement in the desert for forty years before the promise was fulfilled? The Passover *Haggadah* provides us with a brief historical review: "Originally, our ancestors were idol worshippers... And to Isaac I gave Jacob and Esau; and I gave to Esau Mt. Seir to possess it; but Jacob and his children went down to Egypt." [6] Strange! The promise to Esau to possess Mt. Seir was almost immediately fulfilled, but Jacob's inheritance was sidetracked by his descent to Egypt. The *Haggadah* mentions Esau here precisely to draw this contrast, that for the Jew the distance to be traversed between promise and fulfillment is long and circuitous. This is a strange and paradoxical feature of our history.

God told Moses that He had previously identified Himself to the Patriarchs by the name *El Shaddai* (Almighty God) and not by the Tetragrammaton, *Hashem* (Ex. 6:3). Rashi explains the latter name as referring to God fulfilling His promise to enable them to inherit the land in their lifetime.[7] The name *Hashem* signifies realization. The Patriarchs had only been given promises; a long road still lay ahead of them before their descendants would conquer the land. Similarly, the Torah relates, "Now when Pharaoh let the people go, God did not lead them by way of the land of the Philistines, although it was nearer" (Ex. 13:17).[8] Deviations from the straight course and long delays characterize the strange movement of Jewish history; the longest, not the shortest route, seems to be our destiny.

This mystifying pattern of Jewish history is also a *hok*, demanding our loyalty even as it defies our comprehension. It is as irrational as the *Parah Adumah* is in the realm of the individual. Why should *El Shaddai* be separated from *Hashem*, the promise from the fulfillment? And yet the Jew waits patiently, filled with expectancy, with an unshakable faith in the inevitable *ge'ulah*. If rationality, the practical *ratzon tahton*, were our guide, we would never have survived all these detours; we would have given up long ago, even in Egypt. But instead, the Jew makes a total commitment, derived from the *ratzon elyon*, which stubbornly persists irrespective of pragmatic circumstances.

This sovereign will, as it is reflected in the *Korban Pesah*, is expressed in the words, "I firmly believe in the coming of the Messiah; and although he is slow in coming, I daily wait for his coming" (Maimonides' Twelfth Principle of Faith).[9] The enormous capacity of the Jew to wait perseveringly for the *ge'ulah* with a sense of its imminent advent, despite all delays and discouragement, is a unique endowment of our people. This is symbolized by the *hukkah* of *Korban Pesah*; the root word *paso'ah*, semantically, means jumping, leaping, skipping around obstacles and curves in an irregular and impeded movement. (Rashi, Ex. 12:13)

The Midrash Explained

The Midrash cites only these two *hukkim* as representing two levels of total commitment, and with reference to them we pray, "Let my heart be undivided in [observing] Your statutes, so that I may not be put to shame" (Ps. 119:80).[3] The total commitment of the Jew involves his private life as well as his community identification. The injunction of *zot hukkat hatorah* (*Parah Adumah*) means that the Jew will maintain a Torah-true life; he will suspend his questions and will even surrender his *logos*. But the Jew also belongs to a people, is part of its contradictory, zigzagging historical experience, and here he needs the *zot hukkat hapesah*. For both commitments, the Jew employs the *ratzon elyon*, not to ask "why" but only to seek the realization of this sovereign, unmotivated will.

The question the Midrash poses is which of these two total commitments is more significant, the *hukkat hapesah* or the *hukkat hatorah* (*Parah Adumah*)—the commitment to our people's survival or the heroic personal life of *shemirat mitzvot*. The Midrash answers unequivocally that the *hukkat hatorah* takes precedence; she is the mistress, while the *Pesah* is the attendant. First, the Jew must commit himself totally as a single being to a disciplined Torah life. He is to exhibit his commitment daily, in the myriad details of every activity. The *Halakhah* knows nothing of trivial matters; in every detail, the *hukkah* demands absolute obedience.

Next comes the *hukkat hapesah*, the community, the people, the State. The State and the community are important because, through the corporate group, the individual Jew is enabled to act heroically, not only on the collective, history-making level but also in his private life. Yet the relationship between the Jew and God is central. It precedes his relationship with his people, in which God is also involved. The *Korban Pesah* is crucial for Jewish identity and survival, but the *Parah Adumah* endows Jewish existence with meaning and raises national identity to a transcendental level. Such is the decision of the Midrash; we may now inquire about the rationale of this judgment.

Man Needs Purging

Despite his Divine potential, man is frequently brutish, selfish, deceitful, pleasure-hunting, power-oriented. He needs cleansing, purging, redeeming. The fact that he is born with a genetic code does not endow him with dignity and holiness; to earn this status, he must strive for redemption by relating himself to God. How is he to achieve this redemption? We know of *hekhsher kelim*, the cleansing of utensils, which takes place before Passover; this is a simple procedure. The purging of man, however, is much more complex; man succumbs all too readily to that which is, morally speaking, unclean and uncouth. It often seems as if man has just emerged from the jungle, despite his glorious conquests of nature, his technological miracles. Man, too, needs a purging discipline to restore his spiritual identity.

The historical-national experience cannot cleanse the individual man; it is not a cathartic. It might inspire high levels of nationalistic idealism and personal sacrifices, but it will not necessarily cleanse him and sanctify him. It is not *hekhsher adam*. Only the Divine *mitzvah* discipline cleanses the ugliness in man's character and raises him to a new ontological level. We cannot start with the collective experience; we must begin with the individual commitment. As the verse cited by the Midrash indicated, *zot hukkat hatorah* takes precedence because, "And for the unclean, they must take of the ashes of the burnt heifer." [4] In order to be qualified to experience the spiritual unfolding of Jewish history symbolized by the *Korban Pesah*, we must first purge ourselves of all that is unclean and debasing.

Explaining Rabbenu Tam's Tefillin

The duality of Jewish commitment to *shemirat hamitzvot* and to *Keneset Yisrael* may provide a philosophical explanation of the halakhic dispute between Rashi and Rabbenu Tam regarding the sequence of the *parshiyot*, the four paragraphs which are inserted in the four separate compartments of the *tefillin shel rosh* (Men. 34b). It is in each of these four passages (Ex. 13:1–10; 11–16, and Deut. 6:4–9; 11:13–21) that the *mitzvah* of *tefillin* is mentioned.

Rashi regarded the four *parshiyot* as one entity, telling an identical story, all of them conveying the commitment of *kabbalat ol malkhut shamayim*—the acceptance of God's sovereignty and the binding character of His commandments. This being the case, one who faces the wearer of the *tefillin* (*"vehakore"*) should find that the four portions are positioned in the precise order, moving from right to left, that they are situated in the Pentateuch.[10] There is no logical reason to arrange them in any other sequence. Thus, the portion on the extreme right is *Kaddesh* (Ex. 13:1–10); next to it is *Vehayah ki yevi'akha* (Ex. 13:11–16); still moving to the left, we next insert the *Shema* (Deut. 6:4–9); and finally, on the extreme left, *Vehayah im shamo'a* (Deut. 11:13–21).

Rabbenu Tam, however, interpreted the Talmudic text differently, that the order of the last two portions be the reverse of what Rashi had prescribed. The *Shema* (Deut. 6:4–9) should be on the extreme left and *Vehayah im shamo'a* (Deut. 11:13–21) on its right.[11] Rabbenu Tam apparently felt that the Talmudic text speaks of two separate groupings of *parshiyot*, with the two Exodus sections in their sequence starting from the right; and the two Deuteronomy sections in their order, starting from the extreme left. Rashi was concerned with the Pentateuchal sequence while Rabbenu Tam was guided by the philosophic and conceptual messages of these portions.

The excerpts from the Book of Exodus deal with the departure from Egypt and the Passover observance. They challenge the Jew to identify with his people and to commit himself to its historic destiny and survival. The extracts from Deuteronomy, however, are dialogues with the individual Jew, exhorting him to love God and to learn His commandments, "when you stay at home, and when you are away," and to serve Him "with all your heart and with all your soul and with all your might." They declare the observance of the Torah mandatory as well as the teaching of its content "diligently to your children." Our concern here is with the individual Jew as regards *shemirat hamitzvot*.

By placing the *Keneset Yisrael* (Exodus) commitment on the right and the *mitzvah* commitment on the left, Rabbenu Tam emphasizes the two aspects of being Jewish. Each commitment has its own sequence. Support for the view of Rabbenu Tam may perhaps be indicated by the requirement that a *"Shin"* be on either side of the *tefillin shel rosh*. What do these *"Shins,"* situated on the Exodus and the Deuteronomy sides, represent? Perhaps they allude to the two themes of the *tefillin*, implicit in the system of Rabbenu Tam.

Rashi, however, subsumed both commitments under the overall *ol malkhut shamayim* and regarded all the *parshiyot* as conveying one basic theme. He therefore ordained that they be arranged without any change in the sequence of their appearance in the Torah. The accepted halakhic ruling has adopted the view of Rashi, signifying that Jewish nationalism and religious observance are inseparable and constitute a single entity. Both draw their strength from the overall commitment.

הערות לפרק 10

1   עמך עמי, ואלהיך אלהי (רות א, טז).

2   זאת חקת התורה (במדבר יט, ב); זאת חקת הפסח (שמות יב, מג).

3   יהי לבי תמים בחקיך, למען לא אבוש (תהלים קיט, פ).

4   יהי לבי תמים בחקיך. זה חקת הפסח וחקת פרה אדומה. למה ששניהם דומין זה לזה. בזה נאמר "זאת חקת הפסח" ובזה נאמר "זאת חקת התורה" ואי אתה יודע אי זו חקה גדולה מזו. משל לשתי מטרונות דומות שהיו מהלכות שתיהן כאחת, נראות שוות. מי גדולה מזו. אותה שחברתה מלוה אותה עד ביתה והולכת אחריה. כך בפסח נאמר בו חקה ובפרה נאמר בה חקה, ומי גדולה, הפרה שאוכלי הפסח צריכין לה, שנאמר "ולקחו לטמא מעפר שרפת החטאת" (במדבר יט, יז) הוי כל בן נכר לא יאכל בו (שמות רבה יט).

5   זאת חקת הפסח, כל בן נכר לא יאכל בו (שמות יב, מג).

6   מתחלה עובדי עבודה זרה היו אבותינו... "ואתן ליצחק את יעקב ואת עשו, ואתן לעשו את הר שעיר לרשת אותו, ויעקב ובניו ירדו מצרים" (הגדה; יהושע כד, ד).

7   וארא אל אברהם אל יצחק ואל יעקב באל שדי, ושמי ה' לא נודעתי להם (שמות ו, ג). רש"י — לא נכרתי להב במדת אמתות שלי, שעליה נקרא שמי ה', נאמן לאמת דברי, שהרי הבטחתים ולא קימתי.

8   ויהי בשלח פרעה את העם ולא נחם אלהים דרך ארץ פלשתים כי קרוב הוא (שמות יג, יז).

9   אני מאמין באמונה שלמה בביאת המשיח, ואף על פי שיתמהמה, עם כל זה אחכה לו בכל יום שיבא (רמב"ם, שלשה עשר עקרים).

10   והקורא, קורא כסדרן. כסדר שהן כתובין בתורה, מוקדם מוקדם, ומאוחר מאוחר (רש"י, מנחות לד:).

11   הויות לההדי. פירוש, "והיה כי יביאך", "והיה אם שמוע" פנימיות זו אצל זה (תוס' שם, ד"ה והקורא).

CHAPTER XI

THE SINGULARITY OF THE LAND OF ISRAEL

The journey from Mt. Sinai to the Holy Land was to last several days only. Our Sages tell us that "the Holy One, blessed be He, desired to bring them immediately into the Land" (Rashi, Num. 10:33).[1] They set forth, guided by the pillar of cloud and with two trumpets as a signal system of communication. There was a mood of imminent *ge'ulah* as Moses invited his father-in-law, Yitro, to join them in their march.[2]

Just prior to their entry into the Holy Land, God instructed Moses: "Send men to scout the land of Canaan, which I am giving to the children of Israel" (Num. 13.2).[3] Why was there a need for a scouting party to explore the land before the people could enter it? It is generally accepted that these were spies who were sent to acquire military intelligence to facilitate the conquest of the land. The Hebrew word for spies, *meraglim*, does not, however, appear in our text. The verbs used are *veyaturu* and *latur*, which mean "to scout, to tour, to acquaint oneself with" the land. When Joseph accused his brothers of coming to spy on the land of Egypt, the Torah explicitly used the word *meraglim*.[4]

117

In addition, what need was there for military information? When they left Egypt, they had no military reports about the conditions they would encounter in the desert. They understood clearly that the entire Exodus was miraculous, that the Revelation at Mt. Sinai was a supernatural event, and that their being fed daily by the mannah evidenced God's constant concern for them. Surely their entry into the Holy Land would similarly merit God's miraculous intervention! Did they suddenly falter in their faith? What was the need, therefore, for spies?

Also, in noting the precise instructions which Moses gave to them, we find that he primarily asked for demographic and agricultural reports. Only two words may be suggestive of military significance: "Are the towns they live in *open* or *fortified*?" (*ibid.* v. 19).[5] Otherwise, what we have here is a study mission. The first report Moses sought was demographic in nature, about the inhabitants of the land. "And see ... the people who dwell in it; are they strong or weak, few or many?" (*ibid.* v. 18).[6] Rashi amplifies: "There are areas which rear strong [healthy] people and there are those which rear weak people; there are those that produce a large population and there are those that produce a small population."

The second report he sought was of agricultural interest, dealing with fertility and climate. "And the land that they live in, is it good or bad ... is the soil rich or poor? Is it wooded or not? And take pains to bring back some of the fruit of the land—and it happened to be the season of the first ripe grapes" (*ibid.* vv. 19, 20).[7] Of what military value are samplings of grapes or data concerning the land's productivity? Our conclusion, therefore, is that we are dealing with explorers and scouts, not spies.

But why was there a need for this scouting mission? Had they not been previously assured that it was "a land flowing with milk and honey"? Also, what precisely was the sin of these scouts which precipitated mass melancholy and resulted in the children of Israel remaining in the desert for forty years, instead of entering the land immediately?

Another matter warrants elucidation. Rashi asks: "Why is this section dealing with the spies juxtaposed with the section dealing with Miriam's punishment? — [To show the grievousness of their sin] because Miriam was punished on account of the slander which she had uttered against her brother; and these sinners witnessed it, yet they did not take a lesson from her" (*ibid.* v. 2).[8] The sin of the scouts is apparently similar to the sin of Miriam; it is slander, as Rashi indicates here and also in Deuteronomy (24:9). Apparently, Miriam failed to appreciate the special character and status of her brother Moses, just as the scouts were blind to the singular character of the Holy Land. It is this theme that we intend to develop.

The Concept of Singularity

The word "singular" means "being only one," "exceptional," "extraordinary" and "separate." The word *segulah* in Hebrew similarly connotes singularity. In Exodus (19:5), the Torah enunciates the doctrine of the election of Israel as a cardinal tenet of our faith.[9] "And you shall be to Me *segulah* from all other other peoples." The word *segulah* is interpreted by Rashi as referring to "a cherished treasure, comparable to costly vessels and precious stones for which a king has a special regard."

Segulah may also describe relationships between people. For example, Jacob loved Rachel but he did not hate Leah, despite the verse, "And the Eternal saw that Leah was unloved" *(senu'ah)* (Gen. 29:31). His bond to her merely suffered by comparison with Rachel, as in the verse, "And he [Jacob] loved Rachel more than Leah" (*ibid.* v. 30). He had no reason to feel any animosity toward her. But his relationship with Rachel was singular. Similarly, Jacob loved Joseph and Benjamin, Rachel's children, differently than he loved his other sons. Judah described this succinctly:

"his [Jacob's] soul is bound up with the lad's soul" (*ibid.* 44:30). There was a *segulah* dimension in these special loves. It involved an intertwining of souls, a union beyond verbal description. It was more than emotional love; it was a oneness achieved, which is the highest rung of identification. A *segulah* love is an ontological merger.

Similarly, the people of Israel are a *segulah* people, singularly valued by God; this involves no denigration of other nations. It is a specialness—a nation, one of its kind, which God has designated to preserve and disseminate His Divine teachings. This is singularity.

The Singular Land of Israel

A *segulah* people inhabits a *segulah* land. It is "a land which the Eternal your God looks after; on which the Lord your God always keeps His eye, from year's beginning to year's end" (Deut. 11:12).[10] Rashi adds that, although God cares for other lands too, His relationship with Eretz Yisrael is special. The Midrash elaborates: "R. Shimon ben Yoḥai expounded the verse in Hab. (3:6): 'He rose and measured the land,' as meaning: God measured (assessed) all lands but found none suitable for Israel except Eretz Yisrael" (Lev. R. 13).[11]

Jewish destiny is linked with this land; we have no other. Only in this land, our Sages say, does the *Shekhinah* dwell and only therein does prophecy flourish.[12] This *segulah* attribute of the land is no more rationally explicable than the *segulah* of the people. These are qualities certified by our faith, and history has corroborated the singularity of both people and land.

Becoming Acquainted with the Bride

The union of the people of Israel with the land of Israel is comparable to a marriage. The crossing of the Jordan River involved more than geographic movement; it represented 'a marriage between the people and the land, a union of rocky hills and sandy trails with a people whose future destiny is to this day bound up with the state and welfare of the land. Destinies were united, a joint sharing of honors and shame, victory and defeat; for all that transpires there affects the mood and status of Jews everywhere. In a human marriage, divorce or death can sever the relationship. The bond between the land and people, however, is for all time, as Maimonides ruled: its sanctification is for all time (Hil. Bet Habehirah 6:16).[13]

There is a *halakhah* that a man may not marry or even betroth a woman before he knows her, no matter how highly she was recommended to him.[14] This we see illustrated in the story of Isaac and Rebecca.

Eliezer, the trusted servant of Abraham, informed Isaac of the wondrous character of Rebecca, her manners, piety, and wealth.[15] Nevertheless, the Torah tells us that, before Isaac married her, he allowed some time to elapse for them to become better acquainted with each other. The Bible says: "Isaac then brought her into the tent of his mother Sarah, and he took Rebecca as his wife. Isaac loved her, and thus found comfort after his mother['s death]" (Gen. 24:67).[16] Rashi adds: "He brought her into the tent and she closely resembled his mother Sarah; she became Sarah his mother [since the construct "of" in "tent of his mother" does not appear in the Biblical text]. While Sarah was living, a light burned in the tent from one Sabbath eve to the next, there was always a blessing in the [*hallah*] dough, and a cloud was always hovering over the tent [as a Divine protection], but after her death all these had ceased. When Rebecca came, they reappeared."

Isaac believed Eliezer's testimony but he had to learn to value Rebecca himself. Why? Marriage is not a utilitarian transaction, a partnership agreement, a casual relationship. It is an existential commitment, a uniting of two lonely, incomplete

121

souls to share a common destiny with its joys and sorrows. It is not an association but an integration. Such a commitment cannot be based on transmitted data; what is involved concerns one's body and soul, the inner personality finding itself attuned to another. It is a metaphysical fusion. Such a commitment, if it is to be wholehearted, without reservations, and for all time, can only be derived from first-hand knowledge. That explains the prohibition of marrying someone without prior acquaintance and affection.

This, we suggest, was the reason Moses was told to send scouts into the land—not to gather intelligence, but to have the distinguished heads of each tribe explore the land and bring back reports of its singular character. The instructions Moses gave them defined their mission, viz. to make the acquaintance of the land. By entering the land, the people were being wedded to it and, despite Divine assurances of its quality, they had to experience it through their princes before the commitment could be deeply rooted and irrevocably assumed. A commitment granted through proxy information is inevitably limited and qualified.

The Sin of the Scouts

Moses regarded the land not only in a political or physical light, but also as an exalted everlasting union. A singular *segulah* people, special to God, was being joined to a singular land, from which God's attention is never withdrawn.[10] Destinies were being joined. When Jews were exiled, and the land occupied by strangers, it remained desolate and withheld its bounty, even as a loyal wife waits eagerly for the return of her spouse.[17]

Moses expected the scouts to note the *segulah* singularity of the land, to perceive its worthiness in terms of Abraham's covenant with God: "On that day, the Lord made a covenant with Abram, saying, 'To your offspring I give this land' "

(Gen. 15:18). Now the spies, we are told, "went up into the Negev [south] and came to Hebron" (Num. 13:22), but they did not care to explore the Cave of Machpelah in Hebron where the patriarchs and matriarchs were buried, as Caleb did (Rashi). They explored the area from the desert of Zin to Rehob, leading to Hamath, but they viewed the land as one would appraise property. Their report was that of spies, not that of scouts; they balanced debits against credits and declared the entire enterprise hopeless. With grandeur looking down on them, all they could see was the mundane.

The Connection with Miriam

The thematic relationship between the chapter dealing with Miriam's punishment for slander and the serious transgression of the scouts may now be understood.

The Kabbalists urged the daily recital after morning prayers óf six Biblical verses, each of which stipulates zakhor, that it should be remembered. These shesh zekhirot include major historical events, the lessons of which the Jew must keep ever fresh in his mind. They are: (1) the Exodus (Deut. 16:13)—the miraculous birth of our people; (2) the Revelation (Deut. 4:9, 10)—the Divine source of our religion; (3) Amalek (Deut. 25:17)—the importance of vigilance against our enemies; (4) Egel Hazahav (Deut. 9:7)—the preservation of the spiritual integrity of our faith; (5) the Sabbath (Ex. 20:8)—God, the Creator of the world; and (6) Miriam's sin (Deut. 24:9)—emphasizing the gravity of the sin of slander.

We wonder why the Torah singled out slander more than other mitzvot which pertain to ben adam lahavero, such as perjury, stealing, revenge, and shaming. It seems out of place among the pivotal events of Jewish history and the basic principles of our faith that the other five instances commemorate. Superficially, the Miriam episode seems like a passing event of minor significance, certainly unworthy of daily note. We feel compelled to suggest that not slander, but something more basic to Jewish faith, is at stake here.

Since he remained in continual communication with God after the Revelation, Moses had assumed, with Divine approval, a state of celibacy.[18] His sister, Miriam, overheard Zipporah, Moses' wife, complaining of her loneliness and sympathized with her. Miriam questioned the propriety of Moses' separation from his wife. She was loyally devoted to her brother, but insisted that his prophetic status did not require him to relinquish his function as husband and father. "God spoke to us too," she said, "and yet we lead normal family lives" (Num. 12:2).

God's reply to Miriam and Aaron was that the prophetic status and power of Moses was utterly unique and unlike theirs. "My servant Moses is different ... with him I speak mouth to mouth [intimately], plainly, and not in riddles; how, then, were you not afraid to speak against My servant, Moses?" (ibid. 12:7). Miriam had readily conceded Moses' superiority to other prophets, that he possessed greater intellect and saintliness, that he towered over them qualitatively. She failed, however, to discern his *segulah* quality, that he was the only mortal ever to achieve such closeness to God. He was not merely greater; he was different. In Deuteronomy (34:10), the Torah says of Moses: "Never again did there arise in Israel a prophet like Moses." Maimonides lists four distinguishing features, characteristic of Moses' prophecy, which render his status exceptional and the only one of its kind.[19] In his formulation of Thirteen Principles of Faith, Maimonides devotes one principle to prophecy and a second exclusively to Moses—that "he was the chief of prophets, both of those that preceded him and of those that followed." Two separate principles were necessary because the standing of Moses was altogether different from the other prophets. Miriam's sin was her failure to acknowledge this difference. The inclusion of the passage referring to her in the

shesh zekhirot was to emphasize the uniqueness of Moses' prophecy, since acceptance of the authority of his teachings is
the foundation of Judaism.

This, Rashi says, compounded the sin of the scouts. They had
witnessed the punishment of Miriam for not recognizing Moses'
segulah singularity. They knew that Israel possessed a *segulah*
identity. How could they have been blind to the *segulah* quality
of Eretz Yisrael? Moses told them to go up to the Negev proud,
joyful, with an awareness of the great era which was about
to unfold. God's promise to Abraham, Isaac, and Jacob was
about to be fulfilled. A *segulah* prophet was leading a *segulah*
people into a *segulah* land. The response of the scouts, however,
was pedestrian.

The tragedy of Miriam and the scouts was their failure to note
the uniqueness which surrounds the *segulah* dimension of all
aspects of Jewish existence. This explains the inability of non-
Jews to understand the depth of attachment which the Jew, to
this very day, has to this land. They view this bond solely in
secular, nationalistic terms. The intense, passionate involvement
of Jews today throughout the world with the Land of Israel
testifies to an identification which transcends normal devotion
and, instead, reflects a fusion of identities, the *segulah* dimension.

הערות לפרק 11

1 שהיה הקב"ה חפץ להכניסם לארץ מיד (רש"י, במדבר י, לג).

2 נסעים אנחנו אל המקום אשר אמר ה', אותו אתן לכם. לכה אתנו והטבנו לך,
כי ה' דבר טוב על ישראל (במדבר י, כט).

3 וידבר ה' אל משה לאמר: שלח לך אנשים ויתרו את ארץ כנען אשר אני נתן
לבני ישראל (שם יג, א, ב).

4 ויאמר אלהם: מרגלים אתם, לראות את ערות הארץ באתם (בראשית מב, ט).

5 ומה הארץ אשר הוא ישב בה . . . הבמחנים אם במבצרים (במדבר יג, יט).

6 וראיתם את הארץ מה היא, ואת העם הישב עליה, החזק הוא, הרפה, המעט הוא
אם רב (שם יג, יח). רש"י — יש ארץ מגדלת גבורים, ויש ארץ מגדלת
חלשים, ויש מגדלת אוכלוסין, ויש ממעטת אוכלוסין.

7 ומה הארץ אשר הוא יושב בה? הטובה היא אם רעה... ומה הארץ, השמנה
הוא, אם רזה, היש בה עץ אם אין, והתחזקתם ולקחתם מפרי הארץ והימים ימי
בכורי ענבים (שם, יג, יט, כ).

8 "שלח לך אנשים". רש"י — למה נסמכה פרשת מרגלים לפרשת מרים? לפי
שלקתה על עסקי דבה שדברה באחיה, ורשעים הללו ראו ולא לקחו מוסר (שם,
יג, ב).

9 "והייתם לי סגלה מכל העמים" (שמות יט, ה). רש"י — אוצר חביב... כלי
יקר ואבנים טובות שמלכים גונזים אותם, כך אתם לי סגלה משאר אומות.

10 ארץ אשר ה' אלהיך דרש אותה תמיד עיני ה' אלהיך בה מרשית השנה ועד
אחרית שנה (דברים יא, יב). רש"י — והלא כל הארצות דורש... אלא כביכול
אינו דורש, אלא אותה על ידי אותה דרישה שדורשה דורש את כל הארצות
עמה.

11 ר' שמעון בן יוחאי פתח: "עמד וימודד ארץ" (חבקוק ג, ו)... מדד הקב"ה
כל הארצות ולא מצא ארץ שראויה לינתן לישראל אלא ארץ ישראל (ויקרא
רבה יג).

12 "ויקם יונה לברוח תרשישה מלפני ה'" (יונה א, ג). וכי מלפני ה' הוא בורח?
והלא כבר נאמר, "אנה אלך מרוחך ואנה מפניך אברח" (תהלים קלט, ז)...
אלא אמר יונה, אלך לחוצה לארץ, שאין השכינה נגלית שם (ילק"ש, יונה א).

13 ונתקדש בקדושת עזרא השנייה הוא מקודש היום (רמב"ם, בית הבחירה ו, טז).

14 אסור לאדם שיקדש את האשה עד שיראנה (קידושין מא.).

15 ויספר העבד ליצחק את כל הדברים אשר עשה (בראשית כד, סו). רש"י — גלה
לו נסים שנעשו לו, שקפצה לו הארץ, ושנזדמנה לו רבקה בתפלתו.

16 ויבאה יצחק האהלה שרה אמו ויקח את רבקה ותהי לו לאשה, ויאהבה, וינחם
יצחק אחרי אמו (בראשית כד, סז). רש"י — ונעשית דוגמת שרה אמו, כלומר,
והרי היא שרה אמו, שכל זמן ששרה קימת, היה נר דלוק מערב שבת לערב
שבת, וברכה מצויה בעסה וענן קשור על האהל ומשמתה, פסקו, וכשבאת רבקה,
חזרו.

17 "והשמתי אני את הארץ" (ויקרא כו, לב). זו מדה טובה, שלא יהא ישראל
אומרים, הואיל וגלינו מארצנו, עכשיו האויבים באים ומוצאים עליה נחת רוח,
שנאמר, "ושממו עליה איביכם היושבים בה" (שם), זו האויבים הבאים אחרי כן,
לא ימצאו עליה נחת רוח (ספרא, בחקותי) (רש"י, ויקרא כו, לב).

18 תניא, משה פירש מן האשה, והסכים הקב"ה על ידו (שבת פז.) (ראה פ' תורה
תמימה על שמות יט, טו [לא]).

19 רמב"ם, הל' יסודי התורה ז, ו.

126

CHAPTER XII

WHO IS FIT TO LEAD THE JEWISH
PEOPLE?

The Torah is fearful of giving any individual absolute power
to rule over his fellow man. Only God, by virtue of His being
the Creator and all-knowing, is capable of ruling, as a Heavenly
Sovereign, a *Melekh Elyon*. An analysis of the Torah text
and legal codes pertaining to the appointment of a king, *minui
melekh*, clearly shows the Torah's concern about human rulership and the desire to circumscribe its exercise or authority.

"If, after you have entered the land that the Lord your God
has given you, and occupied it and settled in it, you decide,
'I will set a king over me, as do all the nations about me,'
you shall be free to set a king over yourselves, one chosen by
the Lord your God; . . . you must not set a foreigner over you,
one who is not your kinsman" (Deut. 17:14ff).[1]

The Torah commands further that such a king must limit
the size of his royal household (e.g., the number of his wives);
"nor shall he amass silver and gold to excess." He must also
arrange to write his own *Sefer Torah* and thereby become ever
conscious that he is a constitutional monarch, governed by laws
of the Torah, and not an absolute ruler. Thus, "he will not
act haughtily toward his fellows or deviate from the instruction
to the right or to the left, to the end that he and his descendants
may reign long in the midst of Israel" (*ibid.* v. 20).[2]

127

In the Talmud (Sanh. 20b), Rabbi Nehorai explains that the Torah does not command the Israelites to appoint a king; it merely anticipates that they will be tempted to do so in the future. They will ask for a king in precisely these words, as we find in I Samuel (8:5). Although the Torah deplores monarchy or any absolute rulership, it foretells that the Israelites will succumb to the temptation to "be like all the nations that are around me." Most commentators, including Ibn Ezra, Naḥmanides, and Abarbanel, support the view of Rabbi Nehorai—that the appointment of a king in Israel is a concession to human weakness or political reality and is not mandatory. At most, it is a tolerated, but not a religiously desirable, institution. (R. Judah, however, differed with R. Nehorai, declaring it distinctly mandatory, a *mitzvah* of the Torah, to appoint a king [Sanh. *ibid.*]. Maimonides' ruling follows the view of Rabbi Judah.)

Why is Rulership Suspect?

Why does the Torah resist an absolute power structure? Why is delegating rulership to one man over his fellow men not desirable?

It is a well-known axiom that power tends to corrupt the one who wields it. The noblest, best-intentioned ruler is affected by the glory, tribute, and power of his office. This may cause him to step over the boundary of legitimate authority and succumb to arbitrariness and tyranny. The human ego is likely to be distorted and intoxicated by a status which has no external limits. A ruler may develop an insatiable craving for mass acclaim and may shape his policies to curry favor with the masses through pomp, wasteful symbolic expenditures, and expansionist strivings for even greater power. He becomes a slave to the lowest common denominator of mass tastes and vulgar instincts. While his authority is seemingly unlimited, he longs for the "hosannahs" of the crowd and becomes subservient to their mercurial predilections. The balance of the noblest personality can be influenced by such conflicting tensions.

When King Saul was denounced by the prophet Samuel for transgressing God's command, he offered the lame defense that he had to satisfy the people's lust for spoils and submit to their demands. In effect, he conceded that he was a follower, not a ruler (I Sam. 15:15).[3] This tension between an inflated ego derived from unlimited power and the cringing need for popular approval creates conditions which are not conducive to effective leadership. It is difficult for a human being not to succumb to such conflicting pressures.

A second reason for the Torah's reluctance to delegate absolute power is that it is difficult to formulate criteria for ideal leadership. Who should rule? Is the aggressive, brilliant personality superior to the humble, contrite individual? Accidents of birth and circumstance may elevate one person to a more privileged class, endowing him with a regal bearing and an extroverted personality which evoke popular acclaim. Have not many incompetent leaders wreaked havoc throughout history despite their charismatic personalities? Who, therefore, is entitled to rule?

Perhaps no man is ever entitled to rule over his fellow man, precisely because of these considerations. Rulership is, after all, a Divine attribute; only God can exercise it equitably, without abuse. In our prayers we say: "Kingship and rulership belong exclusively to the Almighty," [4] and "Yours, O Lord, is the kingdom and the supremacy as head over all" (I Chron. 29:11).[5] Although we believe that imitating God's ways is a basic Torah guide to morality,[6] this does not apply in the realm of power, a prerogative which is solely His. We do say, "As He is merciful, so should we be," but never, "As He is mighty, so should we be." The *Melekh Elyon*, the Heavenly King, is distrustful of the *melekh evyon*, the earthly king. The latter tends to take himself too seriously.

It was the craving for excessive power that precipitated the first sin of Adam and Eve. The serpent, seeking to subvert man from his obedience to God, cleverly tempted him with the rewards of absolute power: "But God knows that as soon as you eat of it your eyes will be opened and you will be like divine beings who know good and evil" (Gen. 3:5).[7] He assured them that they would become immortal and acquire godlike powers. This was a temptation they could not resist. So avid is man for power and so incapable is he of shouldering it responsibly!

Why was Kingship Permitted?

Social and political reality makes it necessary to entrust power to a king or other ruler, even though, ideally, the Torah would prefer otherwise. Permission to anoint a king may be classified among the *mitzvot* our Sages described in these terms: "Scripture makes this concession to man's evil inclination" [8] (Kid. 21b). Abarbanel relates the concession to appoint a king to the "female war-captive" (*eshet yefat to'ar*) described in Deuteronomy (21:10), where a similar allowance is made for the weaknesses of human nature.

Appointing a king was often a practical necessity, to safeguard the community from dangers both internal and external. Three commandments became obligatory upon the children of Israel as soon as they entered the land: "to appoint a king, to destroy the descendants of Amalek [the enemy], and to build the Temple" (Sanh. 20b).[9] The king was appointed to combat external enemies and to strengthen inner spiritual cohesion. Before the first king was anointed, anarchy prevailed: "In those days, there being no king in Israel, each person acted as he pleased [without restraints]" (Judg. 17.6).[10] This condition, as well as Philistine incursions, motivated the people to demand a king. Maimonides explicitly defines a king's role as follows: "And in all he does, his objective should be heavenly and his goal and thought to enhance the true faith and to fill the world with righteousness, to destroy the arm of wickedness, and to fight the wars of the Lord; for he was crowned specifically to administer justice and to lead in battle, as it says, 'Let our king judge us and go out before us and fight our wars" (I Sam. 8:1; Hil. Melakhim 4:10).[11]

Monarchy, therefore, was permitted not to create symbols of national glory or to forge empires. A king was expected to fulfill a particular *telos,* an objective, an assignment. Saul was anointed to repulse Philistine attacks; David's goal was to unify the loosely federated tribes into a single nation and to complete the conquest of the Holy Land. Solomon's mission was to build the Temple. Other kings were delegated to rid the country of idol worship. Many failed to fulfill their assignment—like Jeroboam, the son of Nevat (I Kings chaps. 12, 13).

The People Must Demand a Ruler

In addition to the requirement of a *telos,* a defined assignment, a Jewish king can only be appointed upon the request of the people. He is not foisted upon them, nor may he seize the throne through a *coup d'état,* even when external and internal dangers threaten. The people must clearly ask for a king; this is a strikingly democratic safeguard. The Torah states: "You shall say, I will set a king over me ... be sure to set a king over yourself, one chosen by the Lord your God." [1] Only in response to the popular will may the Sanhedrin, or a prophet, appoint a king.

The question may be asked: Why was Samuel reluctant to anoint the first king, Saul? The prophet was angry at the people for requesting a king. Since the two preconditions for the *mitzvah* of appointing a king were both present, namely, external and internal dangers and the request of the people, why was God so displeased? Maimonides explains that their motivation was disingenuous and that they simply wanted to rid themselves of the prophet's moral influence. He writes: "They asked mischievously, because they were resentful of the prophet Samuel, and not in the spirit of the *mitzvah*" [12] (Hil. Melakhim 1:2). Had they waited until after Samuel's death, when the prophet was no longer alive to guide them, their request would have been proper. It was religious rebelliousness, not practical exigency, which prompted them. Power structures are illegitimate unless the people seek them for reasons of external or internal security. With Saul, their motivations were impious; they wanted a king to rule them, instead of God. Their timing was wrong.

Even Judicial Power is Suspect

Judicial power is also a form of rulership because it exercises control over others. The Torah is concerned about possible abuses and the human fallibility of judges, just as it concedes the social necessity which requires them—as it acknowledges the compelling need for kingship. In fact, just as only God is entitled to be a king, so, too, only God can truly be a judge. The Divine role and presence in judgment is expressed by the Psalmist: "*Elohim* [i.e. God as judge—*shofet*] stands in the community of the judges [courts]; in the midst of the judges He [also] judges" (82:1).[13] And also, "For judgment is God's" (Deut. 1:17).[14]

This explains the complexities which *Halakhah* has introduced into the judicial process. Though capital punishment is prescribed in the Torah and its detailed application is codified in Jewish Law, very few actual executions have occurred in Jewish history. "A court which implements an execution ... once in seventy years" was considered "a destructive court" (Mak. 7b).[15] Innumerable legal requirements all but precluded the implementation of the death sentence. The same applies to *malkot*, the punishment of lashes. Both represent assaults upon one's fellow man and, because of human fallibility, their execution was reduced to the barest minimum.

The trepidation which should grip the jurist is described by Maimonides: "The judge should always imagine that a sword is at his neck and that Gehinnom is open below to receive him [an awareness of the dire implications if he fails to judge properly]; he must be aware of the person he judges, but [also] before Whom he is judging and to Whom he will be accountable if he veers from the truth" (Hil. Sanh. 23:8).[16] We are concerned not merely with the possible miscarriage of justice, but with a basic principle that, ideally, no man should ever exercise rulership over another. It is with trepidation that the Torah allows kingship and courts as a concession to social necessity, but it does so only within well-defined bounds.

A Power Structure which the Torah Does Encourage

There is one power authority that the Torah not only sanctions but encourages in Jewish society, that of the teacher-student relationship. Our leader is not the king nor the warrior, but the Torah scholar whose authority is that of a *Rebbe* over his *talmidim* (disciples).

Korah, in his rebellion against the authority of Moses, misunderstood the Jewish philosophy of sanctioned leadership. He identified power with kingship in political terms, with a sovereign-subject relationship. Such political structures are based on enforceable authority or implied coercion. He therefore challenged Moses' presumption to kingship, asking by what right any Jew, even Moses, might assume leadership and power over fellow Jews. He said: "You have gone too far! For all the community are holy, all of them, and the Lord is in their midst. Why, then, do you raise yourselves above the Lord's congregation?" (Num. 16:3).[17] The key challenge is *umadu'a titnase'u,* "why do you raise yourselves?" He challenged the presumption of Moses and Aaron to authority, to rule, to judge, and to lead. Every individual possesses intrinsic sanctity, be he Moses or a lowly woodcutter. Korah was echoing the basic Jewish resistance to all presumptions of power.

The authority of Moses, however, derived from his teaching role and his spiritual uniqueness, not his political stature. The *Rebbe* does not raise himself. This was not a case of self-elevation, as Korah had charged, but rather a situation where the entire community had by consensus recognized Moses as leader. It is a spiritual kingship, *malkhut*. The commanding authority of the *Rebbe* has been acknowledged by the Torah in all ages, without reservation. In fact, spiritual authority is often more effective, and its orders more readily obeyed, than political office. The influence of the *Besht* (founder of the Hassidic movement) or the Gaon of Vilna, both during their lifetime and posthumously, extended to and molded the lives of millions. Such a record is hardly matched by political leaders.

Moses is called *Mosheh Rabbenu* (our leader), not *Mosheh Malkenu* (our king), although his authority had qualities of rulership as well. Aaron, too, was not only a *Kohen Gadol* (High Priest) but also, and primarily, a teacher, "for the priest's lips preserve knowledge and the law is sought from his mouth" (Mal. 2:7).[18] The *Kohanim* (priests) were not always charismatic personalities; their sanctity and status were due in large measure to their teaching role. The reflexive form of *titnase'u* (self-elevate), which Korah used, cannot appropriately be applied to Moses and Aaron. These were teachers who, because of their closeness to God and their understanding of His teachings, were freely embraced by the community.

No effort is made by *Halakhah* to limit the authority of a *Rebbe,* as is the case with political officials. The respect due a *Rebbe* is boundless and to the verse, "You must revere the Lord your God" (Deut. 10:20), the Sages append, "this also refers to Torah scholars." [19] In the political realm, God is reluctant to share His *malkhut* (kingship) with men; in the scholarly realm He is willing. He would not share absolute power with a king, but only with Torah teachers. In *Pirke Avot*, Rabbi Elazar b. Shamua is quoted as saying, "[May] the reverence for your teacher be like the reverence for Heaven" (4:15).[20] Why is this authority of man over his fellow man sanctioned? We will cite two reasons.

First, the authority of a teacher is not imposed; no coercion or political instrument is employed. A Torah teacher is freely accepted and joyfully embraced. His authority emerges from his personality; his learning and selflessness are acknowledged. Not fear but affection and respect motivate one's submission. A teacher is a master, like a king. At times, he inspires emulation of his way of thinking and his general deportment, but this does not result in the enslavement of his disciples. The students are not crimped and circumscribed; their souls are not shriveled through fear and conformity. On the contrary, there is an enlargement and growth of the total personality.

Furthermore, authority and ownership go together. An owner can dispose of his property in any arbitrary manner. He can destroy it or give it away. Because a king does not own his subjects, political authority is only reluctantly and partially surrendered to him. The subjects are the equals of the king before God. God's authority, however, is boundless because He is the Creator; therefore, He owns us and legitimately rules over us.

A teacher is not a creator *ex nihilo*; he is a *yotzer*, a fashioner, an artisan, who takes amorphous matter and shapes it into something beautiful. A subject does not belong to a king, but a disciple, in a profounder sense, does belong to his *Rebbe*-master who sensitized his heart and brought out the noblest and finest in him. Similarly, the authority of parents is rooted not only in the fact that the child was physically formed from his parents, but, even more, in the parents' authority as

135

teachers and transmitters of the heritage. A child respectfully calls his father *"avi mori"* (my father, my teacher) and his mother *"immi morati"* (my mother, my teacher). Therefore, a child literally belongs to his parents. The Talmud sums up this idea pithily: "Every man has three partners [in his formation]: God, his father, and his mother" (Nid. 31a).[21]

Teaching and learning are creative activity. When Abraham started his travels, the Torah relates, he took along "the souls they made in Haran" (Gen. 12:5). How does one "make souls?" Rashi explains: This refers to the souls he brought into the faith; Abraham converted the men and Sarah converted the women, and the Torah accounts it as if they had made them." [22]

In the master-disciple relationship. *malkhut* (kingship) finds its fullest realization. The Sages said: "Who are the real kings? —the scholars!" [23] (Git. 62a). It is they who exercise authority ideally. Tradition ascribes Torah scholarship to King David, one of whose descendants will be the future Messiah. Regarding David, our Sages say: "God said to David, 'I value more the one day that you are involved with Torah than the thousands of sacrifices which your son Solomon will offer on the altar'" (Shab. 30a). The authority of the Messiah himself will be primarily that of a teacher, and this, not his political role, will redeem the world. The ideal Messianic king will be a teacher-king, as Maimonides says: "And if a king will arise from the Davidic dynasty, studying Torah, and occupying himself with *mitzvot* like David his ancestor, in accordance with both the Written and Oral law, and compel [lit. "bend"] all Israel to follow him, and fight the wars of the Lord—him we may presume [i.e. there is *ḥazakah*] to be the Messiah" (Hil. Melakhim 11:4).[24]

The Torah has profound respect for the dignity and individuality of man; his rights and free will may not be curtailed or infringed upon. Social reality, however, forces upon us the necessity of entrusting leadership, for otherwise anarchy would ensue. It was Rabbi Ḥanina who said: "Pray for the welfare of the government, since but for the fear thereof, men would swallow each other alive" (Av. 3:2).[25] Kingship is, therefore, sharply circumscribed. This does not prevail in the teacher-disciple relationship, where the exercise of authority is encouraged and submission to teachers extolled.

הערות לפרק 12

1 כי תבא אל הארץ אשר ה' אלהיך נתן לך, וירשתה, וישבת בה. ואמרת אשימה עלי מלך ככל הגוים אשר סביבתי. שום תשים עליך מלך אשר יבחר ה' אלהיך בו. מקרב אחיך תשים עליך מלך. לא תוכל לתת עליך איש נכר, אשר לא אחיך הוא (דברים יז, יד, טו).

2 לבלתי רום לבבו מאחיו ולבלתי סור מן המצוה ימין ושמאול. למען יאריך ימים על ממלכתו, הוא ובניו בקרב ישראל (שם, כ).

3 ויאמר שאול מעמלקי הביאום אשר חמל העם על מיטב הצאן והבקר (שמואל א' טו, טו).

4 המלוכה והממשלה לחי עולמים (תפלת האדרת והאמונה).

5 לך ה' הממלכה והמתנשא לכל לראש (ד"ה א' כט, יא).

6 אחרי ה' אלהיכם תלכו (דברים יג, ה); והלכת בדרכיו (שם, כח, ט).

7 כי ידע אלהים, כי ביום אכלכם ממנו, ונפקחו עיניכם, והייתם כאלהים, ידעי טוב ורע (בראשית ג, ה).

8 לא דברה תורה אלא כנגד יצר הרע (קידושין כא:).

9 תניא, וכן היה ר' יהודה אומר. שלש מצות נצטוו ישראל בכניסתן לארץ, להעמיד להם מלך, ולהכרית זרעו של עמלק, ולבנות להם בית הבחירה (סנהדרין כ:).

10 בימים ההם, אין מלך בישראל, איש הישר בעיניו יעשה (שופטים יז, ו).

11 ובכל יהיו מעשיו לשם שמים. ותהיה מגמתו להרים דת האמת. ולמלאות העולם צדק. ולשבור זרוע הרשעים ולהלחם מלחמות ה'. שאין ממליכין מלך תחלה אלא לעשות משפט ומלחמות. שנאמר, "ושפטנו מלכנו ויצא לפנינו ונלחם את מלחמותינו" (שמואל א' ח, כ) (רמב"ם, הלכות מלכים ד, י).

12 לפי ששאלו בתרעומת. ולא שאלו לקיים המצוה, אלא מפני שקצו בשמואל הנביא, שנאמר "לא אתך מאסו כי אתי מאסו ממלך עליהם" (שמואל א' ח, ז) (רמב"ם, הל' מלכים א, ב).

13 אלהים נצב בעדת אל, בקרב אלהים ישפט (תהלים פב, א).

14 כי המשפט לאלהים הוא (דברים א, יז).

137

15 סנהדרין ההורגת אחד בשבוע נקראת חובלנית. רבי אליעזר בן עזריה אומר,
אחד לשבעים שנה. רבי טרפון ורבי עקיבא אומרים, אילו היינו בסנהדרין לא
נהרג אדם מעולם (מכות ז.).

16 לעולם יראה דיין עצמו כאילו חרב מונחת לו על צוארו וגיהנם פתוחה לו
מתחתיו, וידע את מי הוא דן ולפני מי הוא דן ומי עתיד להפרע ממנו אם
נטה מקו האמת (רמב״ם, הל׳ סנהדרין כג, ח).

17 רב לכם, כי כל העדה כלם קדשים, ובתוכם ה׳ ומדוע תתנשאו על קהל ה׳
(במדבר טז, ג).

18 כי שפתי כהן ישמרו דעת, ותורה יבקשו מפיהו (מלאכי ב, ז).

19 את ה׳ אלהיך תירא (דברים י, כ) — לרבות תלמידי חכמים (פסחים כב:).

20 רבי אלעזר בן שמוע אומר. יהי כבוד תלמידך חביב אליך כשלך, וכבוד חברך
כמורא רבך ומורא רבך כמורא שמים (אבות ד, טו).

21 שלשה שותפין יש באדם, הקב״ה ואביו ואמו (נדה לא.).

22 ״ואת הנפש אשר עשו בחרן״ (בראשית יב, ה). רש״י — שהכניסן תחת כנפי
השכינה; אברהם מגייר את האנשים ושרה מגירת הנשים, ומעלה עליהם הכתוב
כאלו עשאום.

23 דרבנן איקרו מלכים (גיטין סב) ; מן מלכי, רבנן (פרקי היכלות רבתי).

24 ואם יעמוד מלך מבית דוד, הוגה בתורה, ועוסק במצות, כדוד אביו, כפי התורה
שבכתב ושבעל פה, ויכוף כל ישראל לילך בה, ולחזק בדקה. וילחם מלחמות ה׳,
הרי זה בחזקת שהוא משיח (רמב״ם, הל׳ מלכים יא, ד).

25 רבי חנינא סגן הכהנים אומר, הוי מתפלל בשלומה של מלכות, שאלמלא מוראה,
איש את רעהו חיים בלעו (אבות ג, ב).

138

Chapter XIII

THE "COMMON-SENSE" REBELLION AGAINST TORAH AUTHORITY

Jews defer only to recognized Torah scholars in the interpretation of Jewish Law. Today, many individuals claim the right to exercise their own common sense in determining the relevance and format of contemporary Judaism, despite the fact that they are hardly Biblical and Talmudic scholars. Synagogue ritual committees and popular magazine articles debate the continued usefulness of various religious practices and explore the possibilities of reformulating Judaism in line with modern thought. These self-styled *"poskim"* concede their lack of formal training in Jewish texts and sources, but they insist nonetheless on their right to decide fundamental religious questions on the basis of "common sense."

This is not a recent phenomenon. It dates back to the earliest period of Jewish history, to the very generation which received the Torah at Mt. Sinai. Not very long after that event, the Torah (Num. Chap. 16) relates, Korah led a rebellion against Moses and *Ḥazal* imply that he sought to replace Moses as the teacher and leader of Israel. Korah publicly challenged the halakhic competency of Moses and ridiculed his interpretations of Jewish law as being contrary to elementary reason. Citing the *Tanḥuma*, Rashi records the following clever ploy of Korah:

> What did he do? He assembled two-hundred and fifty distinguished men and women ... and he attired them in robes

of pure blue wool. They came and stood before Moses and said to him: "Does a garment that is entirely blue still require *tzitzit* or is it exempt?" Moses replied that it did require *tzitzit*. Whereupon, they began to jeer at him: "Is that logical? A robe of any other color fulfills the *tzitzit* requirement merely by having one of its threads blue. Surely a garment which is entirely blue should not require an additional blue thread!" [1] (Rashi, Num. 16:1).

Likewise, the Midrash tells us of another provocation. "Does a house which is filled with Torah scrolls still require a *mezuzah* on its doorpost?", Korah asked. Moses replied in the affirmative. Korah retorted: "If one brief section of the Torah placed inside the *mezuzah* [*the Shema* and *vehayah im shamo'a*] satisfies the *mitzvah* requirement, most certainly a multitude of scrolls which contain many portions should! Such halakhic decisions do not emanate from God but are fabrications" [2] (Num. R. 18). Korah insisted that to require a *mezuzah* under such circumstances violated elementary logic.

Korah's Rationale

Korah was a demagogue motivated by selfish ambitions. His antagonism began when Aaron and his family were elevated to the priesthood, while the Levites, among whom Korah was prominent, were relegated to mere assistants of the *Kohanim*.[3] Now, we know that every rebellion against authority needs an ideology to arouse the fervor of the people and sustain its momentum. It needs a slogan or a motto which projects a noble ideal to replace the intolerable status quo. The rallying cry which Korah chose was "common sense." He proclaimed that all reasonable people have the right to interpret Jewish law according to their best understanding: "For all the community are holy" [4] (Num. 16:3). In down-to-earth logic, the lowliest woodcutter is the equal of Moses. This appeal to populism evokes considerable support because it promises free-dom from centralized authority; it flatters the people's com-mon intelligence and it approves the right of each Jew or group of Jews to follow their own individual judgment.

The Midrash describes how Korah propagandized his cause. "Korah went about all that night to mislead the Israelites. He said to them: 'What do you suppose—that I am working to obtain greatness for myself? I desire that we should all enjoy greatness in rotation' " (Num. R. 18).[5]

Korah was an intelligent man, *pike'ah hayah* (Rashi, *ibid. v.* 7). He would certainly concede that there were specialized fields in which only experts who have studied extensively over many years are entitled to be recognized as authorities. The intrusion of common-sense judgments in these areas by unlearned laymen would be both presumptuous and misleading. Korah would not have dared to interfere with Bezalel's architectural and engineering expertise in the construction of the Tabernacle, the *Mishkan*, because construction skills were clearly beyond his competence. Today, reasonable people concede the authority of mathematicians, physicists, and physicians in their areas of expertise, and would not think of challenging them merely on the basis of common sense. Why, then, are so many well-intentioned people ready to question the authority of the Torah scholar, the *lamdan*, in his area of specialized knowledge?

Korah's rationale can be understood more readily if we clarify three terms denoting the various levels of reason and intelligence. The Torah says: "He has endowed [Bezalel] with a Divine spirit, with knowledge [*hokhmah*], intellect [*binah*] and intelligence [*da'at*]" [6] (Ex. 35:31). *Hokhmah* refers to the specialized knowledge and scholarship which are acquired by extensive and detailed study. *Binah* is the capacity to analyze, to make distinctions, to draw inferences and apply them to various situations. When *binah* is combined with *hokhmah*, we have the especially gifted and creative thinker. *Da'at* deals with common sense, basic intelligence, and sound practical judgment.

Korah's appeal to common sense in Judaism was basically a claim that only *da'at*, and not *ḥokhmah*, is involved in the application of *Halakhah*. He conceded that the legal aspects of *Halakhah* require expertise, technical and academic. But he maintained that there is also a psychological and emotional aspect in the practice of *Halakhah* and the observance of *mitzvot*. In judging the utility, relevance, and beneficial effects of the *mitzvot*, all intelligent people are qualified to render judgment on the basis of close and informed observation. For this aspect, he argued, common sense, human experience, and basic judgment are the criteria. And on this basis he challenged the authority of Moses.

Korah was committed to the doctrine of religious subjectivism, which regards one's personal feelings as primary in the religious experience. God requires the heart, *Raḥmana liba ba'i* (Sanh. 106b), and it is in the mysterious recesses of his personality that man meets his Maker. The *mitzvot*, by contrast, are physical acts which reflect the inner quest, the hidden feelings of religious emotion. The *mitzvah* is an external form of a spiritual experience; each inner experience has its external correlate in the form of particular *mitzvah* performances.

On the basis of Korah's theory, the *mitzvah* would have to correspond to the mood that prompts it. The value of the *mitzvah* is to be found not in its performance, but in its subjective impact upon the person, its ability to arouse a devotional state of mind. *Tefillin* would be justified, according to Korah's theory, only for their elevating and inspirational quality. The *mitzvah* of *shofar* on Rosh Hashanah would be of value only if it succeeded in arousing the Jew to repentance. If these *mitzvot* ceased having this impact upon people, their observance would be open to question and new rituals, more responsive to changing sensitivities, should perhaps be enacted. What follows from his reasoning is that the *mitzvah* may be modified according to changing times or even according to the individual temperaments of different people. There is, to him, no inherent redemptive power in the *mitzvah* beyond its thera· peutic effects, its capacity to evoke a subjective experience.

Korah argued, using the *mitzvah* of *tzitzit* as an illustration of his point of view, that the blue thread of the *tzitzit* was meant to make us think of distant horizons, of infinity, and of the mysterious link between the blue sea and the blue sky.[7] The *mezuzah*, he argued, is intended to increase our awareness of God and to invoke His protection over our homes. Why, then, is it necessary to limit this symbolism to one thread or to the doorpost? Why not extend it to the whole garment and to the entire house? If blue, in the case of *tzitzit*, is able to evoke feelings of Godliness, then total blueness of the garment should certainly be able to do so. The same reasoning applies to the *mezuzah*. The *mitzvah* is thus reduced to the level of an inspirational means, and not an end in itself. From the standpoint of religious subjectivism and common sense, Korah's argument seems quite cogent.

In response to Korah, we feel it necessary to reaffirm the traditional Jewish position that there are two levels in religious observance, the objective outer *mitzvah* and the subjective inner experience that accompanies it. Both the deed and the feeling constitute the total religious experience; the former without the latter is an incomplete act, an imperfect gesture. We can easily demonstrate that the *Halakhah* values both. In the observance of *keri'at Shema*, of *tefillah*, of *avelut*, of *simhat Yom Tov*, we recite fixed and standardized texts and we perform precise ritual acts. Yet, the real consummation, the *kiyyum*, is realized in the experience, *belev*. The objective *Halakhah* recognizes the emotional response as an essential part of the religious experience.

However, we do not regard the qualitative and subjective experience as primary. Rather, the objective act of performing the *mitzvah* is our starting point. The *mitzvah* does not depend on the emotion; rather, it induces the emotion. One's religious inspiration and fervor are generated and guided by the *mitzvah*, not the reverse. The goal is proper *kavvanah* and genuine *devekut*, but these can be religiously authentic only if they follow the properly performed *mitzvah*. The emotion generated by the *mitzvah* is circumscribed and disciplined by the *Halakhah* and its character is not left open to possible distortion by human desires and fantasies. The halakhically defined *mitzvah* has quantitative dimensions and precise perimeters, and these establish the authenticity of the genuinely Jewish religious experience.

This is a *ḥiddush*, an insight which is not commonly understood. The only solid reality is the *mitzvah*, the integrity of which the *Halakhah* can define and control. It is the *mitzvah* act which has been Divinely prescribed and halakhically formulated; emotional responses cannot be so mandated, because, by their very nature, they are not subject to precise definition.

In teaching the *Halakhah* and its proper application, the *ḥokhmah* dimension of knowledge is decisive; *da'at*, common sense, is insufficient. This was Korah's error, for in the realm of the *Halakhah* only the Torah scholar is the authority and common sense can be misleading.

Why Cannot the Emotions be Trusted?

Why does the *Halakhah* refuse to give primacy to the emotions, to the inner feelings? Why does it not consider *devekut*, religious fervor, a more genuine and authentic experience than the outward act of performing a *mitzvah*? It is because there are three serious shortcomings in making the religious act dependent on human emotion and sentiment.

First, the religious emotion is volatile, ever-changing, and unstable, even within one individual. To correlate the outward act to the inner emotion would require regular adjustments. The *mitzvah* would continually have to be modified and, at times, nullified in favor of new symbolic acts that would correspond to the person's emotional state. The format and identity of the *mitzvah* would be destroyed and no continuity of identifiable performance would be possible.

Second, each person feels an experience differently. Rituals would continually have to be reformulated to correspond to the feelings of different individuals at different times. What was inspiring to one person might not affect another at all. No community (*Kehillah*) service of God would be possible, since group worship presupposes a unifying constancy. What would be appropriate today would be obsolete tomorrow, and what is appreciated in one community may be unintelligible in another.

This kind of ever-changing worship, which responds to varying sensations, is basically idolatrous. That this was a major point of contention in the argument between Moses and Korah is indicated in the *Tanhuma* quoted by Rashi (*ibid.* v. 6): "[Moses] said to them: 'According to the custom of the heathens, there are numerous forms of Divine worship and, consequently, numerous priests, for they cannot assemble for worship in one temple. We, however, have one God, one ark, one Law, one altar, all constituting one form of worship'." [8] Communal worship should be constant and not buffeted by the winds of fashion and subject to varying moods of diverse individuals. Moses contended that Korah's emphasis on the primacy of the emotions would destroy the religious identity of the people and result in fragmented sects. The fact that Jews of all times and from different parts of the world are able to worship together—even allowing for minor variations of liturgical custom—is directly due to the constancy of form which is controlled by the *Halakhah*.

Third, we have no reliable gauge to differentiate secular types of response from the genuinely religious experience. There are many non-religious reactions which claim transcendental qualities of holiness. The love impulse, the aesthetic quest of the

artist, and, nowadays, the indulgence in potent mind-transform-
ing drugs, can easily be confused with the religious experience.
But in fact they are inherently secular and do not reach out
beyond the stimulated sense to God. They never transcend
man's finite limitations. Pagans in ancient times abandoned
themselves to hypnotic trances and orgiastic ceremonies, and
mistakenly identified these as religious experiences. The self
was never transcended; man starts with himself and does not
communicate beyond himself. The Torah, therefore, emphasizes
the *mitzvah*, which reflects God's will; it has the stamp of immutability and universality. The great religious romance of
man with God, the emotional transport, follows one's observance
of the *mitzvah*, not the reverse.

Moses was unquestionably right. If one fulfills the *mitzvah*
of *tzitzit*, recognizing its religious meaning, then a glance at one
blue thread will produce an awareness of God. To this day, the
tallit (even without the blue thread)[9] is religiously inspiring
to the worshipping Jew. Such is the power of the *mitzvah*.
Proceeding from action to feeling, the blue color can remind
one of his link with God. However, if one fails to conform to
halakhic norms and instead, availing himself of common sense,
substitutes a garment that is entirely blue, his response will
be divested of its religious meaning and totally secular. And
if there is a response at all, it will be a mundane, hedonistic
experience, aesthetic appreciation, but not a religious emotion.
The color blue, as an aspect of *kiyyum hamitzvah*, is a source
of religious inspiration; but a blue garment that is not prescribed
by the Torah merely contains a color and may produce many
types of secular associations, some even vulgar and demeaning.

Halakhah as Ḥokhmah

In Judaism, it is the *mitzvah* which initiates the religious
experience. The halakhic legal system, as a *ḥokhmah*, has its
own methodology, mode of analysis, conceptualized rationale,

even as do mathematics and physics. An analogy with science would be helpful here. Aristotelean physics, which dominated the ancient and medieval world, was in some instances faulty precisely because it relied on common-sense experiences. It maintained that an object falls because it has weight, which seems outwardly reasonable but which Galileo and Newton showed to be wrong. They replaced common-sense, surface judgments by scientific laws, a picture of reality which differs from surface appearances. What are heat, sound and matter but creations of the human mind in mathematical terms? These are qualities which we perceive with our senses, but their real identity is defined in conceptual, not empirical terms.

Similarly, the Oral Law has its own epistemological approach, which can be understood only by a *lamdan* who has mastered its methodology and its abundant material. Just as mathematics is more than a group of equations, and physics is more than a collection of natural laws, so, too, the *Halakhah* is more than a compilation of religious laws. It has its own *logos* and method of thinking and is an autonomous self-integrated system. The *Halakhah* need not make common sense any more than mathematics and scientific conceptualized systems need to accommodate themselves to common sense.

When people talk of a meaningful *Halakhah*, of unfreezing the *Halakhah* or of an empirical *Halakhah*, they are basically proposing Korah's approach. Lacking a knowledge of halakhic methodology, which can only be achieved through extensive study, they instead apply common-sense reasoning which is replete with platitudes and clichés. As in Aristotelean physics, they judge phenomena solely from surface appearances and note only the subjective sensations of worshippers. This *da'at* approach is not tolerated in science, and it should not receive serious credence in *Halakhah*. Such judgments are pseudo-statements, lacking sophistication about depth relationships and meanings.

147

The approach of Moses prevailed. The survivors of the cata-
strophe which befell Korah's group later conceded that, in the
words of our Sages, "Moses is truth and his interpretation
of Torah is truth—and we are liars" (B. Bat. 74a).[10] This judgment is still valid. In our day, we are witnessing a resurgence
of strength among those religious groups that are committed
to the Oral Law as a *ḥokhmah*, and who therefore recognize
Torah scholars, *Gedole Yisrael*, as the legitimate teachers of
Israel. Common sense can only spread confusion and havoc
when applied to the *Halakhah*, as it does with all specialized
disciplines.

הערות לפרק 13

1 מה עשה ? עמד וכנס ר"ן ראשי סנהדראות . . . והלבישן טליתות שכולן תכלת.
באו ועמדו לפני משה. אמרו לו, טלית שכולה של תכלת, חייבת בציצית או
פטורה? אמר להן, חייבת. התחילו לשחק עליו. אפשר טלית של מין אחר, חוט
אחד של תכלת פוטרה, זו שכולה תכלת, לא תפטור את עצמה ? (רש"י, במדבר
טז, א).

The Korah rebellion is recorded in the Torah immediately following
the *tzitzit* portion of the preceding *Sidrah*. Korah used the recently
legislated law of *tzitzit* as a pretext for instigating the rebellion.

2 בית מלא ספרים, מהו שיהא פטור מן המזוזה ? אמר לו, חייב במזוזה. אמרו לו,
כל התורה כולה רע"ה פרשיות אינה פוטרת את הבית, פרשה אחת שבמזוזה
פוטרת את הבית ? . . . דברים אלו לא נצטוית עליהן ומלבך אתה בודאן (במדבר
רבה יח).

3 רש"י, במדבר טז, א — ומה ראה קרח לחלוק עם משה ?

4 כי כל העדה כלם קדשים (שם, טז, ג).

5 הלך קרח כל אותו הלילה והיה מטעה את ישראל ואומר להם מה אתם סבורים,
שאני עוסק ליטול את הגדולה לעצמי, אני מבקש שתהא הגדולה על כלנו חוזרת
(במדב"ר יח).

6 וימלא אתו רוח אלהים בחכמה, בתבונה ובדעת (שמות לה, לא).

7 תניא. היה ר' מאיר אומר, מה נשתנה תכלת מכל מיני צבעונין ? מפני שהתכלת
דומה לים וים דומה לרקיע, ורקיע לכסא הכבוד (מנחות מג:). רש"י — ומכח
התכלת מזכיר היושב על כסא.

148

8 כך אמר להם: בדרכי הגוים יש נימוסים הרבה וכומרים הרבה וכולם אין
מתקבצים בבית אחד. אנו, אין לנו אלא ה' אחד, ארון אחד, ותורה אחת, ומזבח
אחד, וכהן גדול אחד (רש״י, במדבר טז, ו).

9 התכלת אינה מעכבת את הלבן, והלבן אינו מעכב את התכלת (מנחות לח).
רש״י — ואע״ג דמצוה לתת תכלת ב' חוטין בציצית . . . אפ״ה, אין זה מעכב את
זה (ואי עביד ארבעתן תכלת או ארבעתן לבן, יצא).

The blue thread of the *tzitzit* was dyed with the secretion of a
hilazon snail. Its identity is uncertain today and it was very scarce even
in the days of the Mishnah. The Tannaim agreed that the absence of
the blue cord does not invalidate the *mitzvah*.

10 משה ותורתו אמת והן בדאין (ב״ב עד.).

CHAPTER XIV

TEACHING WITH CLARITY AND EMPATHY*

(Moses Reluctantly Becomes a "Nursing-Father")

Teaching involves more than the transmission of knowledge and understanding. It requires an empathy between teacher and student, and a sharing of feelings, thoughts, and motives. There is an interaction of personalities, an exchange of values and insights.

Moses, as the teacher *par excellence*, became aware of this broader understanding of the teaching role after the *kivrot hata'avah* episode (Num. chap. 11), when he was called upon to become an *omen*, a "nursing-father," of the newly-founded people. We see this change reflected in Moses' different reactions to the two major sins of the children of Israel in the desert—the *egel hazahav* (Ex. chap. 32) and the *kivrot hata'avah*.

Moses responded to the *egel hahazav* episode resolutely, pleading for Divine forgiveness and dealing forthrightly with the people. Their backsliding into idol worship so soon after the Revelation was a most serious crisis which actually threatened to terminate the relationship between God and Israel. "And

---

* This chapter derives from an address delivered by the Rav on June 10, 1974, celebrating the 25th anniversary of Rabbi Israel Klavan as the Executive Vice-President of the Rabbinical Council of America.

150

the Lord said to Moses ... Now, let Me be, that My anger may blaze forth against them and that I may destroy them; and make of you a great nation" (Ex. 32:9, 10).[1]

Faced with this danger, Moses did not panic. He steadfastly and heroically petitioned the Almighty for forgiveness (*Vayeḥal Mosheh*), arguing the case of the people like a defense attorney. *Ḥazal* suggest that the word *vayeḥal* (and he prayed), instead of *vayitpallel* or *vayitḥanen*,[2] signifies elements of strength, boldness, persistence and daring. There is bold prayer and there is humble prayer; here we have bold prayer, as the Midrash portrays metaphorically: "It is as if Moses were holding on to God, like a person seizing hold of someone's garment, and saying, Master of the Universe! I will not release You until You forgive Israel" (Ber. 32a).[3]

After the *kivrot hata'avah*, on the other hand, Moses complained bitterly of his wretched lot. Instead of defending the people, he seemed to be accusing them. "And Moses said to the Lord: 'Why have you dealt ill with Your servant? And why have I not enjoyed Your favor, that You have laid the burden of all this people upon me? Did I conceive this people? Did I give birth to them, that You should say to me, "Carry them in your bosom, as a nursing-father carries a suckling child" to the land that You have promised on oath to their fathers ... I am not able to carry the burden of this people alone, because it is too heavy for me. If You deal thus with me, kill me rather, I beg You, if I have found favor in Your sight; and let me see no more of my wretchedness' ..." (Num. 11:11–15).[4]

It is simply unlike Moses to become so shaken, so despondent and complaining, to condemn the people out of the depths of resignation. He prefers to be relieved of further leadership; he does not intercede for the people and he even prefers death to further responsibility. Never before had he uttered such words, although the Israelites had rebelled on many other occasions.

It is true that the opening phrase, *lama hare'ota le'avdekha*,

"Why have You dealt ill with Your servant?", is reminiscent of a similar expression by Moses when, as a novice on his first mission to Pharaoh, he had suffered frustration. On that occasion, his initial intervention had caused Pharaoh to intensify the severity of Israel's servitude, whereupon Moses complained to God: "Lord, why have You brought harm upon this people? Why did You send me?" (Ex. 5:22).[5] This was the complaint of a young, inexperienced man, early in his career, who overzealously expected immediate and dramatic results. Moses, however, never again posed this question or gave vent to such a mood until the episode of the *kivrot hata'avah*.

It is also difficult to understand precisely why the sin of *kivrot hata'avah* evoked such an extreme reaction from Moses. With respect to the other sins—the *egel hazahav*, the *meraglim*, *Ba'al Peor*, the immorality of Midian—we know clearly what happened. But what took place at *kivrot hata'avah* is unclear. Superficially, it is the story of a people who were overwhelmed with desire for meat, seemingly a relatively minor infraction. No serious crimes, such as idol worship, murder or sexual immorality, had been committed. Their protests were neither raucous nor violent and threatening. They complained bitterly, nothing more; yet their punishment was cruelly severe. They had aroused God's wrath and Moses, too, resented and denounced their backsliding: "The Lord was very angry and Moses was distressed" (Num. 11:10).[6] What truly constituted the sin which warranted such harsh retribution?

A Contrast Between Egel Hazahav and Kivrot Hata'avah

Moses regarded the golden calf sin as resulting from the terrifying primitive fears of the people. Having miscalculated, they feared that Moses was dead (Shab. 89a; Rashi, Ex. 32:1). They were terrified of being abandoned in the desert. To them the calf was a substitute for Moses. They were misled by the *erev rav,* the "mixed multitude" of gentile sympathizers who had left Egypt with them. Although they had succumbed to idol worship, there were mitigating circumstances in their conduct.

A brief analysis of idolatry, *avodah zarah,* would be helpful.* There is what we call idolatry, which signifies actual worship, ritual and cultic performances, specific acts to propitiate deities presumed to reside within the idols or to be represented by them. In addition, there is also paganism that involves a cultural system, a manner of living. Our Sages were convinced that idol worship inevitably leads to paganism, that worship influences a society's way of life. Yet paganism can persist even after idol worship has been discarded. The later Greeks and Romans, having cast aside idol worship, still lived as pagans, with a pagan life-style and value system. In our day, with idol worship no longer in existence, paganism is still rampant.

What is paganism and how does it contrast with the Torah *hashkafah* (outlook)? The pagan worships deities which represent forces in nature. These deities are themselves without moral norms, and they make no demand of man beyond specific acts of propitiation. For man lustily to partake of nature is, therefore, an act of identifying with such gods. Man actually sees himself as coextensive to nature and therefore craves unlimited indulgence. In Judaism, man's Divine image manifests itself precisely in his self-control, the subordination of his craving and lust to the will of God. It is God the Creator who is to be worshipped, not nature which is merely a creation. To worship God is to submit to a code of "do's and don'ts"; to worship nature is to abandon all norms and restrictions, and to regard all that is possible as permissible, to acknowledge no restraints in the human appetite. The antithesis of paganism is expressed

---

* See Maimonides, *Mishneh Torah, Hil. Avodat Kokhavim* 1:1.2, regarding the development of idol worship.

in the verse, "And follow not the desires of your heart and your eyes, which lead you astray" (Num. 15:39).[7]

The Torah detested the pagan way of life even more than it hated idol worship. The latter is short-lived; even the Greeks and Romans eventually lost faith in it. It eventually collapses; one can teach, persuade, and enlighten against its validity. Yet paganism has a tremendous hold on people long after actual idol worship has been discarded. The sin of the golden calf was idol worship; God's covenant with Israel was almost lost because of it.

The *kivrot hata'avah* episode, however, revealed that, even without idol worship, paganism still exercised its hold upon the people, a vestigial remnant of their long stay in Egypt. The Torah describes the gathering of the quails—an insatiable accumulation of property and the gratification of hungry senses, characteristic of paganism. "And the people rose up all that day and all the night, and all the next day, and they gathered the quails; he that gathered least, gathered ten heaps; and they spread them out all around the camp" (*ibid.* 11:32).[8] We have here desire gone berserk, a craving without any restraint.

The text speaks only of the unlimited gathering of quails. Our Sages, however, tell us that this was a rebellion against all inhibitions. It expressed itself in a repudiation of the sexual code just recently prescribed at Mt. Sinai. On the verse, "And they journeyed from God's mountain" (*ibid.* 10:33), the Sages add: "What does God's mountain [symbolically] signify?" R. Hama, son of Hanina, explained that they turned away from the restrictive disciplines which Sinai had imposed upon them (Shab. 116a),[9] and the *Tanhuma* adds, "as a child runs away from school to avoid studying the Torah." [10]

Their complaint, "Who shall give us flesh?" (*ibid.* 11:4), was merely a pretext, Rashi explains, since they owned large herds of cattle.[11] Perhaps "flesh" is here a euphemism for that which is sensual. The phrase, "we remember the fish which we did eat in Egypt" (*ibid.* v. 5), our Sages explain, refers to sexual immorality, the licentiousness which the Torah now restricted,[12] since fish have a prodigious proliferating capacity. When "Moses heard the people weep among their families" (*ibid.* v. 10), the people were wailing, explains Rashi, because of family matters, because the intermarriage of blood relatives was now forbidden to them.[13] The Oral tradition, as expressed by our Sages, understood *kivrot hata'avah* as an orgy of the senses, an idolization of unrestricted indulgence.

The episode of *kivrot hata'avah* may be contrasted with the Torah approach to self-indulgence, illustrated in the story of the manna. This comparison is even suggested by the text: "Now our gullets are shriveled. There is nothing at all, nothing but this manna to look to" (*ibid.* v. 6).[14] Regarding the manna, we read in Exodus (16:16–18): "Gather as much of it as each of you requires to eat, an *omer* to a person for as many of you as there are; each of you shall fetch for those in his tent. ... he who had gathered much had no excess and he who had gathered little had no lack; they had gathered as much as they needed to eat." [15] We have here controlled acquisition, disciplined indulgence, and a mastering of one's cravings. Such is the Torah approach to material indulgence.

The Changed Role of Moses

Moses had been chosen to be a *Rebbe* (teacher) of *Klal Yisrael*, while Aaron was to be the diplomat, the negotiator. When Moses asked, "Who am I, that I should go to Pharaoh?" (Ex. 3:11), he was doubting his qualifications to deal with protocol and royalty. God replied: Your primary role, Moses, is that of a spiritual and moral teacher, a pedagogue of Torah and *Halakhah*, to prepare the people to receive and become committed to the Revelation. I can find negotiators elsewhere. You were chosen because the main purpose of the Exodus is not the attainment of political freedom but the conversion of a slave society into "a kingdom of priests and a holy nation," *mamlekhet kohanim vegoy kadosh,* and in that role you excel. You are a *Rebbe par excellence.*[16] Moses understood this to be his responsibility and he accepted the mandate.

At the *egel hazahav,* Moses reacted as a teacher. His forceful pronouncements, the powerful impact of the shattering of the *luhot* (two Tablets of the Law), the death of the perpetrators—all this, Moses hoped, would forever eradicate idol worship from Israel. Idolatry was, after all, a deviationist mode of worship and its vacuity and futility are demonstrable. Eventually, it collapses and is discarded as people come to realize its untenability. Effective pedagogy is all that is needed and, for this teaching role, Moses regarded himself as qualified.

Kivrot hata'avah, however, was not idol worship but paganism. The latter is *peritzut,* unlimited lust, sexual wantonness, boundless desire, and sensual indulgence—the hypnotic and the orgiastic, what the Greeks meant by *hedone.* One can argue and persuade effectively against idol worship; but what does one do with paganism, which is morally nihilistic? It is not a competitive and alternative discipline; it is no discipline at all. How does one teach the superiority of a restrictive but ennobling system which wants man to identify with God, not to be a child of nature? In the Garden of Eden, God commanded Adam and Eve to engage in selective indulgence and to maintain self-control over their appetites. To counter paganism, as in the *kivrot hata'avah* episode, the teacher role is insufficient; Moses was now commanded to become an *omen,* a nursing father, a role that he bitterly resisted.

A review of Moses' lament (Num. 11:11–15)[4] indicates that the key words of his protest were "carry them in your bosom, as a nursing-father carries a suckling child" (11:12)[17]—a role that Moses never wanted to assume, which he now found thrust upon him, as the people succumbed to childlike impulses of unrestrained wanting and plaintive wailing.

What is the difference between a teacher and nursing-father (or mother)? A teacher instructs a child and a nursing mother also teaches a child. The latter, however, in addition to teaching, also carries the child in her bosom, *behekekha*; she submerges her identity in that of the child, making her own ambitions secondary or nullifying them completely. The needs of the child take precedence over her own life and she becomes one with the child and finds fulfillment through him. There is an emotional fusion of two identities. A teacher, however, retains his own identity and personality; his is an intellectual communication of specific knowledge.

Moses now became aware that being a teacher was not enough for a leader of Israel, a *manhig Yisrael*. The people, in its early formative years, needed him as a baby needs a nursing mother; they were temperamental, impulsive, filled with uncontrollable desires, restively murmuring. Their complaints were primarily pretexts, *mevakeshim alilah* (Rashi, *ibid.* v. 1). Moses doubted his capacity to become an *omen*; he knew that, in this role, he would be totally submerged in his work. He would not only have to teach and command, but also guide, train, and transform a people inclined to paganism into an *am segulah*. Besides teaching, he would have to reach out emotionally to the people, nurture them through their national infancy, with patient, sympathetic understanding and empathy, as a nursing-father would do. Indeed, as a private individual with a family, personal needs, and pleasures, he would no longer exist; his happiness and fulfillment would no longer be with his wife, children, and personal ambitions. This sacrifice was not expected of other Jewish leaders; his was a one-time historical necessity, an all-consuming responsibility. He was to be totally absorbed in his mission. He was the *av hanevi'im*, forced to withdraw from his ordinary preoccupations and attachments in order to nurture a people in its formative years, a people cardinally important to the Almighty's plan for the world. For this role of an *omen*, Moses felt unqualified, even as he realized that the paganism of *kivrot hata'avah* required this kind of painstaking nurturing; teaching was simply not enough.

* * *

Our age is demonstrably pagan, without idol worship as such. It consists of uninhibited *peritzut* (indulgence). The teaching role may have been sufficient in the past to counter the allurements of other religions, philosophies, and the pseudo-ideologies which still abound nowadays. We could teach and demonstrate the greater credibility of our own way of life; but the paganism of our day requires that elements of the *omen*, the nursing-father, be combined with the teaching role, particularly since the emotional and introspective element is so pronounced in contemporary human relationships. What we require is the warm embrace as much as the brilliant idea; sympathetic understanding, true befriending, and a human reaching-out; a suggestion to our modern *mitonenim* (restless, complaining ones) that "we care"; the teaching role is inadequate.

This is admittedly a demanding responsibility. We need not emulate Moses' total self-effacement, but aspects of the *omen* are necessary. We must have, in addition to teaching: *dedication*, personal commitment, for otherwise the burden is unbearable; *selflessness*, a readiness to subordinate personal career and egotistical ambitions; and *empathy*, an ability to teach with feeling, not only with clarity.

All this must be pursued with dignity and self-respect.

הערות לפרק 14

1 ועתה הניחה לי, ויחר אפי בהם ואכלם, ואעשה אותך לגוי גדול (שמות לב, י).
2 ויחל, ויתפלל, ויתחנן.

3 "ועתה הניחה לי". אמר רבי אבהו, אלמלא מקרא כתוב, אי אפשר לאומרו. מלמד שתפסו משה להקב"ה כאדם שתופס את חברו בבגדו ואמר לפניו: רבונו של עולם, אין אני מניחך עד שתמחול ותסלח לישראל (ברכות לב.).

4 ויאמר משה אל ה': למה הרעת לעבדך ולמה לא מצאתי חן בעיניך, לשום את משא כל העם הזה עלי. האנכי הריתי את כל העם הזה, אם אנכי ילדתיהו, כי תאמר אלי, שאהו בחיקך, כאשר ישא האמן את הינק על האדמה אשר נשבעת לאבותיו... לא אוכל אנכי לבדי לשאת את כל העם הזה, כי כבד ממני. ואם ככה את עשה לי, הרגני נא הרג, אם מצאתי חן בעיניך ואל אראה ברעתי (במדבר יא, יא—טו).

5 למה הרעתה לעם הזה, למה זה שלחתני (שמות ה, כב).

6 ויחר אף ה' מאד, ובעיני משה רע (במדבר יא, י).

7 ולא תתורו אחרי לבבכם ואחרי עיניכם אשר אתם זנים אחריהם (שם, טו, לט).

8 ויקם העם כל היום ההוא וכל הלילה וכל יום המחרת, ויאספו את השלו, הממעיט אסף עשרה חמרים, וישטחו להם שטוח סביבות המחנה (שם, יא, לב).

9 "ויסעו מהר ה'" (שם, י, לג). מאי מהר ה'? א"ר חמא ב"ר חנינא, שסרו מאחרי ה' (שבת קטז.).

This meaning is derived from the fact that Mt. Sinai is referred to in Scripture as *Har Elohim, Har Ḥorev* or *Har Sinai*. The term *Har Hashem* is used exclusively for Mt. Moriah, the site of the Temple, whose holiness, unlike *that* of Mt. Sinai, is for all time.

10 שנסעו מאחרי ה' כתינוק הבורח מבית הספר לבטל מד"ת (רמב"ן; מובא בשם התנחומא בתוס', שבת קטז., ד"ה פורענות).

11 "מי יאכלנו בשר" (יא, ד). פ' רש"י — וכי לא היה להם בשר?... אלא שמבקשים עלילה.

12 "זכרנו את הדגה" (יא, ה) — עריות (יומא עה.) (הכוונה, שנאסרו להם קרובות, ודגה הוא מלשון וידגו לרוב — תורה תמימה).

13 וישמע משה את העם בכה למשפחותיו (יא, י). רש"י — על עסקי משפחות, על עריות הנאסרות להם (ספרי).

14 ועתה נפשנו יבשה, אין כל, בלתי אל המן עינינו (יא, ו).

15 זה הדבר אשר צוה ה', לקטו ממנו איש לפי אכלו, עמר לגלגלת, מספר נפשותיכם, איש לאשר באהלו תקחו... ולא העדיף המרבה, והממעיט לא החסיר, איש לפי אכלו לקטו (שמות טז, טז, יח).

16 וזה לך האות כי אנכי שלחתיך, בהוציאך את העם ממצרים, תעבדון את האלהים על ההר הזה (שמות ג, יב).

Your mission is to prepare the people to worship God at Mt. Sinai.

17 שאהו בחיקך, כאשר ישא האמן את הינק (במדבר יא, יב).

CHAPTER XV

ENGAGING THE HEART AND TEACHING THE MIND*

The Pattern of Dual Leadership

The most authentic form of Jewish leadership is that of the teacher, the Torah scholar, whose power is not political but spiritual. His authority is never imposed; rather, it is eagerly sought. He seeks not the aggrandizement of his personal ego but the transmission of a Divine heritage. The impact of his leadership is more pronounced and enduring than that of political rulers, both during his lifetime and posthumously.[1] The only power structure which the Torah encourages is this non-institutional relationship between teacher and pupil. Indeed, one can say that the role of the political structure of government is to support the teaching community.

A pattern of dual teaching leadership seems to have prevailed during major periods of Jewish history. It began with Moses and Aaron and is exemplified today by the *Rav* (Rabbi) and the Hassidic *Rebbe*. Moses was the teacher *par excellence*. He was not called a king; he was *Mosheh Rabbenu*, not *Mosheh Malkenu*, although he undoubtedly exercised royal authority as well. "And a king [Moses] ruled in Jeshurun [Israel]" (Deut. 33:5).[2] Aaron, who served alongside Moses, was not

---

* This chapter derives from a eulogy delivered by the Rav in 1972 for Rabbi M. Z. Twersky ז״ל, the Talner Rebbe.

only a *Kohen Gadol* but a teacher as well. "And you shall appear before the *Kohanim*—the Levites—or the magistrate in charge at the time, and present your problem; and they shall tell you the verdict in the case... You shall act in accordance with the instructions given you and the ruling handed down to you" (Deut. 17:9, 11).[3] In describing the Kohanite role, the prophet Malachi (2:7) declared: "The lips of the *Kohen* preserve knowledge and Torah is sought from his mouth" (2:7).[4]

Both Moses and Aaron were teachers, but their methods and temperaments differed. Later leadership was divided between the Prophets and the *Kohanim*; and, after prophecy ceased, between *Hazal* and the *Kohanim*. In modern times we have the *Rav* and the *Rebbe*. From the year 70 C.E. until the advent of Hassidism in the eighteenth century, we had only the *Rav*. Then the *Besht*, the founder of Hassidism, appeared. Hassidism was soon accepted by nearly half of European Jewry. The reign of the *Rav* was judged by many as insufficient; only with the *Rebbe* was Jewry restored to the classic dual leadership which characterized major periods of its history.

The two major traditions of Torah teaching may be called that of the King *(Malkhut)*—Teacher and that of the Saint (Kedushah) —Teacher. Moses was the prototype of the king-teacher and Aaron represented the saint-teacher. Both of them enlightened minds, molded characters, and propagated the word of God. Both led their communities along righteous paths and made sacrifices for their welfare. Nevertheless, their methods, their approaches, and the media they employed were different. In terms of ultimate objectives, they were very close to each other, but their emphases varied.

Teaching the Mind and Engaging the Soul

The king-teacher addresses himself to the mind. He engages the intellect, analyzing, classifying, clarifying, and transmitting the details of *Halakhah* with precision. He teaches texts and

161

conceptualized thinking, reconciling seeming contradictions and formulating underlying principles. Moses, Maimonides, the Gaon of Vilna, and Reb Chaim of Brisk reflect the king-teacher *par excellence*. The king-teacher communicates with words because the intellect only grasps ideas clothed in words. He emphasizes study, *limmud*, as the primary means of identifying with God.

This intellectual emphasis is based on the conviction that the human mind reflects in some way the infinite mind of God. Being created in God's image means that we reflect aspects of the attributes of God in a finite, imperfect sense. To know is to identify with His knowledge, to partake of it and, in effect, to identify with Him. A child who shares the knowledge of his father identifies with him. A disciple who absorbs the wisdom of his teacher joins his mind with that of his teacher. To know Torah is to join with the intellect of God. It is God who allows man to partake of His knowledge: "You have endowed man with knowledge and teach mortals understanding" (*Amidah*).[5]

Maimonides emphasizes knowledge as a requisite for loving God. "It is known and certain that the love of God does not become closely knit in a man's heart till he is continuously and thoroughly possessed by it and gives up everything in the world for it ... One only loves God with the knowledge with which one knows him" (Hil. Teshuvah 10:6).[6] He is saying that one can love deeply only a person one knows well. This view reflects the king-teacher outlook of Maimonides, namely, that the intellectual exploration of God's moral (Torah) and cosmic (natural) orders is the bridge spanning the gap between man and God.

The saint-teacher, in contrast, even as he deals with the text, focuses his attention upon the invisible, intangible soul of the Torah. The Torah, like a human being, has—according to the Zohar—both a physical "body", consisting of a thought system and a moral-religious code, and a "soul," an overflowing inward life which can be felt but not understood.

To feel the mysterious heartbeat of the Torah, one has to identify oneself with it. The soul of man, his experiences, must somehow be atuned to the soul of the Torah. The saint-teacher, therefore, communicates with the heart. He tells the heart how to identify its own excited, accelerated beat with the Torah— to feel, not only to understand.

Judaism has a moral code which is concerned not only with actions but with emotions as well. Many commandments in the Torah are exclusively concerned with the inner life of the Jew. The Sabbath, the festivals, represent not just a bundle of "don'ts" but a great experiential reality. What is prayer, if not worship of the heart? And what is the *Shema*, if not an inner act of surrender to the sovereignty of God?

Words reflect the *logos*, but they cannot capture the inner emotions of a religious experience. Intense, soulful excitement cannot be pressed into a verbal framework. Descriptions of love, sorrow or exhilaration only remotely approximate the real experience. They are too fluid, too amorphous, and too sub-jective; the silent word, intuitively transmitted, is more effective. One communicates an experience the way a sick person com-municates an illness. Experiences are contagious and one catches their inner spirit by being in touch with a saint-teacher who is lovesick for God.

The saint-teacher therefore communicates with the heart, through periods of extended, close contact, subtle parables, and ecstatic song and dance. He teaches man not only loyalty to *Halakhah*, but also the art of cleansing the heart of vulgarity, inhumanity, unworthy sentiments, uncouth emotions, and selfish desires. He teaches how a triumph is to be celebrated when the Almighty has granted success, and how to cope with sadness and grief. The saint-teacher creates a society of intense personal piety and subliminal closeness to God.

In the ecstatic and passionate love of God it is the heart, not the mind, which predominates. Prayer, more than study, is the primary emphasis of the saint-teacher. We mentioned earlier that Maimonides felt that an intellectual effort must exist in order to bring forth emotional rapport. Yehudah Halevi (Kuzari, 4), however, expounds the view that the visionary experience is a stronger link than the abstract intellectual experience. Through ethical preparation and mystical transport, not intellectual knowledge, man evokes and inspires emotional communion (*devekut*) with God. Halevi explains that the God of Abraham was apprehended, not merely comprehended. God to him was a reality experience, felt, emotional, and not abstractly intellectual. The God of Aristotle, by contrast, is only comprehended, as a distinct abstract idea; it is not a direct experience but is perceived through the intermediary of the intellect. The Book of Psalms, as an ideal religious work, reflects the emotional and immediate experience of God's reality and providential presence.

The emotional represents the yearning of the soul to return to its origin. Man seeks to root himself in his source "like a tree planted near streams of water" (Ps. 1:3)[7]; "like a gazelle panting after streams of water, so my soul pants after You, O God" (Ps. 42:2).[8] The saint-teacher responds to this craving of the human soul.

Teaching the Few and Reaching the Many

The king-teacher speaks to a select few, for not all are capable of being scholars; not everyone is qualified to understand an abstract halakhic or scientific concept, let alone contribute to it. He must be content with a limited group of the bright and the talented, the select few. The masses feel despondent at being excluded. This was the situation in Eastern Europe prior to the rise of *Hassidut*. Nevertheless, there must be this elite of superior scholars who preserve and interpret the written and oral tradition. Only the *Talmid Hakham* is qualified to distinguish between the authentic and the inauthentic. Yet one simply cannot convert a whole nation into scholars. Only in the Messianic era does Isaiah foresee universal scholarship: "And all your children shall be taught of the Lord" (54:13).[9]

By contrast, the saint-teacher is a leader of the masses, for all Jews have hearts which can be set aflame. All Jews possess sensitive souls and seek God. Every Jew, even the non-scholar, *Hassidut* teaches, is capable of finding God if he seeks earnestly: "But if you search there for the Lord your God, you will find Him, if only you seek Him with all your heart and soul" (Deut. 4:29).[10] This assurance is given to all Jews, not only to the learned few. Hence the teaching of the saint-teacher is democratic, comprehensible, and accessible to the intellectually uninitiated as well as to the philosopher. He presides over an accessible court open to all who seek him for both spiritual and worldly guidance, while the king-teacher confines himself to the *Bet Hamidrash* (academy), speaking primarily to scholars, *lamdanim*.

We should note that there were many Hassidic leaders who chose to combine the role of king-teacher with their saint-teacher responsibilities. They intellectualized *Hassidut*. Similarly, there were king-teachers who enlarged their scope to include wider masses and who allowed greater accessibility. We have simply described the primary traits of each type of teacher's personality, dating from Moses and Aaron in antiquity to the *Rav* and *Rebbe* of modern times.

Hesed and Emet

The king-teacher practices *middat hadin*, criticizing, exhorting, holding people accountable for transgressions and failures. The *am ha'aretz*, the ignoramus, and the lax are censured. *Emet*, truth, demands unbending justice. In the eyes of the *ish emet*, the man of truth, nothing must be given gratuitously. One must be rewarded according to one's merits. If a person is deserving, he should be loved. If he is not deserving, love should be denied him. Any deviation is unpardonable. The sinner is deserving only of reprimand and instruction.

The saint-teacher, however, is primarily guided by *hesed*, limitless compassion and overflowing kindness. The essence of *hesed* expresses itself in its universality and in its ultimate love, from which no one is excluded. The *ish hesed*, the person of unqualified love, does not ask the recipient of his love to present moral credentials. His love is gratuitous as well as boundless. While the king-teacher rebukes the sinner in harsh language, the saint-teacher sheds a tear of sympathy for the sinner when he encounters sin. The king-teacher loudly scorns iniquity, while the saint-teacher, saddened by iniquity, speaks softly. The former fights for *emet* through exhortation and instruction; the latter, by reproaching the sinner the way a loving mother reproaches a mischievous child. The sermon of the king-teacher is often harsh, saturated with prophetic indignation. The sermon of the saint-teacher is subdued, saturated with prophetic love. He teaches through love and concern.

There is a classic story which illustrates, perhaps simplistically, the difference between the two approaches. The coachman who, while greasing his wagon wheels, also decided to *davven Minhah* (recite the afternoon prayers) evoked different reactions from passersby. The *emet*-type exclaimed: "*Sheygetz!* While you *davven*, you grease wheels?" The *hesed*-type said: "Ah, a *sheyner Yid!* [a worthy Jew!] Even when he greases his wheels, he *davvens!*"

Which approach is to be preferred? To be all-loving is to betray truth, to encourage mediocrity, and to allow the inauthentic to distort the teachings of God. This would be inadmissible and a betrayal of our historic trust. On the other hand, to be absolutely truthful is to love only some people and to alienate many who are genuine in their hearts and who are earnestly searching. The reconciliation of *middat hadin* (attribute of strict justice) and *middat harahamim* (attribute of compassion) is achieved only in God. Man can find only a relative solution to this dilemma, depending upon his temperament and outlook. In this, the king-teacher and the saint-teacher part company. They both have discovered a formula to harmonize *hesed* and *emet*, but one emphasizes *emet* and the other *hesed*. They both love and are committed to the truth, yet they act differently.

Moses was a model of the *Rav*; Aaron of the *Rebbe*. Moses was a *k'vad-peh*, a non-verbal person, not given to small talk, easy socializing, and extensive negotiations. He was *Rabbenu*, a scholar, teacher, uniquely spiritually endowed, who communicated tersely what he had to say. He was a teacher primarily to Joshua, the elders of Israel, *zikne Yisrael*, and to others who were qualified to understand the intricacies of Torah and *Halakhah*. The contrast between Moses and Aaron was noted by our Sages: "Moses' guiding principle was—the strict law is immutable. [And yet he loved the people, *Moshe Rabbenu Ohev Yisrael haya* (Men. 65a)] But Aaron loved and pursued peace and sought to reconcile man with his neighbor" (Sanh. 6b).[11] The Midrash adds: *Hesed* and *shalom*—this is Aaron; *emet* and *tzedek*—this is Moses."[12] "The lips of the *Kohen* preserve knowledge"[4] emphasizes Aaron's lips, his persuasive style and closeness to the people. His title was not *Rabbenu* but *Hakohen*, which signifies a minister of God.

We may note their different reactions to the *egel hazahav* incident, the one denouncing, exhorting, and enlightening, the other working along with the people, procrastinating, hoping against hope to defuse the frightened and confused masses in time for Moses' return (see Rashi, Ex. 32:5). Both approaches must somehow be combined.[13] The people must not only be taught by instruction, but also by warm and friendly guidance. A loving permissiveness can only be destructive; a harsh accountability, alienating. We read that when Moses died, *Vayivku bene Yisrael et Mosheh* (Deut. 34:8): only the men, who had studied Torah with him, appreciated his greatness and sensed the extent of their loss. But on Aaron's death, the text reads: *Vayivku kol bet Yisrael,* "all the children of Israel [men and women] wept", united in mourning because, as Rashi explains, "he pursued peace and made peace between man and his neighbor and between wife and husband."

Nowadays, the *Rav,* the contemporary teacher-king, has absorbed many of the qualities of the *Rebbe,* not only teaching but coming close to his people. The *Rebbe,* representing the modern teacher-saint, now also emphasizes scholarship and the teaching role. The classic differences are still there, but the lines of demarcation are at times blurred. Jewish leadership is most effective when it combines the mind and heart in the worship of God.

הערות לפרק 15

1   גדולה תורה יותר מן הכהנה ומן המלכות (אבות ו, ו).

2   ויהי בישרון מלך (דברים לג, ה).

3   ובאת אל הכהנים הלוים ואל השפט אשר יהיה בימים ההם. ודרשת, והגידו לך את דבר המשפט ... על פי התורה אשר יורוך ועל המשפט אשר יאמרו לך תעשה, לא תסור מן הדבר אשר יגידו לך ימין ושמאל (שם, יז, ט, יא).

4   כי שפתי כהן ישמרו דעת, ותורה יבקשו מפיהו (מלאכי ב, ז).

5   אתה חונן לאדם דעת ומלמד לאנוש בינה (תפלה).

6   דבר ידוע וברור שאין אהבת הקב"ה נקשרת בלבו של אדם עד שישגה בה תמיד כראוי ... ועל פי הדעה תהיה האהבה, אם מעט, מעט ואם הרבה, הרבה. לפיכך צריך האדם ליחד עצמו להבין ולהשכיל בחכמות ותבונות המודיעות לו את קונו כפי כח כח שיש באדם להבין ולהשיג (רמב"ם, הל' תשובה י, ו).

7   והיה כעץ שתול על פלגי מים (תהלים א, ג).

8   כאיל תערג על אפיקי מים, כן נפשי תערג אליך אלהים (שם מב, ב).

9   וכל בניך למודי ה' (ישעיה נד, יג).

10   ובקשתם משם את ה' אלהיך, ומצאת כי תדרשנו בכל לבבך ובכל נפשך (דברים ד, כט).

11   משה היה אומר: יקוב הדין את ההר, אבל אהרן אוהב שלום ורודף שלום ומשים שלום בין אדם לחבירו שנאמר, "תורת אמת היתה בפיהו ועולה לא נמצא בשפתיו" (מלאכי ב, ו) (סנהדרין ו:).

12   "וילך ויפגשהו בהר האלהים וישק לו" (שמות ד, כז). זהו שאמר הכתוב "חסד ואמת נפגשו. צדק ושלום נשקו" (תהלים פה, יא). חסד ... ושלום, זה אהרן. אמת ... וצדק, זה משה (תנחומא).

13   "הוא אהרן ומשה" (שמות ו, כו). רש"י — יש מקומות שמקדים אהרן למשה ויש מקומות שמקדים משה לאהרן, לומר ששקולין כאחד.

168

Chapter XVI

A STRANGER AND A RESIDENT

The first patriarch, Abraham, introduced himself to the inhabitants of Canaan with the words, "I am a stranger and a resident among you" (Gen. 23:4).[1] Are not these two terms mutually exclusive? One is either a stranger, an alien, *or* one is a resident, a citizen. How could Abraham claim both identities for himself?

Abraham's definition of his dual status, we believe, describes with profound accuracy the historical position of the Jew who resides in a predominantly non-Jewish society. He was a resident, like other inhabitants of Canaan, sharing with them a concern for the welfare of society, digging wells, and contributing to the progress of the country in loyalty to its government and institutions. Here, Abraham was clearly a fellow citizen, a patriot among compatriots, joining others in advancing the common welfare. However, there was another aspect, the spiritual, in which Abraham regarded himself as a stranger. His identification and solidarity with his fellow citizens in the secular realm did not imply his readiness to relinquish any aspects of his religious uniqueness. His was a different faith and he was governed by perceptions, truths, and observances which set him apart from the larger faith community. In this regard, Abraham and his descendants would always remain "strangers."

Single and Dual Identities

Like other people, the Jew has more than one identity. He is a part of the larger family of mankind, but he also has a Jewish identity which separates him from others. Each identity imposes upon him particular responsibilities. As a citizen of a pluralistic society, the Jew assumes the social and political obligation to contribute to the general welfare and to combat such common dangers as famine, corruption, disease, and foreign enemies. Where the freedom, dignity, and security of human life are at stake, all people—irrespective of ethnic diversity—are expected to join as brothers in shouldering their responsibilities. These are concerns which transcend all boundaries of difference.

Years ago, the prophet Jeremiah counseled the Jewish inhabitants of Babylonia to "seek the welfare of the city whither I have caused you to be carried away captive, and pray unto the Lord for it; for in its prosperity you shall prosper" (29:7).[2] In Talmudic days, Samuel of Nehardea promulgated the enduring rule that, in civil matters, the law of the land is as binding upon Jews as are the religious commandments of their own faith (Git. 10b).[3] Even under the cruel oppression of Rome, Rabbi Ḥanina enjoined: "Pray for the peace of the realm, since but for the fear thereof, men would swallow each other alive" (Avot 3:2).[4]

The Jew, however, has another identity which he does not share with the rest of mankind: the covenant with God which was established at Mt. Sinai over 3,000 years ago. All of Jewish history only makes sense in terms of the validity of this covenant, which entrusted the Jewish people of all generations with a particular national destiny and a distinctive religious heritage. This identity involves responsibilities and a way of life which are uniquely Jewish and which, inevitably, set the Jew apart from non-Jews. It is particularistic, rather than universalistic. As fellow human beings, the Jew and the non-

Jew are members of a broad-based fraternity. Jews, however, must often confront others and insist on their right to be different and not to be derogated. The political and social structure of society must not interfere with the religious, cultural, and social institutions which the Jew finds necessary to preserve his separate identity. Here, the emphasis is not on similarity but on difference, not on togetherness but on apartness.

There is an inevitable tension in trying to uphold these two identities. Many Jews maintain that the universal and the covenantal cannot be combined in our relationship with other faiths. It is absurd, they argue, to claim unity in the secular realm, and the next instant to make an about-face by emphasizing our distinctiveness and separateness in the religious sphere. There is something contradictory and psychologically discordant in maintaining this dual role. They feel the need to choose between being human and being Jewish, and very frequently it is the secular reality which becomes their dominant concern. They become ardent supporters of humanistic and philanthropic causes and they passionately identify with efforts to enhance the moral and aesthetic quality of life, while neglecting the spiritual-religious element as far as they themselves and the Jewish people are concerned.

Among these one-identity proponents one can find many who persist in expressing an unabashed pride in their heritage. Their total immersion in secular affairs has not severed their Jewish connections. Yet they often tend to redefine their Judaism in universal terms, to dilute its aspects of distinctiveness, and to present it as not very dissimilar from the majority faith. Their reformulation of the theology, worship, and rituals of Judaism tends to de-emphasize the religious differences that are deemed to form barriers to full social and political integration.

Such misrepresentation of one's identity betrays cowardice and self-delusion. In fact, both identities are compatible and, in most instances, they are inescapable. The secularized Jew who

171

either denies or distorts his faith is purchasing his acceptance and integration into the general society at the expense of his intellectual honesty. There is something fraudulent and disingenuous in the effort to deny one's roots and one's soul. It scars the psyche and, in fact, is rarely successful. While this group loudly proclaims its exclusive human identity and its denial of all sectarian loyalties, the non-Jewish world adamantly regards all Jews, including the assimilated, as members of a separate and distinct community with its own specialized interests and concerns. The concept of a totally shared humanity is a utopian ideal which is rarely fully achieved.

Where Judaism Differs

From its very inception, Judaism has been strikingly different from other faiths. It has embodied ideas, a way of life, and aspirations for the future which set the Jewish people apart from other groups. Even a rather unfriendly observer, Balaam felt compelled to characterize the Jews as a "people that shall dwell alone, and shall not be reckoned among other nations" (Num. 23.9).[5]

There are three primary areas of distinctiveness without which Judaism would lose its essential character.

Commandments. These are the *mitzvot*, behavioral imperatives, which are derived from the Divine Will. They find their precise formulation in the *Halakhah*, Jewish Law, and have been codified by Torah scholars over the centuries. These commandments are very personal to the observant Jew and they reflect the inner mystery of Israel's commitment to God. They have suggestive meanings and emotional overtones which are known only to the two partners of the covenant. To equate these *mitzvot* with the ritual observances of another faith is to belie the distinctiveness of both. To declare these *mitzvot* as no longer obligatory is to divest Judaism of its primary mark of singularity. Such acts of reductionism are basically fraudulent.

Doctrines. Judaism regards its dogmas and values as verities which are rooted in the Torah tradition and whose authority is ultimately Divine. Our theological and philosophical premises about God, man, and creation are uniquely Jewish and, through the course of centuries, have been preserved despite efforts at dissuasion, ridicule, and torture. We, in modern times, have not been authorized by our millennia-old history to revise these historical attitudes or to trade the fundamentals of our faith for the illusory pursuit of interfaith goodwill. Such would be a betrayal of our great tradition and would, furthermore, produce no practical benefits. A cringing readiness to barter away our identity will never evoke the respect of any who confront us. Only a staunch and unequivocal bearing, reflecting our firm commitment to God and a sense of pride and privilege in being what we are, will impress other faith communities.

Future Expectations. Judaism foresees and eagerly awaits the coming of the Messiah, the vindication of Jewish singularity and chosenness, the ingathering of the dispersed in the Holy Land, the reestablishment of the Temple, the universal acknowledgment of ethical monotheism, and the realization of world peace. These beliefs have sustained us for countless centuries in periods of trial. They are called eschatological expectations, since they represent our vision of the future which we anticipate with exultant certainty. Other faiths define their eschatological expectations in other terms.

Adopting the religious practices of others, the dilution of dogmatic certitudes, and the waiving of eschatological expectations would spell the end of the vibrant and great faith experience of our four-thousand-year-old history.

We have been critical of the one-identity proponents who choose the universal-human response at the expense of their Jewish identity. One can equally question the parochialism of

173

those whose Jewish identity excludes any interest in the larger concerns of society and who seem to live insulated from all that is beyond their immediate group. In all fairness, however, we insist that this self-involvement is frequently due to the fact that, for centuries, the non-Jewish world has reduced its Jewish inhabitants to a subordinate level of bare toleration and has excluded them from equal citizenship and opportunities, regarding them, until modern times, as being bereft of noble instincts and creative abilities. Jews should not be held responsible for this cruelty and blindness, which precluded any possibility of their joining others in advancing the progress of society. When given equal status, they were always ready to fulfill the Divine challenge to "fill the earth and to subdue it" (Gen. 1:28).[6] As demonstrated in most modern Western societies, Jews, when given the opportunity, have contributed far more than their proportionate share to the welfare of humanity.

The Confrontation of Jacob and Esau

The confrontation of Jacob and Esau, after twenty years of separation, has been interpreted by our Sages and commentators as a paradigm, guiding future generations of Jews in their relation to other groups. Many years earlier, the two brothers had parted under threatening circumstances and now, hopefully mellowed by the passage of time, the two old adversaries were about to meet. The text is remarkably incisive: "And he [Jacob] commanded those at the front, saying, When Esau my brother meets you and asks you, saying: '*Whose* are you and where are you going? And whose [animals] are these ahead of you?' Then you shall answer that they are your servant Jacob's: 'It is a present sent to my lord, Esau, and behold he [Jacob] is right behind us' " (Gen. 32:17-18).[7]

Jacob anticipated that Esau would ask three questions of him and his family as they approached to take up residence in Canaan. "Whose are you?"—To whom do you pledge your ultimate loyalty? "And where are you going?"—What objectives and goals do you seek for yourself in the future? Who is your God and what manner of life and discipline will He require of you and your descendants? These two inquiries relate to Jacob's soul and spiritual identity. Consequently, Jacob commanded his representatives to reply boldly, clearly, and precisely that their souls, their personalities, their metaphysical identities, their spiritual future and social commitment were the private concerns of Jacob. "They are your servant Jacob's," and no human power may interfere or attempt to sever this eternal bond with God which had been established in the covenant with Abraham.

Jacob anticipated, however, that Esau would also ask a third question: "And whose are these [cattle, gifts, etc.] ahead of you?" —Are you ready to contribute your talents, capabilities, and material resources toward the material and cultural welfare of the general society? Are you ready to give of your oxen, goats, camels, and bulls? Are you willing to pay taxes, to develop and industrialize the country? This third question is focused on secular aspects of life. To this question Jacob instructed his agents to answer in the affirmative: "It is a present to my lord, Esau." Yes, we are determined to participate in every civic, scientific, and political enterprise. We feel obligated to enrich society with our creative talents and to be constructive and useful citizens.

This testament handed down to us by Jacob is particularly relevant in our day when, after millennia of separation, various gestures of rapprochement are being made. The identical questions are implicitly being heard: "Whose are you? Where are you going? Whose are these before you?" A millennia-old history demands of us that we meet these challenges courageously and give the same answers which were entrusted to Jacob's messengers several thousand years ago.

Interreligious Discussion and Activity

It is self-evident that meetings between two faith communities are possible only if they are accompanied by a clear assurance that both parties will enjoy equal rights and full religious freedom. No relationship even remotely suggestive of subordination would be tolerable. A democratic confrontation certainly does not demand that we submit to an attitude of self-righteousness on the part of the majority faith community which, while debating whether or not to absolve the Jewish community of some mythical guilt, completely ignores its own historical responsibility for the suffering and martyrdom inflicted upon the few, the weak, and the persecuted.

Two basic ground rules must govern such group contacts. First, Judaism is not to be regarded as validating itself in history by virtue of its being the precursor of another faith. Any suggestion that the historical worth of our faith is to be gauged against the backdrop of another faith, and the mere hint that a revision of basic historical attitudes on our part is anticipated, are incongruous with the fundamentals of religious liberty and freedom of conscience and can only breed discord and suspicion. Such an approach is unacceptable to any self-respecting faith community that is proud of its past, vibrant and active in the present, and determined to live on in the future, and which intends to continue serving God in its own unique way. Only a full appreciation of the singular role, inherent worth, and basic prerogatives of each religious community will help promote the spirit of cooperation among faiths.

Secondly, the discussion should concern itself not with theological but with secular matters of mutual concern. In the private religious realm, each faith has its own "words" and forms which are uniquely intimate, reflecting its philosophical character, and are totally incomprehensible to people of other faiths. The claims of supernatural experiences on the part of each group differ, and an attempt to achieve dialogue on this level can cause more friction than amity, more confusion than clarity, and thereby prove harmful to the interrelationship. The areas of joint concern should be outer-directed, to combat the secularism, materialism, and atheistic negation of religion and religious values which threaten the moral underpinnings of our society. As far as religion is concerned, we should be guided by the words of Micah (4:5): "Let all people walk, each one in the name of its god, and we shall walk in the name of the Lord, our God, for ever and ever." [8]

Our approach to the outside world has always been of an ambivalent character. We cooperate with members of other faiths in all fields of human endeavor but, simultaneously, we seek to preserve our distinct integrity which inevitably involves aspects of separateness. This is a paradoxical situation. Yet, paraphrasing the words of our first ancestor, Abraham, we are very much residents in general human society while, at the same time, strangers and outsiders in our persistent endeavor to preserve our historic religious identity.

הערות לפרק 16

1   גר יתושב אנכי עמכם (בראשית כג, ד).

2   ודרשו את שלום העיר אשר הגליתי אתכם שמה והתפללו בעדה אל ה', כי בשלומה יהיה לכם שלום (ירמיה כט, ז).

3   אמר שמואל: דינא דמלכותא דינא (גיטין י:).

4   רבי חנינא סגן הכהנים אומר, הוי מתפלל בשלומה של מלכות, שאלמלא מוראה, איש את רעהו חיים בלעו (אבות ג, ב).

5   הן עם לבדד ישכן ובגוים לא יתחשב (במדבר כג, ט).

6   ומלאו את הארץ וכבשה (בראשית א, כח).

7   ויצו את הראשון לאמר: כי יפגשך עשו אחי ושאלך לאמר, למי אתה ואנה תלך ולמי אלה לפניך, ואמרת, לעבדד ליעקב, מנחה היא שלוחה לאדני לעשו והנה גם הוא אחרינו . . . (בראשית לב, יז—יח).

8   כי כל העמים ילכו איש בשם אלהיו, ואנחנו נלך בשם ה' אלהינו לעולם ועד (מיכה ד, ה).

177

CHAPTER XVII

LESSONS IN JEWISH SURVIVAL

The Purim *Megillah* insists that "these days should be remembered and kept throughout every generation, every family, every province and every city; and these days of Purim should not fail from among the Jews, nor the remembrance of them perish from their descendants" (Esth. 9:28).[1] Apparently, it is important for Jews of all generations to derive crucial lessons from the *Megillah,* a book whose mood reflects the basic vulnerability of the Jew.

The entire Persian episode involved the absurd and the unexpected, seeming coincidences and capricious events. Mordecai suddenly found himself saved from the gallows and elevated to the august post of Prime Minister. Overnight, a doomed people found itself dramatically triumphant over its enemies. Even as we celebrate, though, we are aware that the pendulum can swing in reverse. Had Haman not previously enjoyed the king's trust? Yet suddenly he was executed. Why delude ourselves that Mordecai would be any more secure as Prime Minister? Were Jews previously not confident about their security and then, without prior warning, found themselves facing annihilation? What if Esther were suddenly deposed because of some irrational provocation, as was Vashti before her? Who is clairvoyant enough to assure us that such absurd changes of men and moods will not repeat themselves?

178

The *Megillah*, therefore, portrays the instability and uncertainty that govern the fate of the Jew. The Egyptian *galut*
taught the Jew ethical sensitivity (see Chapter XVIII), but the
Persian *galut* apparently was meant to provide lessons on how
to survive as a people. The former made an imprint upon the
character of the Jews, while the latter was concerned to per-
petuate the physical entity of the people. Until the destruction
of the Temple in 586 B.C.E., the First Commonwealth was
nourished by the lessons of the Egyptian sojourn. For the Second
Commonwealth, an additional inspirational experience was necessary in the face of threats to the survival of the people.

Four significant lessons may be derived from the Persian
galut. First, our faith in man must not blind us to the demonic
within him; the question, "Can it happen here?", must be
faced soberly, not naively. Second, every upheaval, every major
movement and event in history has dire possibilities for the
Jews. Third, a common destiny unites all Jews. And finally, God
intercedes whenever total destruction faces the Jewish people.

First Lesson: Man Can Become Satan

Our faith in man's goodness should not blind us to the
latent demonic in man. Evidently, civilized men can become
the personification of evil. The thin veneer of social restraint
can suddenly be lifted, exposing the ugly, brutish potential of
man. Created "in the image of God," man can also assume a
satanic identity. He is capable, from time to time, of going
berserk, of turning into a monster.

"The emissaries went forth in haste to carry out the king's
bidding. The edict had been announced in the capital city of
Shushan. The king and Haman were dining, but the city of
Shushan was cast into bewilderment" (Esth. 3:15).[2] Their
bewilderment was due to the traditional naivety of the Jew who
cannot believe that human beings may act like predatory

179

beasts of the jungle. This was a traumatic discovery for the Jews of Persia. The Jew believes intuitively in man's inherent goodness, that a Divine spark inhabits every human being, even the habitual sinner and criminal. This is the basis of *teshuvah*, that the kernel of man's soul ever remains uncontaminated, and may yet induce a moral regeneration. The sudden confrontation with total "Amalek-style" cruelty was, therefore, a painful and rude awakening.

In Haman, the Jews of Persia met a descendant of Amalek. Who is Amalek? He is the personification of total evil, for whom immorality has become the norm. The Torah says, "The Lord will be at war with Amalek throughout the ages" (Ex. 17:16).[3] Does it not seem undignified for the Lord to declare war on a Bedouin tribe? Rashi adds that "God swore that His name and throne would not be complete until the name of Amalek was obliterated." Furthermore, our Sages taught that the final triumph over Amalek will occur in the days of the Messiah.

Amalek is obviously more than a Bedouin tribe. He is more than a particular group, nationality or people. He is Everyman gone berserk, who has shed his Divine image for that of Satan. Any nation which declares that its policy is to destroy the Jewish people is Amalek, for it has emblazoned on its banner the slogan of impassioned hatred: "Come, let us destroy them as a nation, that the name Israel may no more be remembered" (Ps. 83:5).[4] This is the persistent villainy that the Lord bids us combat and against which He has sworn eternal enmity. It is for this reason that there is a positive Torah commandment: "Remember what Amalek did to you when you were on your journey, after you left Egypt . . . Do not forget!" (Deut. 25:17, 19).[5] This Scriptural reading is appropriately prescribed for the Sabbath preceding Purim.

In our generation, Hitler and Stalin are clearly Amalek personified. Jews in Germany, and even in concentration camps, discounted rumors of mass killings until it was too late. In Communist Russia, many Jews continued to support Stalin, despite his demonstrated tyranny and anti-Semitism. The Jew is naive in his faith in man and is therefore particularly vulnerable. "Can it happen here?" the Jews of Persia probably asked themselves, incredulously.

The first lesson of Purim is that Jews everywhere, even those dwelling under benign conditions, must answer decidedly: "Yes, it can happen here and elsewhere, as it has occurred in the past." The ethical sensitivity and respect for man, which was so successfully imprinted upon the Jewish personality by the Egyptian experience and reinforced by the preachings of the Prophets, should not blind Jews to stark realities. A sober awareness of dire possibilities will, hopefully, lead to vigilance and to precaution. Amalek is an historic phenomenon; *Lo tishkah*—the lesson must never be forgotten.

Second Lesson: The Jew is More Vulnerable than Others

Human monsters, though an enemy and threat to all mankind, somehow specialize in the hatred of Jews. They may be proponents of particular ideologies of the left or right, agnostic secularists or reactionary clericalists, yet they strangely become preoccupied with the Jew and derive particular delight from tormenting him. This hatred of the Jew emerges from any economic or political spectrum. Hitler's national ambitions need not have involved Jews as a central obsession. There was nothing in his policy of expansionist nationalism which required his annihilation of East European Jewry. Similarly, Communism, as an economic and political ideology, could have functioned without adopting any particularly repressive policies against Jews. Yet the Jew is continually caught up in the thick of events which are completely unrelated to him. At times, great empires vie with each other and the Jew is forced to cast his lot with the less objectionable, thus unwillingly becoming involved.

It was a rude awakening for the Jews of Persia to discover that the main preoccupation of the new Prime Minister was to annihilate them. He was even willing to bribe the king in order to win his approval. Suddenly, the Persian Jew discovered that he was hated with concentrated passion. No one has a virulent hatred for the United States or France, although particular policies may be vehemently decried. The mere existence of the Jew, however, irritates Amalek and his hatred can suddenly and violently erupt and be translated into mass murder. Why is this so? There is no answer; it is an absurd situation which has accompanied the Jew since the dawn of his history. Our Sages suggest that it is, somehow, related to the singular religious destiny which was assigned to him at Mt. Sinai.[6]

The Persian *galut* taught the Jew that the very presence of a Mordecai irrationally arouses the animal in a Haman. He expressed this uncontrollable hostility in these words: "Yet all this [honor] is worthless to me, so long as I see Mordecai, the Jew, sitting at the king's gate" (Esth. 5:13).[7] The Jew must therefore be alert to a second area of vulnerability, that satanic men will, regardless of their other primary interests, somehow implicate the Jew in their destructive activities. To believe reassuringly that, "if we do not make waves, they might not notice us" is a dangerous illusion.

Third Lesson: All Jews Share a Common Destiny

This hatred of the Jew is an animosity directed against the entire group. It is not necessarily confined to religious or ethnically conscious Jews who are more conspicuous by their separateness. The hatred of Haman is commodious enough to embrace the Jew with a *mezuzah* on his doorpost as well as the Jew whose home is devoid of all symbols of Jewishness. The distinctive garb and striking appearance of the *Ḥassid* did not make him a more likely victim of the Nazis than westernized Jews who were outwardly indistinguishable from non-Jews. The assimilated and the nationalist Jew evoke the same venom from the tyrant. At Ahasuerus' banquet, many thousands of assimilated Jews were present. They undoubtedly regarded themselves as secure. Yet, when the decree was promulgated, all Jews were subject to a common destiny; no one was exempted.

The formal transfer of authority to Haman took place when "the king removed his ring from his hand and gave it to Haman . . . the oppressor of the Jews" (*ibid.* 3:10).[8] The Talmud poignantly elaborates: "The transfer of the ring was more effective in uniting the Jews in religious repentance than the forty-eight prophets and seven prophetesses, who were unable to turn Israel to better courses" (Meg. 14a).[9]

During the First Commonwealth, the Jews were divided into two kingdoms, Yehudah and Yisrael, which at times even warred with each other. God now wanted a united people. Who united them?—Haman! That they shared a common, inescapable destiny became clear to all classes of Jews. Haman's hatred was vented against the entire people and not toward particular Jews. He intended to spare no one; he did not select anyone for preferential treatment. He said, "There is a certain people scattered abroad, and dispersed amongst [other] peoples in all the provinces of the kingdom" (3:8).[10] They are one people, despite their varied stations in society, their outward dissimilarities, and their scattered habitations. It was Haman who imposed a oneness, a cohesiveness upon the Jewish people.

For the Second Commonwealth, God wanted a united people, and this the Persian experience accomplished. Mordecai told Esther (who seemed initially hesitant about interceding): "Think not that you will escape in the royal house, more than other Jews" (4:13).[11] Resolutely, she immediately replied: "Go, gather together *all* the Jews" (4:16)[12]—Inform them that a common

183

threat confronts all Jewry and that no group can afford the luxury of imagined security. A concerted and vigilant response is imperative if Jewish survival is to be ensured.

Fourth Lesson: God Does Not Abandon His People

The previous lessons somberly alert us to the fearful possibilities which forever threaten the Jew. The fourth lesson, however, is reassuring and inspiring and may very well be the primary purpose of the Persian galut.

There the Jew discovered a basic existential condition which protects him whenever he is threatened by satanic enemies. When imminent annihilation confronts the Jew, God always sends His agent(s), shelihe Hashem, to save His people. Mordecai and Esther assùmed this role in Persia, just as Moses was mandated to do when God said to him: "Come, now, and I will send you to Pharaoh, and you shall free My people, the Israelites, from Egypt" (Ex. 3:10).[13]

Paradoxically, man—any man of flesh and blood—can presume to represent God. Prophets ordinarily transmit messages or perform acts dictated by God, but they do not represent God. Nevertheless, it is a basic Jewish concept that God functions primarily through man. Ge'ulah, the redemption of the Jew, is always achieved through a sheli'ah Hashem. In the awaited Messianic era, the redemption will come about through the agency of an endowed human being, the Melekh Hamashi'ah. In the Talmud, Rabbi Hillel (not Hillel the Tanna) expressed the view that there will not be an individual Messiah in the future, but that God Himself will bring about the Messianic era (Sanh. 99a). Rabbi Joseph denounced this view, declaring it to border on heresy. Apparently, the belief that ge'ulah is always achieved through a sheli'ah Hashem is an article of faith.

In the Ani Ma'amin, the Principles of Faith formulated by Maimonides, we read: "I believe with perfect faith in the coming of the Messiah, and though he delays in coming, I will wait for him daily." [14] The expectation is for a personal Messiah and not merely a Messianic era. In Exodus (2:23) we note that God heard the cries of the suffering Israelites and, in one verse after another (23 to 25), it is clear that God was ready for the *ge'ulah*. What delayed it? The next verse explains that "Moses was a shepherd of sheep for his father-in-law, Yitro" (*ibid.* 3:1). Moses was not yet ready for his mission and so God waited, because He only works through a *shali'ah*. It took seven days of persuasion, our Sages say, before Moses, in his overwhelming humility, could be induced to accept the assignment. Similarly in Shushan, an old man, Mordecai, and his young niece, Esther, had to work out their sense of mandate and the strategy to be employed, before the *ge'ulah* process could unfold.

To retain a vivid awareness of these four lessons of the Persian exile is critically important for Jewish survival at all times. Even as we marshal all our human resourcefulness in face of hovering physical dangers, we have an unswerving faith that God will intercede to frustrate the wickedness of Amalek. The final triumph will be His, and ours also.

הערות לפרק 17

1   והימים האלה נזכרים ונעשים בכל דור ודור, משפחה ומשפחה, מדינה ומדינה,
     ועיר ועיר, וימי הפורים האלה לא יעברו מתוך היהודים, וזכרם לא יסוף מזרעם
     (אסתר ט, כח).

2   הרצים יצאו דחופים בדבר המלך, והדת נתנה בשושן הבירה, והמלך והמן ישבו
     לשתות, והעיר שושן נבוכה (שם, ג, טו).

3   מלחמה לה׳ בעמלק מדר דר (שמות יז, טז). רש״י — נשבע הקב״ה שאין שמו
     שלם ואין כסאו שלם, עד שימחה שמו של עמלק כולו.

4   לכו, ונכחידם מגוי, ולא יזכר שם ישראל עוד (תהלים פג, ה).

5   זכור את אשר עשה לך עמלק בדרך, בצאתכם ממצרים . . . לא תשכח (דברים
     כה, יז, יט).

6   מדבר סיני, שירדה שנאה לאומות העולם עליו (שבת פט:).

7   וכל זה איננו שוה לי, בכל עת אשר אני ראה את מרדכי היהודי יושב בשער
     המלך (אסתר ה, יג).

8 ויסר המלך את טבעתו מעל ידו, ויתנה להמן בן המדתא האגגי צרר היהודים
(שם ג, י).

9 אמר רבי אבא בר כהנא, גדולה הסרת טבעת יותר מארבעים ושמונה נביאים
ושבע נביאות, שנתנבאו להן לישראל, שכולן לא החזירום למוטב ואילו הסרת
טבעת החזירתן למוטב (מגילה יד.).

10 ישנו עם אחד מפזר ומפרד בין העמים בכל מדינות מלכותך (אסתר ג, ח).

11 אל תדמי בנפשך, להמלט בית המלך מכל היהודים (שם, ד, יג).

12 לך כנוס את כל היהודים הנמצאים בשושן (שם, ד, טז).

13 ועתה, לכה ואשלחך אל פרעה והוצא את עמי בני ישראל ממצרים (שמות ג, י).

14 אני מאמין באמונה שלמה בביאת המשיח, ואף על פי שיתמהמה, עם כל זה אחכה
לו בכל יום שיבא (רמב״ם, שלשה עשר עקרים).

CHAPTER XVIII

THE ETHICAL EMPHASIS IN JUDAISM

The Jewish people endured two major exiles (*galuyot*): Egypt and in Persia. In both instances, the entire Jewish people was subjugated by a threatening tyrant whose nefarious plans could have spelled the end of Jewish history. During other periods of persecution, even under Nazidom in modern times, Jews were dispersed among different sovereignties and their destruction in one area did not necessarily threaten them with extinction elsewhere. The Egyptian and Persian exiles, however, were unique in that each encompassed the totality of the Jewish people.

There are striking similarities between *galut Mitzrayim* (Egypt) and *galut Paras* (Persia).* In both, God sent messengers, *shelihe Hashem*, to save His people: Moses in Egypt and Mordecai and Esther in Persia. After each of these redemptions, the Israelites publicly affirmed their acceptance of the Torah. Our Sages inform us that, after Haman's downfall, the Jews of Persia recommitted themselves to the Torah in a mass expression of gratitude at a public convocation. Commenting on the verse, "the Jews ordained and took upon themselves" (Esth. 9:27),

---

* The exile from the Land of Israel in 586 B.C.E. was actually to Babylonia and is called *Galut Bavel*. Babylonia was later absorbed into the Persian Empir

187

our Sages added: "They reaffirmed their commitment to the Torah as they had done previously [at Sinai]" (Shab. 88a).[1]

Equally noteworthy are the injunctions that the events of both exiles are to be kept fresh in the national memory and never forgotten. The *Seder* observance is basically a reliving of the Exodus experience, and during the rest of the year we are required to recall the event daily. Similarly, the *Megillah* prescribes that "these days should be remembered and kept throughout every generation, every family, every province, and every city; and these days of Purim should not fail from among the Jews, nor the remembrance of them perish from their descendants" (*ibid.* 9:28).[2] Apparently, God wanted Jews of all generations to recall significant lessons of the Egyptian and Persian exiles.

Why Providence ordained the Egyptian and Persian exiles can only be conjectured. Many *Midrashim* ascribe a variety of purposes to both events. Judaism does not accept the existence of the irrational in human life, and certainly not where the entire Jewish people is involved. Events which we call accidents and are seemingly inexplicable at the time of their occurrence may begin to make sense and to show logical patterns when viewed in retrospect, from the vantage point of later years. Looking back, we can discern moral lessons and enduring impressions which the Egyptian and Persian exiles left upon the Jewish historical memory. In hindsight, many events become intelligible.

In answer to Moses' plea, "Oh, let me behold Your Presence", God replied: "You cannot see My face, for man may not see Me and live ... But as My Presence passes by, I will put you in a cleft of the rock, and will cover you with My hand until I have passed by. And I will take away My hand, and you will see My back; but My face shall not be seen" (Ex. 33:18–23).[3] What Moses learned here was that God's Presence (involvement) on earth is not always discernible while the events themselves occur. As His presence is passing by, we are, as it were, thrust into a narrow cleft of rock with His hand obscuring our understanding. The "frontal" view, *lir'ot et panai*, is not illuminating.[4] But in retrospect, years later, when God has already passed by, interpretations suggest themselves and understanding is frequently possible. Glancing backward, *ahorai*, we can discern contours of meaning.

Only from the vantage point of historical distance, as we study the Jewish past, may we arrive at some appreciation of the enduring influences which *galut Mitzrayim* and *galut Paras* have had upon the Jewish personality.*

Molding Jewish Character

What was the purpose of the first exile of the Jewish people 3500 years ago? Of course, it welded twelve tribal families into one nation through their shared suffering. They entered Egypt fragmented, and emerged united. The Exodus also dramatically manifested God's involvement in the birth of the Jewish people and demonstrated His concern with their destiny. In Deuteronomy (4:20) another reason is suggested: "But *you* the Lord took and brought out of Egypt, that iron furnace, to be His people of inheritance as you are this day." [5] Rashi explains that the "iron furnace" here designates a vessel used for refining gold. The suffering in Egypt apparently was intended to refine and cleanse the Jewish character, to remove the dross of moral impurities and to heighten their ethical sensitivity. This metaphor was echoed by the prophet Isaiah: "Behold, I have refined you, but not as silver; I have tried you in the furnace of afflictions" (48:10).[6] The Egyptian exile may thus be viewed as a necessary experience which molded the moral quality of the Jewish people for all time.

---

* The lessons of the Persian exile are explored in Chapter XVII.

Whenever the Torah wishes to impress upon us the *mitzvah* of having compassion and sympathy for the oppressed in society, it reminds us of our similar helplessness and lowly status during our bondage in Egypt. The most defenseless elements in society are usually the slaves, strangers (proselytes), widows, and orphans, and we are repeatedly enjoined by the Torah to be sensitive to their plight: "You shall not pervert the justice due a stranger or to the fatherless; nor take a widow's garment in pawn. Remember that you were a slave in Egypt, and the Lord your God redeemed you; therefore, I command you to observe this commandment" (Deut. 24:17-18).[7] The stranger, in particular, personifies the helpless one who has no family or friends to intercede on his behalf. For this reason, as the Talmud indicates, the Torah exhorts us in thirty-six Scriptural references to treat the stranger kindly (B. Metz. 59b).

The Egyptian experience may therefore be regarded as the fountainhead and moral inspiration for the teaching of compassion which is so pervasive in Jewish Law. It sharpened the Jew's ethical sensitivity and moral awareness. The Midrash has R. Nehemiah say this explicitly: "The Egyptian bondage was of great value for us, since it served to implant within us the quality of kindness and mercy" (Mekhilta de-R. Shim'on ben Yoḥai Ex. 13:3). Ours is a singularly ethical culture, which expresses itself through a heightened regard for human rights and dignity. *Kevod haberi'ot* (respect for human dignity) and social justice are implicit in the Biblical concept that man was created in God's image.

To this day, even Jews who are alienated from religious practice seem more responsive than gentiles to causes which affect mankind. There are crimes which come harder to a Jew than to others. This may sound chauvinistic, but it is statistically true. Murder and physical violence were unheard of among Jews in the past, and are still proportionately rare among those who have any roots in their heritage. Embezzlement and cheating in financial matters may entice Jews vulnerable to the temptations of money and riches; but rarely homicide, which occurs so frequently in other cultures. To the extent that a Jew becomes estranged from Jewish values, however, he begins to manifest behavioral tendencies which prevail in the dominant culture.

The *Halakhah* has formulated many regulations designed to prevent one from hurting others by word or deed, wittingly or unwittingly. This is illustrated in its abhorrence of slander (*rekhilut*) and evil gossip (*leshon hara*).[8] The prohibition, "Do not put pitfalls before the blind" (Lev. 19:14),[9] has been broadly interpreted by our Sages as prohibiting contributory actions which are harmful to others, even to those who are not physically blind but are misguided by their ignorance. The Torah expects us to protect society from situations liable to cause damage, such as roofs without railings[10] and uncovered pits. Jewish Law is also insistent on the moral obligation to perform positive acts of charity and helpfulness, even for our enemies.[11] Such injunctions—to be highly solicitous of the welfare of others— are not as finely developed in other legal systems as they are in ours.

Our Sages regard compassion as the distinguishing characteristic of the Jewish people.[12] Yet, we may ask, is not compassion a natural expression of man's being created in God's image (*betzelem Elohim*), an endowment which all mankind possesses in common? Why, then, was the Egyptian enslavement necessary for the Jews? The answer is that *betzelem Elohim* signifies only a capacity to love, not the necessity of loving. This capacity, which all people possess, can be and is frequently suppressed; but when it becomes a necessity, it cannot be suppressed. It then flows naturally and is indigenous to one's character. The Egyptian experience sought to transform the Jews into a people to whom compassion would be a necessity, not merely a capacity.

There are two words which are often used interchangeably, but are not synonymous: *merahem* and *rahaman*. *Merahem* is verbal in form, a participle, and accordingly places emphasis on the deed. The person described as a *merahem*, then, is one who performs many charitable acts. He may at times be cold and unfeeling, but he does nevertheless manage to perform many deeds of compassion. In each situation he hesitates, deliberates whether to respond compassionately or not. If he decides to perform the noble deed, we regard him as worthy, but we would not go so far as to call him a compassionate person, since although he may have the capacity and inclination to love his fellow man, he feels no dominant compulsion to do so.

Rahaman, on the other hand, is an adjectival form describing an attribute, a characteristic. The *rahaman*, then, is a person who has only one choice—to act compassionately. His attitude flows naturally from his personality. He does not hesitate; he is not self-conscious. He cannot act otherwise; he is able only to love, and is unaware of any alternative. No one would describe the *Hafetz Hayim*,[13] for instance, as a person who performed acts of *tzidkut* but as a *tzaddik*, since his goodness was inseparably bound up with his character. He could not be otherwise. Hence, the *rahaman* is superior to the *merahem*.

Ideally, the Jewish people have been described as *rahmanim bne rahmanim*, a people from whom compassion and communal responsibility flow naturally. In its detailed legal development, the *Halakhah* is the embodiment of this sensitivity. A person who is uncertain how to act in face of human need may readily engage in rationalization and be diverted by self-serving considerations. But the *Halakhah* directs him to act with compassion and gradually transforms him into a *rahaman*, a person who spontaneously responds with compassion.

This, in retrospect, seems to be the dominant lesson to be derived from *galut Mitzrayim*. It taught the Jew ethical sensitivity, what it truly means to be a Jew. It sought to transform the Jew into a *raḥaman*, one possessing a heightened form of ethical sensitivity and responsiveness.

Faith and Morality are Indivisible

Since morality is basic to Judaism, it follows that to be regarded as a religious Jew, one must also be ethical.

The Ten Commandments (Decalogue) were, as we know, inscribed upon two tablets of the Law. The first five commandments deal with acts of faith which relate man to his Maker, *ben adam Lamakom*, while the latter five prohibit anti-social acts, *ben adam laḥavero*. The Torah introduces the Decalogue with the verse, "And God spoke all [*kol*] these words saying" (Ex. 20:1).[14] Rashi notes that the verse would be entirely meaningful without the redundant word *kol*, stating simply that "God spoke these words saying, etc." He therefore explains: "This teaches us that the Holy One, blessed be He, pronounced all these words in a single utterance, an impossibility for human beings."

What is the significance of God's simultaneous utterance of the entire Decalogue? It teaches us that all Ten Commandments constitute an indivisible, organic unity. We have not ten commandments but one, with ten aspects. The word "all" in this context does not mean "all of them," which characterizes a numerical sum total of independent teachings, but rather a totality, an interdependent oneness of all its seeming parts. Faith and morality are integrally one and inseparable.

Can There Be Morality Without Faith?

Can a secular state nurture a moral society? Can a culture which is indifferent to the transcendental imperative inspire ethical performance in private and public life? In past decades, secular humanists were certain that man could be induced and motivated to pursue ethical norms without the absolute imperative of the

Divine. Our thesis is that in the long run, and for the masses of society, there can be no such thing. Either man accepts the authority of God as the Legislator of the moral norm, or he will eventually fail in all attempts to create a moral society. A relativistic man-made moral order will simply not endure, and the inability of modern secularism to motivate ethical behavior in private or public life is evidence of this truth.

The verse, "When a person sins and commits a trespass against the Lord by dealing falsely with his neighbor" (Lev. 5:21),[15] is homiletically interpreted by our Sages as follows: He who commits a trespass against the Lord will eventually also deal falsely with his neighbor. Morality without faith cannot sustain itself.

An interesting Midrash supports this idea: Rabbi Reuven was asked by a philosopher in Tiberias: "Who is the most hateful [morally dangerous] person in the world?" He replied, "He who denies his Creator, because the denial of all norms follows if one rejects God. No man violates a law unless he first repudiates the legislative authority of the law" (Tosefta Shevu'ot 3:5).[16]

Rabbi Reuven felt that the non-believer constitutes a danger to the moral fabric of society. The philosopher was astonished by his answer because faith, after all, is the private affair of the individual; and, furthermore, are not many atheists teachers of morality? The Rabbi insisted, however, that eventually atheism leads to the demoralization of the individual and society. Man can easily rationalize his crime, declare norms to be relative, and proclaim himself the arbiter of right and wrong. With most people, the baser part of their natures will tend to dominate. Indeed, the moral bankruptcy of secularism is apparent to all students of our contemporary world.

By declaring the indivisible unity of both tablets of the Decalogue, God declared that, without faith, morality cannot be sustained.

THE ETHICAL EMPHASIS IN JUDAISM

Can One Have Faith Without Morality?

It is equally true that there can be no faith (*emunah*) without lovingkindness (*ḥesed*). People who are ritualistically observant but ethically deficient distort Judaism. Their self-righteousness and presumed piety are hypocritical. Here, too, the *bedibbur eḥad*, God's combined utterance, proclaims the indivisibility of the entire Decalogue. It is moral schizophrenia to separate ethics from God.

In the final analysis, authentic Judaism will prevail over secularists and deviationists only if it results in a superior value system of ethical behavior. God may be worshiped only if we first make peace with our fellow man. There can be no Judaism without morality.

This ethical emphasis may be the primary lesson to derive from the Egyptian *galut* experience.

הערות לפרק 18

1 קימו וקבלו היהודים עליהם ועל זרעם (אסתר ט, כז). אמר רבא . . . הדור קבלוה בימי אחשורוש . . . קיימו מה שקיבלו כבר (שבת פח.).

2 והימים האלה נזכרים ונעשים בכל דור ודור, משפחה ומשפחה, מדינה ומדינה, ועיר ועיר, וימי הפורים האלה לא יעברו מתוך היהודים, וזכרם לא יסוף מזרעם (אסתר ט, כח).

3 ויאמר הראני נא את כבדך . . . ויאמר, לא תוכל לראת את פני, כי לא יראני האדם וחי . . . והיה בעבר כבדי, ושמתיך בנקרת הצור, ושכתי כפי עליך עד עברי. והסרתי את כפי וראית את אחרי, ופני לא יראו (שמות לג, יח—כג).

4 "הראני וכו'" — אמר משה להקב"ה, הראני נא מדה שאתה מנהיג בה את העולם. א"ל, אין אתה יכול לעמוד על מדותי (מדרש שו"ט כה).

5 "ואתכם לקח ה', ויוצא אתכם מכור הברזל, ממצרים, להיות לו לעם נחלה כיום הזה" (דברים ד, כ). רש"י — כור הוא כלי שמזקקים בו את הזהב.

6 הנה צרפתיך ולא בכסף, בחרתיך בכור עוני (ישעיה מח, י).

7 לא תטה משפט גר יתום, ולא תחבל בגד אלמנה. וזכרת כי עבד היית במצרים ויפדך ה' אלהיך משם, על כן אנכי מצוך לעשות את הדבר הזה (דברים כד, יז, יח).

8 לא תלך רכיל בעמיך (ויקרא יט, טז).

195

9 ולפני עור לא תתן מכשל (שם, יט, יד); לפני סומא בדבר. היה נוטל ממך עצה,
אל תתן לו עצה שאינה הוגנת לו... שמא תאמר, עצה טובה אני נותן לו, הרי
הדבר מסור ללב, שנאמר ויראת מאלהיך, אני ה' (תו"כ).

10 כי תבנה בית חדש, ועשית מעקה לגגך, ולא תשים דמים בביתך, כי יפל הנפל
ממנו (דברים כב, ח): רבי נתן אומר, מנין שלא יגדל אדם כלב רע בתוך ביתו,
ולא יעמיד סולם רעוע בתוך ביתו, שנאמר, ולא תשים דמים בביתך (כתובות
מא:).

11 שמות כג, ד, ה.

12 כל המרחם על הבריות, בידוע שהוא מזרעו של אברהם אבינו (ביצה לב:);
שלשה סימנים יש באומה זו: הרחמנים והביישנים וגומלי חסדים (יבמות עט.).

13 Rabbi Yisrael Meir Hakohen (1838—1933), popularly known as the
Ḥafetz Ḥayim from the title of his major work on the evils of gossip
and slander, is universally acknowledged as the tzaddik ("Saint and
Sage") of the immediate past and present generations. His ethical
works have become classics, while the rulings of his Mishnah Berurah
commentary on Shulḥan Arukh, Oraḥ Ḥayyim, are accepted as
authoritative in all Ashkenazi communities throughout the world.

14 וידבר אלהים את כל הדברים האלה לאמר (שמות כ, א). רש"י — מלמד שאמר
הקב"ה עשרת הדברות בדבור אחד, מה שאי אפשר לאדם לומר כן.

15 נפש כי תחטא ומעלה מעל בה' וכחש בעמיתו (ויקרא ה, כא).

16 חנניא בן חכינאי אומר: "וכחש בעמיתו" — אין אדם כופר בעמיתו עד שכופר
בעיקר. פעם אחת שבת ר' ראובן בטבריה. מצאו פלוספוס. אמר לו, איזה הוא
שנוי שבעולם? א"ל, זה הכופר במי שבראו... דהא אין אדם כופר בדבר עד
שכופר בעיקר, ואין אדם הולך לדבר עבירה אלא אם כפר במי שצוהו לו עליה
(תוספתא, שבועות ג, ה).

196

CHAPTER XIX

REFLECTIONS ON FREEDOM
AND SLAVERY

We begin our recitation of the Passover *Haggadah* with the words: "We were slaves to Pharaoh in Egypt and the Eternal, Our God, took us out from there" (Deut. 6:21).[1] We intend to interpret this verse, with particular emphasis on three aspects: (a) The Psychology of Slaves (*Avadim Hayinu*); (b) On Being Pharaoh's Slaves (*LeFar'oh*); (c) Becoming Servants of God (*Elohenu*).

Juridic and Typological Slavery

There are two aspects of slavery which need not always coincide. The first is *juridic*, a political condition which reduces man to a chattel, a form of private property, to *kinyan kaspo*, an object belonging to an owner. The slave's body and skills belong to his master by virtue of a legal system which so degrades his status. He is a "thing" and is subject to the whim and caprice of his master's will, to physical coercion, exploitation, and humiliation.

The second type of slavery is *typological*, a mental state of servility rather than a physically imposed enslavement. There are people who think, feel, act, and react in a distinctively docile manner which suggests that their will has been broken, their ego effaced, and their freedom warped and constricted. This is an emotional condition, a crushing of one's initiative, a submersion of one's individuality, and a distortion of one's judgment. This slave mentality can be found even among politically emancipated people. The scouts sent by Moses to survey the Holy Land summed up their dispiritedness in the words: "And we were in our own sight as grasshoppers" (Num. 13:33). Such feelings of inferiority, God decided, could not inspire the initiative and confidence required to succeed in the conquest of the Holy Land.

Appropriately, then, the blessing in the *Haggadah* of gratitude for redemption from Egyptian servitude expresses a twofold appreciation: "And we shall chant unto You a new hymn about our redemption [juridic] and the liberation of our soul [typological]." [2]

The Psychology of Slaves (*Avadim Hayinu*)

Slaves are significantly excluded by the *Halakhah* from three aspects of Jewish life. They are: 1. *pasul le'edut*—a slave is disqualified from giving testimony in court; 2. *patur mimitzvot aseh shehazeman geraman*—while a slave serving a Jewish master may, with his assent, be converted to Judaism, his religious status during his slavery is considerably circumscribed. He must observe all Torah prohibitions, *mitzvot lo ta'aseh,* but he is exempt from performing such positive commandments for which a particular time has been set; and 3. *issur hithatnut*—a slave may not marry, and thereby bind himself to another, while he is still a slave. [3]

These three regulations are inherent in the typological characterization. They are deficiencies imbedded in the slave's psyche. The scars upon his personality are due to his extended subjugation to the arbitrary will of a master. Slavery imposes psychological effects which transform the human personality and prevent it from exercising its free will. We will now elaborate each of these disqualifications.

1. *Pasul Le'edut.* A slave's testimony is not trustworthy, for

198

two reasons: his conception of truth is distorted and he also lives in a perpetual state of intimidation.

A slave is a man without options. He cannot make his own decisions, except in insignificant areas. His discernment in substantive matters is consequently impaired. He never develops faith in his own judgment because it is never tested and sharpened pragmatically. Trial-and-error experiences which build confidence and refine perception are absent. Only the free man is continually challenged by the many-faceted possibilities inherent in all aspects of life. Those who are restricted in the scope of their choices or participation tend to develop illusions: they see truth subjectively; they observe things not as they are, but as they (the slaves) would like them to be. Being ever unable to intervene or take judgmental initiatives, they view matters passively. Truth and falsehood are sharpened for the one to whom such distinctions are useful; maimed and confined people, however, find their distinctions blurred and are surrounded by unrealities. Rendering testimony, however, is an exercise of discernment, an awareness of nuances, a keenness of perception, and a breadth of judgment. A slave lacks these qualifications.

A slave also lives in a constant state of fear because he is subject to the mercurial will of his master. Thus, anxiety persists even if there is no overt threat or actual attempt at intimidation. It is a perpetual tension inherent in his status and brought on by his awareness that, at any moment, he may be subject to arbitrary directives. He will therefore intuitively desist from ever contradicting his master, for fear of provoking his anger. It becomes a reflex act of fear and distrust. Inmates in concentration camps reported that they grew docile, readily submissive, and ever fearful of assertive personal judgments. An automatic concurrence prevailed. Such fears may be neurotic and non-sensible in a particular context, but they nevertheless persist. In the *tokhaḥah* (the section listing the punishments meted out for abandoning the *mitzvot*), the Torah characterizes this condition as follows: "The life you face shall be precarious; you shall be in terror, night and day, with no assurance of survival" [4] (Deut. 28:66).

During the *Seder,* the practice of "leaning," *hesebah,* in the performance of various rituals is intended to demonstrate our liberation from slavery and the disabilities it entails. Leaning connotes a state of complete relaxation, a relief from all tension or anxiety—casting off the yoke. Leaning is the antithesis of standing at attention: it denotes independence and fearlessness. We thus demonstrate a change of status, from fear-ridden slavery to the relaxed state of the free man—*me'avdut leherut.*

2. *Mitzvot Aseh Shehazeman Geraman.* A slave is relieved of the requirement to observe time-related *mitzvot* because he lacks time consciousness. Everything organic or inorganic exists within the dimension of time. There is an inexorable cycle of birth, life, and death, the attrition of change which is most clearly discernible in the organic world. The ebb and flow of time also take their toll of the inorganic world, continually transforming and reshaping. The only creature that can experience time, that feels its passage and senses its movement, is man. This is called time-awareness.

There are three dimensions of time, each of which is part of the time-experience. These are retrospection, anticipation, and appreciation. Retrospection refers to man's ability to re-experience the past, to feel deeply that which is only a memory, to transport an event of the distant past into a "creative living experience" of the present. Anticipation is man's projection of visions and aspirations into the future. Indeed, his present life is regulated in expectation of the fulfillment of these dreams. His present is shaped by his vision of the future. Appreciation embraces the present as a precious possession, as inherently worthy.

If there is no retrospection, there can be no *mitzvah* of *sippur yetzi'at Mitzrayim.* The *Seder* itself is a recreation and a reliving of the past as a present reality. We recite "In every generation, each person should feel that he personally experienced the Exodus from Egypt." History becomes part of our present time-awareness. Memory is more than a storehouse; it can become a present-day experience, a part of the "I" awareness. Rabbi Akiba is not a figure of the past; he guides us in the present, as do Maimonides and Rashi. They are daily companions and they vivify our everyday lives. Tragically, many Jews nowadays, ignorant of their past, find themselves rootless, alienated, and adrift. They are Jews who live only in the present.

In anticipation, man moves from reminiscing to expectation, from memories to visions. To live fulfillingly in time requires both a worthy past and a promising future. Time-awareness is not only for dreaming. This, in turn, suggests that we have the freedom to make decisions and the moral commitment to intervene. We derive from retrospection the moral imperative to act now in order to realize our visions for the future. The *Haggadah* opens with *Avadim Hayinu* (retrospection) and it concludes with *Nishmat Kol Ḥai*, which is an anticipatory vision of the future, moving from hindsight to foresight.

The third time-awareness dimension is "appreciation", which means valuing the present and prizing each moment as a precious gift. Retrospection and anticipation are significant only insofar as they transform the present. In every fraction of a second, visions can be realized or destroyed.

The *Halakhah* is very time-conscious. A time differential of even one minute or less determines the *sheki'ah*, the onset of the Sabbath, the *zeman keri'at Shema* (the period when the *Shema* may be recited), and *notar* in *Kodashim* (Temple sacrifices). A large number of halakhic regulations hinge on the passage of minute segments of time. In science, too, imprecision in time can spell disaster for astronauts approaching the moon, or cause intricate experiments to go awry.

Time-awareness is the singular faculty of the free man, who

can use or abuse it. To a slave, it is a curse or a matter of indifference. It is not an instrument which he can harness to his purposes. The free man wants time to move slowly because, presumably, it is being employed for his purposes. The slave may want to accelerate time, because it will terminate his oppressive burdens. Not being able to control time, the slave grows insensitive to it; inexactitude and unawareness characterize his schedule. This too, one may add, is the misery of many who retire in later years into idleness. They no longer feel needed; they have no further valued contributions to make, so no great anticipation moves them excitedly through the day. A bland, emotionless life ensues. Parenthetically, a *Talmid Ḥakham* in his old age is not stricken by this malady.

In the concentration camps, night and day became indistinct and blurred. What was not done one day could be done the next; opportunities lost or anticipated generated no great excitement. Time was loosely and meaninglessly structured. This is the condition of the slave. Any *mitzvah*, therefore, which is defined within a time context does not devolve upon a slave. These *mitzvot* are meaningful only in their being related to what preceded their performance and to what will follow thereafter. They are time-structured. Their significance is derived from their association with a particular segment of time.

The *Kiddush* on the first *Seder* cup of wine fulfills the requirement of *Kiddush Hayom*, to declare the sanctity of the festival season. It concludes with the words, *Mekaddesh Yisrael vehazemanim*, "Who sanctifies Israel and the festive seasons." Time is thereby declared a holy entity; but only a free man can make *Kiddush*, designate a span of time as of special significance. Time exists only for the one who is responsive to its ebb and flow. The Sephardi *Haggadah* adds the word *beḥipazon* to the text of *Ha Laḥma Anya*, indicating a hurried departure from Egypt, a time-consciousness which governed the Exodus.

3. *Issur Hithatnut.* Marriage is more than a social institution

202

for the purpose of satisfying particular personal and social needs. Marriage raises man above the singular; a spiritual relationship is established. In the *Sheva Berakhot* (Seven Marriage Blessings), we first proclaim *Yotzer ha'adam*, that God is man's creator; no reference is made here to woman. The next blessing, however, referring to *binyan adé ad* (a perpetual fabric), points to Eve. Only here is *Betzalmo*, the Divine nature of man stressed. The first blessing refers to the "type" man; the second sees him in a relationship, having transcended his egocentricity. Only now does he reflect a Divine image.

Only he who possesses himself, a *ben horin*, can relate himself to another in a free reciprocity. A slave is obviously not a free agent; he cannot exercise this initiative and therefore cannot marry. The paschal lamb sacrifice required a family togetherness, a *seh levet avot, seh labayit*, "a lamb for each family, for each household" (Ex. 12:3). Prior to the sacrifice, each Jew was consciously aware of his group association. Such social or group interrelatedness is a *herut* (freedom) experience. Marriage is not for a slave personality.

To summarize our analysis of slavery: we indicated that the slave is a frightened personality whose truth-discernment is impaired; he is insensitive to time and is also incapable of establishing relationships.

On Being Pharaoh's Slaves (LeFar'oh)

Why the emphasis, "to Pharaoh"? Is it not enough to say "we were slaves in Egypt"? The text emphasizes that the Israelites were slaves to Pharaoh in a corporate state, but were not owned by individual Egyptian masters. Slave systems vary. In ancient Greece or in early American history, slaves were bound to individuals; in Nazi Germany, Soviet Russia, and other absolute totalitarian states, the national entity itself enslaves the people. The distinction is significant.

203

In private slavery, some form of human relationship exists between the slave and his master. Two human beings interact, despite the difference in their station. It is possible for human empathy to enter their relationship, with occasional feelings of sympathy, confidence, identity, and trust. Such was the relationship of Joseph and Potiphar. It is a subordination, but not necessarily a subjugation. In corporate slavery, however, an impassive oppression precludes all human association; there is no friendship or human emotion. It is a depersonalized, faceless prison, with the inmates reduced to number identification.

In Egypt, Jews were owned by the state—*Velo avadim la'avadim,* they were not subservient to Egyptians who were themselves oppressed like slaves. The total State operated as a technological machine, with all people reduced to useful cogs. This was the plight of the Israelites and the text wishes to emphasize this additional dimension of their misery.

Becoming Servants of God (*Elohenu*)

The pronominal suffix in *Elohenu* seems redundant. The words, "and the Eternal took us out", clearly ascribe the redemption to Divine intervention. *Elohenu,* however, indicates an ongoing, continuing relationship, the suffix connoting a reciprocal interaction. The Exodus from Egypt was not a one-time confrontation and intervention. Rather, even after their liberation, God did not retreat from His intimate association with the Israelites. There is here a persistence of relatedness which is unlike His sporadic intervention with other nations. The term *am segulah* means "a precious treasure" which is continually valued.

Elohenu also signifies that the redemption from Egypt was not from slavery to freedom, *me'avdut leherut,* but rather from being slaves to man to becoming servants of God, *me'avdut le'avdut.* To the verse, *Ki li bene Yisrael avadim,* "You are servants unto Me" (Lev. 25:55), our Sages append the command: *Velo avadim la'avadim*, "And not slaves to slaves" (fellow man). Liberation, therefore, meant throwing off man's yoke and willingly embracing God's yoke, *Ol Malkhut Shamayim*. The Torah does not believe in absolute freedom, that man should be free from all norms and duties. Relieved of man's oppression, the Israelites were now free to choose voluntarily to surrender this freedom, but to God. It is as if God said: "Give up your freedom to Me, and only then will you be free." [5]

This may seem paradoxical. How can man be free if he surrenders his freedom? An analysis of man's existential condition will be helpful. Is man ever truly free? Is he not a prisoner of natural law, subject to the caprices of his state of health, the intrusion of accidents, and the ever hovering spectre of possible death? These are physiological constraints. Man is also subject to social pressures: the mores of his society, the biases of his family, and the prejudices of his class. In reality, supposedly free man is buffeted, pressured, coerced, and restricted in his options, even if no human taskmaster hovers over him. These forces warp his initiatives and deprive him of real freedom.

In surrendering to God, man truly achieves freedom. He is no longer tormented by psychologically depressing anxieties about his health or the spectre of death. The world is under the rulership of a beneficent God and we achieve an identification with Him by following His teachings. Man is thereby equipped to cope with all hostile and threatening forces. He is bolstered by his faith in the transcendental orderliness of things and in God's ultimate compassion. The ravages of life no longer terrorize him, This one basic fear of God (more precisely, awe-inspiring reverence) removes all other fears. To surrender to God therefore brings more freedom, not less.

We can now appreciate that *vayotzi'enu* (mere "bringing forth") without *Elohenu* would constitute bondage once again, namely, to physiological, psychological, and social constraints.

הערות לפרק 19

1   עבדים היינו לפרעה במצרים ויוציאנו ה׳ אלהינו ממצרים (דברים ו, כא).

2   ונודה לך שיר חדש, על גאולתנו ועל פדות נפשנו.

3   פסול לעדות, פטור ממצות עשה שהזמן גרמא, איסור התחתנות.

4   והיו חייך תלאים לך מנגד, ופחדת לילה ויומם, ולא תאמין בחייך (דברים כח, סו).

5   והלחות מעשה אלהים המה והמכתב מכתב אלהים הוא, חרות על הלחת (שמות לב, טז); אל תקרי חָרוּת אלא חֵירוּת (עירובין נד.). פ׳ רש״י — בשביל הלוחות היו בני ישראל בני חורין; אין לך בן חורין אלא מי שעוסק בתלמוד תורה (אבות ו, ב).

CHAPTER **XX**

THE MITZVAH OF SIPPUR YETZI'AT MITZRAYIM

The *mitzvah* of *Sippur Yetzi'at Mitzrayim* requires the recitation of the *Arami oved avi* passage (Deut. 26:5) both when offering the first fruits in the Temple and on *Pesaḥ*. It is essentially a capsule review of early Jewish history, with particular reference to the wanderings of the patriarch Jacob, his sojourn in Egypt, the subsequent enslavement of the people, the miraculous Exodus, the settlement in the Holy Land (*Yishuv ha'aretz*), and the presentation of the first fruits (*Bikkurim*) in the Temple.

The purpose of *Sippur* is to express our gratitude and thanksgiving (*hakkarat tovah*) to God for granting us the two basics of Jewish nationhood: freedom from foreign oppression, which culminated in the Revelation at Mt. Sinai, and settlement in *Eretz Yisrael*. The pilgrim bringing his first fruits thanked God for his crops and acknowledged that his presence and good fortune in possessing this land was not an accidental quirk of history, but rather the culmination of a series of miraculous events, starting with the patriarch Jacob. Similarly, on *Pesaḥ*, the Jew recognizes the Divine hand in the beginnings of his peoplehood and this betokens a special relationship between God and Israel for all of history.

The thanksgiving motivation of *Sippur* is clearly indicated by

Maimonides. Regarding the *Bikkurim*, he writes: "We are commanded to recount (*lesapper*) the story of His goodness and salvation; we begin with our patriarch Jacob and conclude with the slavery in Egypt ... and we are to thank Him and to beseech Him for future blessings whenever we bring the *Bikkurim*" (Sefer Hamitzvot 132).[1] A similar characterization is found with respect to *Pesah*: "We are commanded to tell the story (*lesapper*) at the beginning of the fifteenth of Nisan ... and we are to thank Him for all the goodness He has bestowed upon us" (*ibid.* 157).[2]

The text of *Arami oved avi* is recorded in Deuteronomy (26:5 ff.), in the *Bikkurim* chapter. "An Aramean sought to destroy my father, and he went down into Egypt and sojourned there, few in number; and he became there a nation, great, mighty and populous. And the Egyptians dealt ill with us, and afflicted us, and laid upon us hard bondage. And we cried unto the Lord, the God of our fathers, and the Lord heard our voice and saw our affliction, and our toil, and our oppression. And the Lord brought us out of Egypt with a mighty hand and with an outstretched arm and with great terror, and with signs and with wonders. And He brought us unto this place and gave us this land, a land flowing with milk and honey. And now, behold, I have brought the first fruits of the land which You, O Lord, have given me." [3]

The *mitzvah* of *Sippur* on *Pesah*, observed at the *Seder*, is mandated by the verse, "You shall tell your son on that day, saying, this is done [the *Pesah* observance] because of what the Eternal did for me when I came out of Egypt" (Ex. 13:8).[4] The precise text for the fulfillment of the *mitzvah* on *Pesah* is not indicated in the Torah, as in the ritual of *Bikkurim*, but our Sages concluded that just as *Arami oved avi* suited the *mitzvah* of *Sippur* in the case of *Bikkurim*, it would also be appropriate at the *Seder* (Mishnah Pes. 10:4; Maimonides, Hil. Ḥametz Umatzah 7:1, 4).[5] Although it is a *mitzvah* to recall the Exodus from Egypt every day of the year, and not only on *Pesah*,[6] this requirement may be fulfilled merely by a perfunctory reference, *zekhirah*, without the elaboration which *Sippur* entails at the *Seder*.

Why was the Seder Sippur Abbreviated?

The *Bikkurim* text of *Arami oved avi* extends over six verses, concluding with a reference to *Yishuv ha'aretz* and the *Bikkurim*. In the *Haggadah*, however, the last two verses are omitted and the recitation concludes with "And the Lord brought us out with a mighty hand," etc. We can appreciate the inappropriateness of the reference to the offering of *Bikkurim* at the *Seder*, but the omission of *Yishuv ha'aretz* is perplexing. Two explanations may be given.

The purpose of the Exodus was to create "a kingdom of priests and a holy nation" (Ex. 19:6). *Pesaḥ* and the Revelation at Sinai are bound to each other because the full purpose of the Exodus was only realized at Mt. Sinai. Physical liberation without a spiritual identity would hardly be considered a fulfillment of God's promise to the Patriarchs. Indeed, Moses' assignment was to lead the Exodus and arrange for the Revelation, and nothing more. "And this shall be your sign that it was I who sent you. When you have freed the people from Egypt, you shall worship God at this mountain" (Ex. 3:12).[7] It was not his mission to bring them into the Land, as indeed he did not. *Eretz Yisrael* was their physical destination, but not their spiritual identity. *Pesaḥ* celebrates the achievement of their singularity as a people, and the verse pertaining to *Yishuv ha-'aretz* was therefore omitted from the *Arami oved avi* in the *Haggadah*.

Maimonides suggests that it is the festival of *Sukkot*, in addition to its other themes, which commemorates *Yishuv ha'aretz*, Israel's settlement of the Holy Land. He writes: "I believe that the Four Species are a symbolic expression of our rejoicing, that the Israelites changed [their habitation] from the wilderness, which is 'no place of seed, or of figs, or of vines, or of pomegranates, or water to drink' (Num. 20:5), to a country full of fruit trees and rivers. In order to remember this, we take the fruit which is the most pleasant of the land, the branches which smell best, the most beautiful leaves and also the best of the herbs, i.e., the willows of the brook" (Guide 3:43). *Pesaḥ*, therefore, did not have to provide for *yishuv ha-'aretz* in its observance.

This may explain the ruling of those who drink only four cups of wine at the *Seder*. These commemorate the four Biblical expressions (Ex. 6:6-7) which denote redemption: *Vehotzeti* ("I will bring you out from under the burdens of the Egyptians"), *Vehitzalti* ("And I will deliver you from their bondage"), *Vega-'alti* ("And I will redeem you with an outstretched arm"), and *Velakaḥti* ("And I will take you to Me for a people"). A fifth term, *Veheveti* ("And I will bring you into the land"), is not celebrated by a fifth cup of wine. It is not intended to denigrate the importance of settling the land or the pivotal place *Eretz Yisrael* occupied in our religious life, but merely to indicate that *Pesaḥ* encompasses a specific period, from the Exodus to the Revelation. It celebrates the formation of a people with its own spiritual personality.

The above explanation for the omission of *Yishuv ha'aretz* is only partially satisfactory. Both the Mishnah and Maimonides clearly stipulate that the *Arami oved avi* text was to be read in its entirety at the *Seder* (*sheyigmor kol haparashah*). Why, then, was the recitation abbreviated? A more plausible explanation is that these last verses were omitted only after the destruction of the Temple and the exile from the land; but they were very much part of the *Arami oved avi* text in the *Haggadah* when the Jews resided independently in their own land. It seemed incongruous to thank God at the *Seder* for the wonderful land from which they were exiled. In omitting these verses, the *Haggadah* highlights our sense of deprivation, strengthening our prayers and efforts to restore Jewish sovereignty in the land and, once again, to be able to recite the *Arami oved avi* in its entirety. The absence of these verses is, therefore, only temporary and will be happily restored in Messianic days.

Declarations of Relevance

Because the event being commemorated is over 3500 years old, one can easily come to regard oneself as so remote from the entire episode as to be completely detached from it. This poses a problem, since the *mitzvah* of *Sippur* is not truly fulfilled unless we personally identify with the Exodus, suffering its anguish and exulting in its triumphs. What relevance, therefore, can *Arami oved avi* have for us today?

To solve this problem, the compiler of the *Haggadah* inserted arguments for its relevance both before and after the *Arami* portion. Preceding its recitation, we say: "And if God had not taken our ancestors out of Egypt, we and our children and our children's children would still be enslaved in Egypt." [8] The thesis is set forth that, were it not for the redemption from Egypt, there would be no Jewish people today. We are not recalling an historical curiosity, but rather are accounting for our present-day identity.

The theme of relevance is even further developed: "For not only one tyrant has risen up against us to destroy us, but in every generation tyrants have sought to destroy us and the Holy One, blessed be He, has delivered us from their hands." [9] Not only does the Exodus account for our present Jewish identity, but we are also experiencing similar persecution in our own day. We not only know history but relive it. The battle to affirm the right of the State of Israel to live securely is a contemporary version of the Egyptian experience. The Pharaohs of our day are more dangerous than ancient tyrants because the means of destruction at their disposal are more fearful. Reading

211

the Exodus narrative, we realize more poignantly our contemporary plight. It is with this in mind that, immediately after the *Arami* section, we add: "In every generation a person should look upon himself as if he personally had come out of Egypt. Not our ancestors alone did the Holy One, blessed be He, redeem, but us also has He redeemed with them." [10]

The past is not only relevant but current as well. The liberation from tyranny, and the fight for freedom, is the story of Jewish history as a whole. It is only by identifying personally with the Exodus that we can proceed with the *Haggadah* and truly be grateful to God for His past and present miracles.

Six Requirements for Relating the Haggadah

1. *Reading (Mikra).* This is fulfilled through a recitation of the Scriptural text of *Arami oved avi*, without any interpretation, elaboration or reflection. Scholars and the unlearned engage in an identical verbal performance. In this aspect, the *Pesaḥ* and *Bikkurim* recitations are alike (except for the last two verses), since the *Bikkurim* too required no elaboration beyond the actual text.

2. *Studying (Limmud).* Here, the *Sippur* requirement for *Pesaḥ* extends beyond the obligations of the *Bikkurim* pilgrim. We are challenged to become students, not merely readers, to probe the Biblical text in depth and to interpret it in accordance with the teachings of the Oral Law, the *Torah shebe'al peh.* These include not only the expositions and derivations which were transmitted orally through the generations together with the Written Law, but also teachings which were derived through the hermeneutic rules of logic whereby the Torah is expounded—the *middot shehaTorah nidreshet bahen.* Through these rules of analytical exegesis, the words of the Biblical text were subjected to extension, limitation, analogy, textual parallelism, logical inference, as well as other modes of interpretation.

The word *Haggadah* connotes more than the act of "telling"

or "narrating." It suggests an elaborate form of study. "Thus shall you say to the house of Jacob and tell (*vetaggid*) to the children of Israel" (Ex. 19:3)[11] entails more than a perfunctory recital of a particular narrative. The word *vetaggid* stems from the same root as *Haggadah*.

The Oral Law is subdivided into three parts: *Midrash*—the interpretation of the text using hermeneutic rules of logic; *Mishnah*—the halakhic process which determines the final law; and *Gemara*—the employment of halakhic thinking, analysis, and application [*sevara*]. In the *Haggadah*, all three types are used. The *Arami oved avi* is interpreted by the Midrash. *Halakhah* is set forth by Rabban Gamliel's formulation, "Whoever has not explained these three items has not fulfilled his requirements. These are *Pesaḥ*, *Matzah*, and *Maror*," [12] Logical inferences are inherent in "Therefore, it is our duty to thank, adore, laud," etc., "In every generation a person should look upon himself as if he personally had gone out of Egypt," etc., and in many other instances in the *Haggadah*.

3. *Teaching* (*Talmud*): In addition to the role of students, we are asked to become teachers, *melamdim*; to impart and to implant Jewish knowledge and loyalties in the next generation. From *Barukh Hamakom* onward, we become pedagogues, adapting teaching methods to the needs of various types of students: the wise, the wicked, the naive, and the simple. In all generations, including our own, the *Seder* experience has been a most potent influence in capturing the hearts and minds of children, thereby ensuring a continuation of our *Massorah*. God made His covenant with Abraham because "I have known him, that he will command his children and his household after him, that they may keep the way of the Lord, to do righteousness and justice" (Gen. 18:19).[13] Parents are not only biological progenitors but also teachers, and they are traditionally referred to as *avi mori* ("my father, my teacher") and *immi morati* ("my mother, my teacher").

4. *Teaching Methodology—Verbal.* The *Haggadah* uses the interrogative dialogue as the most effective means of stimulating children's participation and instruction. It begins with the Four Questions; the remainder of the *Haggadah* comprises the answer. Intellectual curiosity to know and to understand must be stimulated, and questions must be encouraged. The whole of Jewish history is a long search for God, and we want our children to become part of this quest by asking questions which will evoke the teacher in all of us.

In Deuteronomy (4:29) we read: "But if you search there for the Lord your God, you will find Him, if only you will seek Him with all your heart and soul." The exegete, R. Ovadiah Sforno, comments: "The reason you will find Him is that you seek Him with all your heart." [14] Curiosity and the eagerness to know are prerequisites for real learning. When Yitro asked Moses why he was tediously involved with the people all day, Moses replied: "Because the people come unto me to seek [*lidrosh*] after God" (Ex. 18:15).[15] Inquisitiveness must be stimulated, and the interrogative method is an effective means of establishing an educational relationship.

5. *Teaching Methodology—Audio-Visual.* Teachers are aware that audio-visual aids are helpful supplements to the educational process. Suggestive symbols and rituals affect the child emotionally and imaginatively, as well as intellectually. The *Seder* evening is richly endowed with such educational tools. The *ke'arah* plate, with its *matzah, maror, haroset, karpas,* egg, and shankbone, captivates the mind and heart with its historical suggestiveness and curious observances. The requirement to lean as an expression of relaxed emancipation, the four cups of wine, and the meal (*se'udah*) with its concluding *afikoman,* inspire questions and supply answers. *Pesah, matzah,* and *maror,* Rabban Gamliel taught, must be both visually presented and verbally explained.[12]

A meal is basically a biological act, although modern man has

214

made of it a social experience with table manners and aesthetic enhancements. Judaism, even as it acknowledges the social aspect of eating (*zimmun, seh levet avot,* etc.), also tries to elevate it further, to make of it a holy experience. Rabbi Shim'on said: "Three who have eaten at one table and have not spoken words of Torah, it is as if they had eaten of the sacrifices of the dead; but three who have eaten at one table and have spoken words of Torah are as if they had eaten from the table of God" (Av. 3:4).[16]

Transforming an animal need into an act of worship is a uniquely Jewish idea. The table is referred to in our tradition as an altar, and meals which are associated with religious observances are called *se'udot mitzvah.* On the verse, "And Aaron came with all the elders of Israel to partake of the meal before God with Moses' father-in-law" (Ex. 18:12), Rashi comments: "From this we learn that he who partakes of meals at which scholars sit may be regarded as though he partakes in the splendor of the *Shekhinah.*" [17] The *Seder se'udah* is an integral part of the *Sippur* performance because it, too, teaches the story of the Exodus.

6. *Thanksgiving (Shevah).* Gratitude to God is the most dominant motif of the Jewish liturgy. It is expressed through *shevah,* songs of praise to God. Its most exultant forms are the *Hallel* (Ps. 113–118) and *Hallel Hagadol* (Ps. 136). The latter *shevah* was chanted publicly in the Temple with its rhythmic response, "For His lovingkindness endures forever," *ki le'olam hasdo.*

Hallel is recited on Festival days, but it was omitted from the Purim liturgy because, as R. Nahman explained, "Its reading [i.e. the *Megillah*] fulfills the requirement to recite *Hallel.*" [18] *Shevah* is implicit in the very recital of the Purim narrative and no additional *Hallel* was necessary. If so, why was *Hallel* included in the *Haggadah* when the narrative of the Exodus itself should have satisfied the *shevah* requirement?

It seems that *shevah* is not enough for the *Seder* night. We are expected to rise to higher levels of exultant praise, to a *shirah hadashah*. It is a night when the Jew is in love with God, a night of passionate romance which is reflected in the tradition of reading the Song of Songs after the *Haggadah*. We move from the *Hallei Hagadol* to *Nishmat kol hai*, "the breath of every living being shall bless Your name." We ecstatically see all of creation joining in a grand symphony of homage to God for all the blessings of life. From the *ge'ulat Mitzrayim* we are gripped with an appreciation that God is also the ultimate salvation of all mankind. The concluding note of the *Haggadah* is an eschatological vision of a glorious future, when "every mouth shall give thanks and every tongue shall swear allegiance unto You; every knee shall bow to You." [19] To highlight this added dimension of gratitude, the *Hallel* and the *Hallel Hagadol* were included in the *Haggadah*.

הערות לפרק 20

1 שצונו לספר טובותיו אשר היטיב לנו והצילנו . . . ולשבחו על כל זה ולבקש ממנו להתמיד הברכה כשיביא הבכורים (רמב"ם, ס' המצות, עשה קלב).

2 שצונו לספר ביציאת מצרים בליל ט"ו בניסן בתחלת הלילה כפי צחות לשון המספר . . . ולהודות לו, יתעלה על כל טוב שגמלנו (רמב"ם, ס' המצות, עשה קנז).

3 ארמי אבד אבי, וירד מצרימה, ויגר שם במתי מעט, ויהי שם לגוי גדול עצום ורב; וירעו אתנו המצרים ויענונו ויתנו עלינו עבודה קשה; ונצעק אל ה' אלהי אבתינו וישמע ה' את קלנו וירא את ענינו, ואת עמלנו ואת לחצנו; ויוציאנו ה' ממצרים ביד חזקה ובזרע נטויה ובמרא גדול ובאותות ובמופתים; ויבאנו אל המקום הזה ויתן לנו את הארץ הזאת, ארץ זבת חלב ודבש; ועתה הנה הבאתי את ראשית פרי האדמה אשר נתתה לי ה' (דברים כו, ה-י).

4 והגדת לבנך ביום ההוא לאמר, בעבור זה עשה ה' לי בצאתי ממצרים (שמות יג, ח).

5 מצות עשה של תורה לספר בנסים ונפלאות שנעשו לאבותינו במצרים בליל חמשה עשר בניסן, שנאמר, זכור את יום הזה אשר יצאתם ממצרים . . . והוא שידרוש מארמי אובד אבי עד שיגמור כל הפרשה. וכל המוסיף ומאריך בדרש פרשה זו, הרי זה משובח (רמב"ם, ה' חמץ ומצה ז, א, ד).

6 למען תזכר את יום צאתך מארץ מצרים כל ימי חייך (דברים טז, ג).

216

7 וזה לך האות כי אנכי שלחתיך, בהוציאך את העם ממצרים תעבדון את האלהים על ההר הזה (שמות ג, יב).

8 ואלו לא הוציא הקדוש ברוך הוא את אבותינו ממצרים, הרי אנו ובנינו ובני בנינו משעבדים היינו לפרעה במצרים.

9 שלא אחד בלבד עמד עלינו לכלותנו, אלא שבכל דור ודור עומדים עלינו לכלותנו, והקדוש ברוך הוא מצילנו מידם.

10 בכל דור ודור, חייב אדם לראות את עצמו כאלו הוא יצא ממצרים ... לא את אבותינו בלבד גאל הקב״ה, אלא אף אותנו גאל עמהם.

11 כה תאמר לבית יעקב ותגיד לבני ישראל (שמות יט, ג).

12 רבן גמליאל היה אומר: כל שלא אמר שלשה דברים אלו בפסח לא יצא ידי חובתו, ואלו הן, פסח, מצה ומרור.

13 כי ידעתיו, למען אשר יצוה את בניו ואת ביתו אחריו, ושמרו דרך ה׳, לעשות צדקה ומשפט (בראשית יח, יט).

14 ״ובקשתם משם את ה׳ אלהיך ומצאת, כי תדרשנו בכל לבבך ובכל נפשך״ (דברים ד, כט). פ׳ ספורנו — והטעם שתמצאנו הוא כי אמנם תדרשנו בכל לבבך.

15 כי יבא אלי העם לדרש אלהים (שמות יח, טו).

16 רבי שמעון אומר: שלשה שאכלו על שלחן אחד ולא אמרו עליו דברי תורה, כאלו אכלו מזבחי מתים. אבל שלשה שאכלו על שלחן אחד ואמרו עליו דברי תורה, כאלו אכלו משלחנו של מקום (אבות ג, ד).

17 ויבא אהרן וכל זקני ישראל לאכל לחם עם חתן משה לפני האלהים (שמות יח, יב); פ׳ רש״י — מכאן שהנהנה מסעודה שתלמידי חכמים מסבין בה, כאלו נהנה מזיו השכינה (ראה דברים יד, כג, ״ואכלת לפני ה׳ אלהיך״).

18 רב נחמן אמר: קריתא זו הלילא (מגילה יד).

19 נשמת כל חי תברך את שמך ה׳ אלהינו ... כי כל פה לך יודה, וכל לשון לך תשבע וכל ברך לך תכרע.

IN HIS OWN WORDS — מפי הרב

"Reason does not lay down the path along which the man of faith walks. Only after the fact, can reason describe it. The latter walks behind, not in front of the man of faith."

"The Lonely Man of Faith," *Tradition*, Vol. 7, No. 2, p. 56.

"We certainly have not been authorized by our history, sanctified by the martyrdom of millions, to even hint to another faith community that we are mentally ready to revise historical attitudes, to trade favors pertaining to fundamental matters of faith, and to reconcile "some" differences. Such a suggestion would be nothing but a betrayal of our great tradition and heritage and would, furthermore, produce no practical benefits . . . We cannot command the respect of our confronters by displaying a servile attitude. Only a candid, frank, and unequivocal policy reflecting unconditional commitment to our God, a sense of dignity, pride, and inner joy in being what we are, believing with great passion in the ultimate truthfulness of our views, praying fervently for and expecting confidently the fulfillment of our eschatological views when our faith will rise from particularity to universality, will inspire the peers of the other faith community among whom we have both adversaries and friends."

"Confrontation," *Tradition*, Vol. 6, No. 2, p. 25.

"We [Jews] are rooted in the here and now reality as inhabitants of our globe, and yet we experience a sense of homelessness and loneliness as if we belonged somewhere else. We
are both realists and dreamers, prudent and practical on the
one hand, and visionaries and idealists on the other. We are,
indeed, involved in the cultural endeavor and yet we are committed to another dimension of experience."

Ibid., p. 26.

"The essence of the Halakhah . . . is the creation of an ideal
world and the perception of the relationship that exists between
it and reality, in all its manifestations . . . There is no phenomenon,
event, creature for which *a prioristic* Halakhah does not have
an idealistic standard of judgment."

"Ish Hahalakhah — Galui V'nistar," p. 28.*

"Holiness, according to the viewpoint of the Halakhah, is
created by the appearance of a distant, lofty transcendence in
the midst of our physical world, by the "descent" of God, who
is totally incomprehensible, to Mt. Sinai, by the imposition of
a hidden, concealed world upon the face of reality . . . An
individual does not become holy through metaphysical attachment to the hidden, nor through mystical union with the infinite . . . but, rather, through his corporeal existence, his bodily
actions, and through fulfilling his task of realizing Halakhah
in the sense world . . . Holiness is realized through a life ordered
and fixed in accordance with the Halakhah, is manifested in the
observance of laws governing illicit relations, forbidden foods,
etc. . . . The synagogue is not the center of the Jewish religion . . .
[It is] the Halakhah which brings the Divine presence into the
midst of the world of the senses, of physical concrete reality . . .
The true Temple is the sphere of our daily, mundane activities
and existence, for it is there that the Halakhah is realized."

Ibid., p. 47.

* This and the following two excerpts were translated by Lawrence
Kaplan.

220

Once Rabbi Ḥayyim was asked what was the function of a Rabbi. He replied: "To redress the grievances of those who are abandoned and alone; to protect the dignity of the poor and to save the oppressed from the bonds of the oppressor."

Ibid., p. 80.

Quite often a man finds himself in a crowd among strangers. He feels lonely. No one knows him, no one cares for him, no one is concerned with him. It is an existential experience. He begins to doubt his ontological worth. This leads to alienation from the crowd surrounding him. Suddenly someone taps him on the shoulder and says, "Aren't you Mr. So and So? I have heard so much about you." An alien turned into a fellow member of an existential community. What brought about the change? The recognition by someone, the word!

To recognize a person is not just to identify him physically. It is more than that: it is an act of identifying him existentially as a person who has a job to do that only he can do properly. To recognize a person means to affirm that he is irreplaceable. To hurt a person means to tell him that he is expendable, that there is no need for him.

The Halakhah equated the act of publicly embarrassing a person with murder. Why? Because humiliation is tantamount to destroying an existential community and driving the individual into solitude. It is not enough for the charitable person to extend help to the needy. He must do more than that; he must try to restore to the dependent person a sense of dignity and worth. That is why we have developed special sensitivity regarding orphans and widows, since these persons are extremely sensitive and lose their self-confidence at the slightest provocation. The Bible warned us against afflicting an orphan and widow.

"The Community", *Tradition*, Vol. 17, No. 2, p. 16.

Jacob had emerged victorious from a most awesome encounter; he had held fast his mysterious foe, through a night of sorrow, fear, and loneliness, until the new day dawned. Was Jacob's victory something to be expected; could it have been predicted logically? Was he certain of victory? Of course not. He was alone, weak, and unarmed, a novice in the art of warfare. Why did Jacob not surrender to the foe who attacked him in the dark? Jacob acted "absurdly," and contrary to all rational practical consideration. In other words, he acted heroically. He, the lonely and helpless Jacob, dared to engage a mighty adversary in combat. He who had displayed so much business acumen and the keenness of a pragmatic mind, during his long sojourn in Laban's household, suddenly, in the darkness of a grisly, strange night, made the leap into the "absurd." He refused to yield to a superior force and declared war upon an invincible enemy. What Jacob manifested was not *ko'aḥ* but *gevurah,* heroism, which is always employed when reason despairs and logic retreats. With daybreak, the helpless, lonely, non-logical Jacob found himself unexpectedly the victor, the hero.

The impossible and absurd had triumphed over the possible and logical; heroism, not logic, won the day. Is this merely the story of one individual experience? Is it not in fact the story of *knesset Israel,* an entity which is engaged in an "absurd" struggle for thousands of years?

"Catharsis," ibid., p. 41.

Man is a dialectical being; an inner schism runs through his personality at every level. This schism is not due to man's revolt against his Maker, as Christian theology has preached since the days of Augustine. Unlike this view, according to which it was man who, by his sinful rebellion against his Maker, precipitated the split in human nature, the Judaic view posits that the schism is willed by God as the source of man's greatness and his election as a singular, charismatic being. Man is a great and creative being because he is torn by conflict and is always in a state of ontological tenseness and perplexity. The fact that the creative gesture is associated with agony is a result of this contradiction, which pervades the whole personality of man.

"Majesty and Humility," *ibid.*, p. 25.

The error of modern representatives of religion is that they promise their congregants the solution to all the problems of life —an expectation which religion does not fulfill. Religion, on the contrary, deepens the problems but never intends to solve them. The grandeur of religion lies in its *mysterium tremendum*, its magnitude and its ultimate incomprehensibility. To cite one example, we may adduce the problem of theodicy, the justification of evil in the world, that has tantalized the inquiring mind from time immemorial till this last tragic decade. The acuteness of this problem has grown for the religious person in essence and dimensions. When a minister, rabbi, or priest attempts to solve the ancient question of Job's suffering, through a sermon or lecture, he does not promote religious ends, but, on the contrary, does them a disservice. The beauty of religion with its grandiose vistas reveals itself to men, not in solutions but in problems, not in harmony but in the constant conflict of diversified forces and trends.

"Sacred and Profane," *Gesher*, Vol. 3, No. 1, p. 7.

INDICES

מפתח העינים לפי פרשות השנה והחגים

(המספרים מציינים את הפרקים בספר זה)

Index of topics according to *Sidrah*; numbers denote chapters of this book.

226

INDEX OF BIBLICAL AND RABBINIC SOURCES*

References marked * occur in footnotes.

*Thanks are due to Dr. Marvin Ring, who compiled the indices of Biblical and Rabbinic Sources, commentators and authors, and subjects.

228

230

INDEX OF COMMENTARIES AND AUTHORS

Index of Subjects

Din (court verdict) — 53ff, 60, 62.
Divine attributes — 13f, 129.
Divine imperative (*ḥukkah*) — 42, 75, 108ff.
Divine Presence — 84, 188.
Divine Retribution — 64ff.

Egypt — 37, 80, 111, 115, 117f, 154f, 184, 187, 189f, 197, 204, 208, 211.
R. Elazar — 89.
R. Elazar b. Shamua — 135.
Election of Israel — 119f.
Eliezer — 121.
Elisha ben Avuya — 66.
Elohim — 13ff, 62.
Eretz Yisrael — 26, 64, 67, 120, 125, 207, 209f.
Esau — 95, 111, 174f.
Esther — 178, 183ff, 187.
Euthanasia — 104.
Eve — 14, 18f, 24, 130, 156.

Free will — 40f, 46, 50, 77, 198.

Rabban Gamliel — 33, 213f.
Ge'ulah — 96, 111f, 117, 184.
God — Man cannot perceive real essence of—13; Sustainer of creation—16, 33; both *yotzer* and *boré*—17; forgives man's sinfulness because He acknowledges human vulnerability to changing fortunes—45f; universal and eternal as His law—101.
Golden Calf — 52, 101, 123, 150, 152ff, 167.

R. Haim of Volozhin — 75.
Halakha — 17, 54ff, 59, 61, 65, 74f, 93, 121, 132, 142ff, 155, 161, 163, 172, 191f, 198, 201, 213; main objective is to achieve performance—75f; primacy of mitzvah over emotions—142ff; practice of—142.
R. Ḥama, son of Ḥanina — 154.
Haman — 44f, 178ff, 187.
R. Ḥanina — 137, 170.
Hattarat nedarim — 94.
Havayah — 13ff.
Ḥazakah — 65.
Hefker — 18.

Korah — 133f, 139ff, 144f, 147f.
Korban Pesah (Paschal-Lamb Sacrifice) — 108ff, 203.

Leah—119.
Limmud — 71f, 75f, 162, 212; joining with the intellect of God—71f.
Logos — 90, 104f, 147, 163.
Lots — 42ff.

Manna — 155.
Marriage — 121f, 202f.
Mezuzah — 140, 143, 182.
Middat Hadin — 34ff, 165f.
Middat Harahamim — 167.
Mimahorat — 51f.
Miriam — 119, 123f.
Mishpatim — 51ff, 96, 99f, 103ff, 110.
Mitzvot — 16, 19f, 41, 53, 80, 96f, 99, 103, 107, 109, 114f, 123, 142ff, 172, 199f, 202.
Moab — 95.
Moral will — 76f.
Mordecai — 45, 68, 178, 182ff, 187.
Moses — 13, 24f, 51f, 57, 61, 66, 77f, 80, 111, 117f, 122, 133f, 139f, 142, 145f, 148, 150ff, 160f, 167, 185, 187f, 209, 214; convened first Jewish court in history — 53; distinguishing features of his prophecy — 124f.
Mt. Seir — 111.
Multiple creations — 27f.

R. Nahman — 215.
R. Nehemiah — 190.
R. Nehorai — 128.
Nineveh — 20.

Parah Adumah (Red Heifer) — 100, 108ff.
Passover — 44, 115, 197, 207ff.
Peritzut — 156, 158.
Philistines — 37, 111, 130f.
Plato — 33.
Prayer — uncertainty of life is primary motive for — 41; motivated by man's feeling of *tzarah* — 49, 80f; as dialogue — 77ff; Biblically mandatory or Rabbinically imposed — 79ff; structure of — 82f; resolves existential depth crisis — 87.

240

ABBREVIATIONS

Biblical References		Talmudic References	
Gen.	Genesis	Ber.	Berakhot
Ex.	Exodus	Shab.	Shabbat
Lev.	Leviticus	Pes.	Pesaḥim
Num.	Numbers	Meg.	Megillah
Deut.	Deuteronomy	Yev.	Yevamot
Judg.	Judges	Ket.	Ketubbot
Sam.	Samuel	Git.	Gittin
Isa.	Isaiah	Kid.	Kiddushin
Mic.	Micah	B. Kam.	Bava Kama
Hab.	Habakkuk	B. Metz.	Bava Metzia
Zech.	Zechariah	B.. Bat.	Bava Batra
Mal.	Malachi	Sanh.	Sanhedrin
Ps.	Psalms	Mak.	Makkot
Prov.	Proverbs	Av.	Avot
Eccles.	Ecclesiastes	Men.	Menaḥot
Esth.	Esther	Nid.	Niddah
Chron.	Chronicles		

Note. — "Gen. R.", "Ex. R.", etc. indicates *Midrash Rabbah* commentary.

PARTIAL BIBLIOGRAPHY

A. WRITINGS OF THE RAV
(in English)

"Confrontation," *Tradition*, Vol. 6, No. 2, p. 5; published by the Rabbinical Council of America, New York.

"The Lonely Man of Faith," *Tradition*, Vol. 7, No. 2 (1965).

"Sacred and Profane," *Gesher*, Vol. 3, No. 1 (1966), published by Student Organization of Yeshiva University.

"The Community," *Tradition*, Vol. 17, No. 2, pp. 7–24.

"Majesty and Humility" (*ibid.*, pp. 25–37).

"Catharsis" (*ibid.*, pp. 38–54).

"Redemption, Prayer, Talmud Torah" (*ibid.*, pp. 55–72).

"A Tribute to the Rebitzen of Talne" (*ibid.*, pp. 73–83).

(in Hebrew)

איש ההלכה — גלוי ונסתר (המחלקה לחינוך ולתרבות תורניים בגולה של ההסתדרות הציונית העולמית), ירושילם, תשל"ט; כולל את המסות: "איש ההלכה", "ובקשתם משם", ו"רעיונות על התפילה".

B. TRANSLATIONS AND RECONSTRUCTIONS
(in English)

Hashkafah Lessons, adapted by Rabbi Abraham R. Besdin, xeroxed; distributed by the Rabbinical Council of America (15 units).

Shi'ure Harav — a Conspectus of Public Addresses, Hamevasser, Yeshiva University (1974), ed. by Joseph Epstein.

(in Hebrew)

על התשובה — דברים שבעל־פה (המחלקה לחינוך ולתרבות תורניים בגולה של ההסתדרות הציונית העולמית), כתב וערך והוסיף אחרית־דבר פינחס ה. פלאי, ירושלים, תשל"ה.

בסוד היחיד והיחד, מבחר כתבים עבריים מאת הרב יוסף דב הלוי סולובייצ'יק (הוצאת "אורות"), ירושלים תשל"ו ערך והוסיף מבוא פינחס הכהן פלאי.

חמש דרשות, תירגם דוד טלזנר, ירושלים, מכון טל אורות, תשל"ד.

243

C. CRITICAL STUDIES

Ahron Lichtenstein, "Rabbi J. B. Soloveitchik," in *Great Jewish Thinkers of the Twentieth Century* (ed. S. Novick); Washington, B'nai B'rith, Pub., pp. 281–97.

Lawrence Kaplan, "The Religious Philosophy of Rabbi J. B. Soloveitchik," *Tradition*, Vol. 14, No. 2 (1973), p. 43.

Arych Strikovsky, "The World of Thought of Harav J. B. Soloveitchik," *Gesher* (1966).

Eugene Borowitz, "The Typological Theology of Rabbi J. B. Soloveitchik," *Judaism*, Vol. 15 (1966).

Morris Sosevsky, "The Lonely Man of Faith Confronts the *Ish Hahalakhah*," *Tradition*, Vol. 16, No. 2 (1976).

Breinigsville, PA USA
05 November 2010
248742BV00002B/2/P